F.V.

Hitchcock's America

HITCHCOCK'S AMERICA

Edited by
Jonathan Freedman *and*
Richard Millington

New York   Oxford • Oxford University Press   1999

Oxford University Press

Oxford   New York
Athens   Auckland   Bangkok   Bogotá   Buenos Aires   Calcutta
Cape Town   Chennai   Dar es Salaam   Delhi   Florence   Hong Kong   Istanbul
Karachi   Kuala Lumpur   Madrid   Melbourne   Mexico City   Mumbai
Nairobi   Paris   São Paulo   Singapore   Taipei   Tokyo   Toronto   Warsaw

and associated companies in
Berlin   Ibadan

Copyright © 1999 by Oxford University Press, Inc.

Published by Oxford University Press, Inc.
198 Madison Avenue, New York, New York 10016

Oxford is a registered trademark of Oxford University Press.

Library of Congress Cataloging-in-Publication Data
Hitchcock's America / edited by Jonathan Freedman and Richard
Millington.
p. cm.
Includes bibliographical references and index.
ISBN 0-19-511905-3; ISBN 0-19-511906-1 (pbk.)
1. Hitchcock, Alfred, 1899–   —Criticism and interpretation.
2. National characteristics, American, in motion pictures.
3. United States—In motion pictures.   I. Freedman, Jonathan, 1954– .
II. Millington, Richard H., 1953– .
PN1998.3.H58H575 1999
791.43'0233'092—dc21   98-19329

Robert J. Corber, "Hitchcock's Washington," first published in *In the Name of National Security:
Hitchcock, Homophobia, and the Political Construction of Gender in Postwar America,* © 1993.
Reprinted with permission of the author and Duke University Press.

Paula Marantz Cohen, "Hitchcock's Revised American Vision: *The Wrong Man* and *Vertigo,*"
first published in *Alfred Hitchcock: The Legacy of Victorianism,* © 1995.
Reprinted with permission of the University Press of Kentucky.

Amy Lawrence, "American Shame," first published as "Jimmy Stewart in Being Beaten: *Rope* and the
Postwar Crisis in American Masculinity," in *Quarterly Review of Film and Video* 16:1 (1995): 41–58.
Reprinted with permission of the *Quarterly Review of Film and Video.*

1 3 5 7 9 8 6 4 2

Printed in the United States of America
on acid-free paper

Contents

Contributors

Dana Brand is associate professor and chair of the Department of English at Hofstra University. He is the author of *The Spectator and the City in Nineteenth-Century American Literature* (Cambridge University Press, 1991) and of essays on writers from Hawthorne to Nabokov.

Paula Marantz Cohen is a professor of humanities and communication at Drexel University. She is the author of *The Daughter's Dilemma: Family Process and the Nineteenth-Century Domestic Novel* (University of Michigan Press, 1993) and *Alfred Hitchcock: The Legacy of Victorianism* (University Press of Kentucky, 1995). She has written essays on Victorian culture and literature, on Helen Keller, and on Conrad's *Secret Agent* and Hitchcock's *Sabotage*.

Robert J. Corber's most recent book is *Homosexuality in Cold War America: Resistance and the Crisis of Masculinity* (Duke University Press, 1997). He is the author of *In the Name of National Security: Hitchcock, Homophobia, and the Political Construction of Gender in Postwar America* (Duke University Press, 1993) and is coediting, with Donald E. Pease, an anthology of essays by the New York Intellectuals for Duke University Press. He is a member of the core faculty at the New School for Social Research.

Jonathan Freedman is an associate professor of English and American studies at the University of Michigan. He is the author of *Professions of Taste: British Aestheticism, Henry James, and Commodity Culture* (Stanford University Press, 1990) and *The Temple of Culture: Anti-Semitism, Assimilation, and the Making of American Intellectual Life, 1880–1980* (Oxford University Press, forthcoming).

Debra Fried is an associate professor of English and director of graduate studies at Cornell University. She has published essays on poetics, puns, Millay, and George Cukor's *The Women*.

Amy Lawrence is an associate professor of film studies at Dartmouth College and director of the program. She is the author of *Echo and Narcissus: Women's Voices in Classical Hollywood Cinema* (University of California Press, 1991) and *The Films of*

Peter Greenaway (Cambridge University Press, 1997); she has also written on sound, feminism, stardom, and animation.

Elsie B. Michie is an associate professor of English at Louisiana State University. She has written *Outside the Pale: Cultural Exclusion, Gender Difference, and the Victorian Woman Writer* (Cornell University Press, 1993) and essays on gender, economy, and race in the nineteenth-century English novel.

Richard H. Millington is an associate professor of English at Smith College. He is the author of *Practicing Romance: Narrative Form and Cultural Engagement in Hawthorne's Fiction* (Princeton University Press, 1992) and of essays on Hawthorne and Willa Cather.

Michael Wood is a professor of English at Princeton University. Author of widely praised books on Stendahl, Marquez, and Nabokov and many reviews and essays, he has also written *America at the Movies* (Basic Books, 1975) and essays on Buñuel.

Hitchcock's America

Introduction

Jonathan Freedman and Richard Millington

At a certain moment, early in *Shadow of a Doubt*, the two lumpish detectives who have been trailing Uncle Charlie—whom they, and we, know to be the infamous Merry Widow Murderer—pay a call on the home of Charlie's sister Mrs. Newton, in the hypernormal town of Santa Rosa, California. The detectives disguise themselves as reporters for a major American magazine, there to pay tribute to the perfection of the "average" American home. It is all a cover, of course, for their attempts to get to the back of the house and learn all they can about Charlie, who has taken refuge there; but before they are able to do so, they are forced to watch Mrs. Newton—whose husband is obsessed with homicide, whose brother is a psychopath—eagerly pose for their cameras, breaking eggs for an iconic American cake. The perfect American wife, in other words, is being shown by the film to be a perfectly clueless ditz whose obtuseness about her male relations mimics the willed ignorance of human desires enacted throughout her self-idealized small town. But something more is at work here as well. Her very normativeness is being demonstrated to be wholly simulacral, both a pose for and the creation of the media who ostensibly record it—and, it hardly needs to be added, a pose for and a creation of Hitchcock's self-conscious, self-mocking camera as well.

This moment succinctly registers and prophesies, as do few we can think of from contemporary films or literature, transformations then rapidly under way in American life and intensifying in the years to follow. The film understands and comments on the increasing power of interconnected media like the middlebrow magazine and the Hollywood film not merely to record the expectations or the fantasies of the mass American audience but also to shape its very behavior. Too, it would seem to anticipate, and critique in advance, the policing of gender identities that marked the later 1940s—especially by those cultural forces urging women to return from factories to homes very much like the Newtons' in the

Hitchcock's "suburbia"

years immediately following the end of the war. It is prescient as well in its understanding of the ways that the small-town ideal of American midwestern life was being imported on a mass scale to that most congenial of locales, California, and the ways this hybrid constructed a model for America's newly hegemonic social artifact, the suburb. And, perhaps most important, it depends for its essential structure on a set of narrative devices familiar to Americans and Americanists alike: the opposition between the city—home of crime, sexual depravity, and lonely, familyless women to be preyed on by the likes of the Merry Widow killer—and the small town—home of family values, republican virtues, and quiet evenings at home spent reading gruesome accounts of murder. And as that last image suggests, the film deconstructs this culturally resonant dichotomy by importing the sexuality and madness culturally associated with the former to the seeming innocence and purity of the latter and watching its shadows get cast on the ostensibly—if not ostentatiously—normative structures of American life.

To be sure, *Shadow of a Doubt*'s screenplay was written by the author of *Our Town*, the definitive middlebrow examination of the persistence of small-town pastoralism in the American imaginary; but its thematics are hardly absent in Hitchcock's other work. Consider, for example, *Psycho*, which translates *Shadow*'s narrative pattern into the tale of a young, love-seeking embezzler who leaves the corrupt city to meet her Gothic doom in the twisted heart of the nuclear family, at the hands of a madman taxidermist cum transvestite. Remarkably witty and powerfully critical, too, is the film's creation of a new primal scene for the American Gothic: the motel. (The Gothic, it is worth remembering here, has been a narrative particularly favored by American writers from Charles Brockden Brown through Poe through Faulkner and Flannery O'Connor through Stephen King). Or consider *The Trouble with Harry*, which does to the New England countryside what *Shadow of a Doubt* and *Psycho* do to California and motel-culture respectively, or the ironic tour Hitchcock conducts of the most resonant iconography of American cultural life in *North by Northwest*. And consider the insistence, in so many of his American films from *Rope* through *Psycho* through *Frenzy*, on the presence of alternative or "deviant" forms of sexuality at the very center of the middle-class sensibility and its cultural institutions—or, in the case of *Strangers on a Train* (as Rob Corber argues), at the center of the national security state itself.

It is our contention in this volume that Hitchcock's varied deployments of American public spaces, cultural narratives, literary traditions, iconography, and ideological crosscurrents are not adventitious, accidental, or marginal. Rather, we suggest that at the center of Hitchcock's Hollywood films stands a sustained, specific, and extraordinarily acute exploration of American culture. In doing so, we hope to help fill a considerable gap in the criticism of this most often studied of filmmakers, and to see his work in a new light. For while the formal precision and psychological power of Hitchcock's art have generated brilliant readings of individual films and provided the occasion for important theoretical arguments about the experience of film spectatorship, there has been surprisingly little published criticism that looks in a focused way at Hitchcock as an interpreter of American culture. For the most part, Hitchcock emerges from the critical tradition as a Jamesian master, as a psychological "case," as a (perhaps *the*) conduit for the male gaze, as the site through which ideology plays. We would suggest, to the contrary, that he might be viewed as an indispensable historian, critic, and analyst of American middle-class culture from the 1940s through the 1970s.

As the essays we have gathered here demonstrate, to see that the condition of American culture is the prevailing subject of Hitchcock's Hollywood films is to discover a new way to describe and value his work. It is to notice, for example, the consistent way in which individualism and domesticity, the interdependent and conflicting ideals of American middle-class ideology from Tocqueville to Dan Quayle, serve as the focus of his films. (One need only think about how different Hitchcock's American families are from their British counterparts to see his com-

mitment to rendering the distinctive social textures of the culture he examines.)
It is to see his movies as a series of lucid interrogations of the totems of American
life—the cult of motherhood, the mythology of the masterful male—and the institutions that celebrate, interpret, and patrol our cultural terrain: advertising, the
judicial system, psychiatry, the police, the movies themselves. Indeed, it is to describe in a new way Hitchcock's notorious self-referentiality: No other director has
used the conditions of Hollywood movie-making—the star, the special effect, the
set, the equation between camera and film audience—to comment so richly on
what films do and what we have come (and have been taught) to expect of them,
and through them, of ourselves. From the perspective we offer here, many of the
elements of Hitchcock's art—the yearnings of the private self, the shape of gender
roles, the deep strangeness of the normal, the rich self-consciousness about the
social or psychic meanings of film technique—emerge not simply as discrete themes
or issues but as parts of an ongoing enterprise of cultural diagnosis. Working at
a time when the ideological web that composes the sign "America" was being reconstructed and recodified with particular intensity, Hitchcock, we are suggesting,
was engaged simultaneously in a rich interpretation of the American middle-class
culture that was the object of this social project and in providing the "thick description" that makes such interpretation convincing and generative.[1]

Let us be clear at the outset, however, that our goal is not to produce an
"American" Hitchcock—a naturalized, or even nationally identified, version of that
distinctive figure. For one thing, we write from a perspective that calls into question
the naturalness of the category "American," seeing it (as we see Hitchcock seeing
it) as a constructed or produced artifact of discordant, competing, and complicating
social forces and ideological pressures. For another, we want to place Hitchcock
in the long and distinguished tradition of responses to a relentlessly self-defining
nation by travelers to its shores. Thus, we propose that one should think of Hitchcock as something of a twentieth-century Tocqueville, anatomizing the lineaments
of American culture and society, testing and contesting the "habits of the heart"
that make America America. Indeed, like Tocqueville, Hitchcock renders as he
interrogates the varied forms taken by a complex democratic society—except that
in Hitchcock's case, this culture has engendered formations that Tocqueville would
never have imagined, like the suburb, the roadside, the motel, the advertising industry; and except that Hitchcock's meditation on their cultural effects are implicit,
suggestive, and mordant.

Or, to cite a slightly different analogue, Hitchcock might be placed alongside
the exiles from European persecution and unrest who flocked to Los Angeles during
the war, especially those German directors and actors who reshaped the visual and
narrative practices of the American film industry. (Hitchcock learned the elements
of his craft quite literally alongside many of these figures: apprenticing at UFA,
the German film studio, he brought with him many of the same techniques that
the *noir* writers, actors, and directors imported first into the British,

then more directly into the American cinema.) More specifically, and as Fredric Jamerson has noticed, Hitchcock's encounter with America might be seen as resembling that of the European artists, philosophers, and novelists who joined him in exile in America and who found an ironic haven in southern California. Indeed, this latter analogy is perhaps the most fruitful one, and not only because Hitchcock could have bumped shoulders with Mann, Brecht, Schoenberg, Adorno, and Horkheimer in the Los Angeles of the 1940s. Like the last two of these in particular, Hitchcock never lost his sense of thorough alienation from the country and culture in which he found himself, manifested in small ways and large. In his personal life, Hitchcock delighted in playing the stereotypical Englishman: high tea at the Hitchcocks' was a Hollywood institution, and frequently only fellow English exiles were invited, on the theory that only such people could appreciate the tea ceremony. (This gesture was of course a highly equivocal one, since Hitchcock's lower-middle-class origins made his attempts to play the aristocrat in exile an oddly American gesture of class conquest through personal reinvention.) And in his filmmaking, as in the arguments mounted by Horkheimer and Adorno, Hitchcock understood—and in his case, exploited—the central role that the entertainment industry increasingly took in remaking social, cultural, and affectional life within the American public sphere.

Which suggests our last possible comparison between Hitchcock and other cultural observers: not as a Frankfurt-style cultural critic but as a variant of the anthropological or ethnographic participant observer, living among people who are profoundly "other" the better to fathom their manners, mores, and culture. In making the comparison, we don't mean to invoke the vision of the hypercivilized European recording the doings of benighted "natives"—although at times this is an element of Hitchcock's self-presentation, particularly in the ways he mischievously played on American cultural insecurities by embodying the droll, deadpan English observer. Rather, the vicissitudes of Hitchcock's response to the cultural apparatus in which he was enmeshed places him in the midst of the ethnographic problems of participant observation—of how one is to be a part of the culture that one claims to observe; of how one is to observe a culture one affects by being there; and of how the means of representation themselves can register these problematics. The anthropologist's practice of participant observation is of course central to Hitchcock's self-presentation—to his witty appearances in his own films, to the irony he brought to their advertising campaigns, to the arch commentary he offered as part of his own television programs, even to the marketing of the *Alfred Hitchcock Mystery Magazine*. A particularly campy but resonant variant of this strategy may summarize its self-incriminating wit: in the theatrical trailer for *Frenzy*, Hitchcock offers his American audience a tour of London, with special attention to the places where the murders of the film are committed; then shows himself lurking outside one crime scene; then steps into the shot to take a tie off the neck of a strangled woman and tie it firmly around his own.

But as that last example suggests, in all of these venues, Hitchcock performed a keen and knowing transformation of himself into "Hitchcock"—a commodified distillation of his own personality, a readily vended version of his own readily recognized profile, a light-hearted embodiment of the very perversity he analyzed so powerfully in his films. And to make the matter even more complex, Hitchcock placed himself in the midst of that cultural formation by adopting this stance of the detached observer—a stance that works precisely by disavowing such partic- ipation even while indulging it to the hilt. Which suggests one last metaphor for Hitchcock's self-presentation: not just anthropologist or European culture critic but avid participant in a distinctive American tradition of narrative address. Like Haw- thorne's Miles Coverdale or Faulkner's Quentin Compson or, in a powerfully pos- itive vein, the speaker of Whitman's *Song of Myself*, he crafts a position for himself "both in and out of the game and watching and wondering at it"; but Hitchcock's is a game, we are repeatedly forced to remind ourselves, whose rules he himself wrote and profited from. And it is finally this double sense, we would suggest, that needs to be brought to the analysis of Hitchcock's American films. At once maker and beholder, insider and outsider, canny participant and critical observer, Hitch- cock needs to be approached with the same wary sophistication and cultural spec- ificity that he brings to his own magisterial participant observation, not only in the American film industry but in American culture itself.

THERE ARE PRESENTLY as many voices and positions within Hitchcock criticism as within film studies generally, and in emphasizing the need for this project, we don't want to overstate its uniqueness. To a certain extent, the very fact that we have been able to gather the essays in this volume from contributors in a number of different fields suggests that this kind of historicizing work—whether undertaken under the sign of American studies, cultural studies, or film studies—is coming increasingly to the fore. But it is no accident that it is in relation to film that this work is taking place: for here the imperative felt within all these fields toward a more historically specific and culturally alert criticism is registered with the greatest—and most ramifying—power. For film offers not only, as critics since Benjamin (and Vachel Lindsay) have been reminding us, a radically new form of apprehension for a radically new kind of audience—one organized by the logic of the mass, in Benjamin's influential terms—but also a new way of thinking about the powers of visual representation at the moment of modernity. And this new framework has led to fresh conceptions of cinema and history alike. As far as the former is concerned, Leo Charney and Vanessa Schwartz have recently put the matter succinctly: "Cinema . . . must not be conceived as simply an outgrowth of such forms as melodramatic theater, social narrative, and the nineteenth-century realistic novel. . . . Nor can technological histories sufficiently explain the emer- gence of cinema. Rather, cinema must be reunderstood as a vital component of a broader culture of modern life which encompassed political, social, economic, and cultural transformations."[2] But as that last sentence suggests, this "reunderstanding" works both ways. Even as cinema historians extend the vocabulary with which they speak of this new cultural form—and here we might think not only of Charney and Schwartz's volume but also of the pathbreaking work of Miriam Hansen and Tom Gunning on early cinema, or of the works included in a recent anthology edited by Vivian Sobchack on film and history—so too cultural historians have had to reckon increasingly with cinema's emergence. Thus, historians like Lary May, Lizabeth Cohen, and Michael Rogin have devoted rich and sustained attention to movies as they attempt to tell new stories about consumerism, working-class culture, racial narrativity. Others have extended film theory's concern with spectatorship into accounts of other cultural formations: Robert Allen and Eric Lott have sought to reorient our understanding of burlesque and blackface mistrelsy, respectively, with explicit reference to 1970s feminist film theory. Still others have understood that this new medium poses problems to the historical enterprise itself: one thinks here of a recent anthology edited by Robert Rosenstone, *Revisioning History*, in which twelve historians respond to the challenge posed not only by the presence of film *in* history but to the very narrative and epistemological assumptions *of* history.[3]

The authors of this volume come from a number of different disciplines—film studies, American studies, English—that have been touched by the developments we have outlined above. While they have different responses to the imperatives that shape film studies and cultural history alike, they understand and seek to participate in this newer understanding of film's complex and entangled relation with the cultural and the historical, not only with respect to Hitchcock but also with respect to to his milieu and moment. To be sure, they have had ample precedent. The way toward such a view of Hitchcock was—like so many other kinds of attentiveness toward his films—first pointed out some time ago by Robin Wood, in his seminal essay on the cultural embeddedness of film genres, "Ideology, Genre, Auteur" (1976). The work of Tania Modleski, with its lucid and concrete identification of the social stakes of Hitchcock's complex representation of women, can be read simultaneously as a work of feminist engagement and of cultural history, as can that of other feminist critics who have broken away from a too predictable concern with a reified and monolithic Lacanian lingo of "the gaze." From a Marxist perspective, Virginia Wexman has challenged the social myopia of academic Hitchcock criticism, while Leonard Leff and Robert Kapsis have studied the material circumstances that shaped his filmmaking and established the trajectory of his reputation.[4]

Even as one acknowledges this powerful, still emerging body of work, to look back upon the history of Hitchcock criticism is to be struck by how long it took for Wood's insight to bear fruit. Instead, a classic ideological battle—between a Lacan-derived account of Hitchcock's films as unintentional dramatizations of an inevitable ideological entrapment and the Hitchcock who, for Stanley Cavell and associates, instantiates in his heroic authorship a rich and untrammeled personal agency—has paradoxically obscured the extent to which ideology itself might be understood as the *subject* of Hitchcock's work.[5] It was thus, from the point of view of this volume, an important moment when Fredric Jameson, in a review of William Rothman's *The Murderous Gaze*, again suggested that we should ask, What are Hitchcock's films (not the celebration, not the instrument, but) the history of? And the answers that both Jameson and Slavoj Žižek—operating, it seems, as a loosely organized intellectual "firm"—have proposed have been no less valuable and suggestive. One thinks, for instance, of Jameson's suggestion that we might set aside the "banalities" of plot and theme and "admire Hitchcock's eye for the peculiarly invisible yet material nodes in which daily life can be detected," or that we might glimpse via *North by Northwest*'s "spatial system" the ideological configurations of late capitalism. Or one might instance Žižek's similarly striking linking of the phases of Hitchcock's work to—simultaneously—the three stages of twentieth-century cultural history (realism, modernism, postmodernism), the three types of twentieth-century male character (the "autonomous" subject, the insipid organization man, and the "pathological narcissist"), and three Lacanian "objects," or his identification of "the ultimate social-ideological lesson of *Psycho*" as "the collapse of the very field of intersubjectivity as medium of Truth in late capitalism, its disintegration into the two poles of expert knowledge and psychotic 'private' truth."

Yet as these citations perhaps indicate, when Jameson and Žižek "do" history, they do it in the manner of the Recording Angel: sweepingly, as from a great height, and already furnished, one surmises, with a pretty clear sense of what patterns are likely to emerge.[6] And herein lies the occasion of our volume. While our essayists share with Jameson and Žižek their central historicizing question, readers will discover that these essays are disposed to perform their historical work more from the ground up than from the sky down; and if Jameson and Žižek show us Hitchcock doing the work or serving the turn of a magisterial cultural analysis, these essays will suggest that he fulfills no less interestingly the social and cultural historian's dictum that historical "cases" become significantly representative only by being fully particular.

"I do not mean to prescribe rules to strong and valiant natures," wrote Thoreau in *Walden*. While all of the essays we have gathered participate energetically in the project we have been defining, we have not dreamed of prescribing or selecting for a particular view of the complex relation between Hitchcock's movies and American ideology. All of our essayists perform that task in ways distinctively their own. In our opening essay, "Love, American Style: Hitchcock's Hollywood," Debra Fried takes an ingeniously concrete approach to Hitchcock's "Americanness," proposing that America presented itself to Hitchcock, most directly, as a specific set of working conditions—intrusive management, stock shots, stars, genres—associated with the Hollywood studio system. Through a careful discussion of his use, in the earlier American films, of the workaday and conventional elements of the established Hollywood style, Fried shows how Hitchcock deploys these apparently constraining practices to deepen the expression of his characteristic themes. He thus, paradoxically, makes his films more intensely individualistic and, as he does so, conducts an oblique and implicit meditation on the questions of individual freedom and social constraint so central both to his own work and to the American ideology he encounters. Fried's interest in the thematic reverberations of "technical" choices returns in our final essay, Michael Wood's "Fearful Cemetery." Wood's analysis of *Family Plot*, Hitchcock's last film, begins with the director's claim that what really interested him about this project was plottedness itself, the "structural image" of two inevitably converging narratives. Wood shows how the experience of inhabiting a plot, made visible in several key shots, becomes crucially expressive in the film, eliciting more fully than any episode the fantasies and paradoxes that compose American freedom.

Four of the essayists look to the movies they discuss for insight about some of the central cultural transformations and ideological tensions of the postwar years. In "Unveiling Maternal Desires: Hitchcock and American Domesticity," Elsie B. Michie places *Shadow of a Doubt* and the American remake of *The Man Who Knew Too Much* in relation to vigorous attempts to shore up the ideology of domesticity in the aftermath of World War II. She presents these films not as participating in that ideological enforcement but as themselves interested in and revealing about the figure of the "good mother" and the tensions latent within that cultural icon—tensions expressed especially in "liminal" scenes (at the border between the domestic sphere and the world it defends against), where the films' maternal characters find ways to express the costs of their fulfillment of that role. In "From *Spellbound* to *Vertigo*: Alfred Hitchcock and Therapeutic Culture in America," Jonathan Freedman examines Hitchcock's attitude toward American culture through his changing response to the massive popularization of psychoanalysis in America, in which proliferating mass media advertised that therapeutic regime as a cure for all ailments, personal or social. While *Spellbound* powerfully celebrates and helps establish the cultural authority of psychoanalysis, with *Vertigo* Hitchcock dismantles the edifice he has helped to construct, demonstrating the inadequacy of both psychoanalysis and detection—Hollywood's twin schematics of solution—to do more than exacerbate the very irrationalities they pretend to cure.

For both Michie and Freedman, Hitchcock is a formidable analyst of American culture not because he is above ideology in some heroic way but because he is so deeply enmeshed in it: Indeed, for Freedman, it is precisely because Hitchcock acknowledges his own role in the "psychoanalysis boom" of the 1940s that he is able to diagnose its proliferation in the 1950s. For the next two essayists, in contrast, his films are presented as sites of intense historical interest precisely because they do not or cannot fully acknowledge the meanings they contain. In

"American Shame: *Rope*, James Stewart, and the Postwar Crisis in American Masculinity," Amy Lawrence interprets *Rope* not as a technical tour de force but as obliquely exploring and confronting, through the figure of Jimmy Stewart, the guilt generated by World War II—guilt produced by the difficulty of distinguishing between "moral" and "immoral" acts of murder. Her argument is doubly contextual, proposing that Stewart's meaning within the film—and for his culture—is shaped both by the distinctive version of masculinity expressed in the history of his previous roles and by the audience's knowledge of his immediate personal history: his experience as a bomber pilot (never publicly described, but powerful precisely because of that reticence). Robert J. Corber's "Hitchcock's Washington: Spectatorship, Ideology, and the 'Homosexual Menace' in *Strangers on a Train*" interprets that film as an intricate exercise in the ideological enforcement so characteristic of the 1950s. In making his argument, Corber complicates the customary Oedipal model of spectatorship, proposing that *Strangers* is shaped, most crucially, by its structuring of the male viewer's much more fluid identification with its two main characters. He shows how the film plays out, in its narrative and its orchestration of audience response, the construction of a "homosexual menace" in medical and legal discourse—and the attempt to control such "deviance" in the social drama of government purges. And he argues that the massive effort at social discipline the film participates in is, finally, less an attempt to punish homosexuals than to instruct its audience in their need to discipline themselves against the dangers of unstable identities and the lure of social upheaval more generally. Indeed, its most crucial target may be not a menacing homoerotic desire but unruly women, resisting their postwar return to domesticity.

Three essays in the collection explore Hitchcock's engagement with American culture through his examination of "the American character," the analysis of which was one of the central intellectual preoccupations of his era. In "Rear-View Mirror: Hitchcock, Poe, and the Flaneur in America," Dana Brand connects L. B. Jeffries, via Hitchcock's intense interest in Poe, to two cultural fantasy figures who embody strategies for mastering the city: the flaneur and his more active counterpart, the detective. Brand reads the film, in the tradition of Poe, as a profound critique both of the reductiveness of prevailing American schemes for understanding reality and of the narcissistic masculinity—callous, lonely, and figuratively violent—that sponsors it. Richard Millington's "Hitchcock and American Character: The Comedy of Self-Construction in *North by Northwest*" sees the work of that film as at once diagnostic and curative. As the movie sends Cary Grant's Roger Thornhill on a tour of the mythic landscape of American individualism, it analyzes the mechanisms by which American character is mass produced, separates Thornhill from his own evacuated identity, and suggests a strategy for the reclamation of something that might be understood as freedom. The film emerges from this analysis as a canny, consciously paradoxical attempt to use the movies—perhaps the most powerful of the engines of American self-production—to disrupt that very process. Paula Marantz Cohen's "Hitchcock's Revised American Vision: *The Wrong Man* and *Vertigo*" sees a shift in Hitchcock's way of representing character as an articulation of a large-scale cultural change: the decline of the explanatory and emotional power of a nineteenth-century, "novelistic" model of character growth and gender complementarity, in which full selfhood is achieved through the creation of the couple. While in his earlier films Hitchcock had labored to translate this model to the movies, in *The Wrong Man* and *Vertigo*, Cohen argues, he begins its dismantling.

These brief summaries demonstrate the range of interest and versatility of approach of our contributors' work; at the same time, similarities emerge that, taken together, begin to define a new direction for the study of Hitchcock. First, the essays exemplify, in their way of going about their work, a conviction that the ideological force of Hitchcock's American films—and, along with that, inferences about Hitchcock's degree of control over what his films enable us to see—can only emerge from the most careful scrutiny of the individual films, rather than from the application of a prior, abstract narrative about ideology's "operation." Second, a shared interest in Hitchcock as a historian—or as providing materials through which history might distinctively be written—emerges in a common emphasis on the ways his films both enact and register central cultural transformations of the postwar years. Finally, there is a common move, unsurprising in its intellectual logic but quite striking in its results, toward contextualization as an interpretive strategy. Readers of this volume will thus find the meanings of Hitchcock's films illuminated by an extraordinary range of materials—the actualities of the studio production system, a Senate Appropriations Committee report on homosexuals in the State Department, a *Life* magazine tribute to the power of psychoanalysis, the plot structure of the cigarette ad, a J. Edgar Hoover essay on domesticity, to take a handful of examples—that in themselves testify to the richness and particularity of Hitchcock's encounter with America.

THREE OF OUR ESSAYS have been previously published. Robert J. Corber's "Hitchcock's Washington" is taken from his book *In the Name of National Security: Hitchcock, Homophobia, and the Political Construction of Gender in Postwar America*, copyright © 1993, reprinted with permission of the author and Duke University Press. Paula Marantz Cohen's essay comes from her *Alfred Hitchcock: The Legacy of Victorianism*, copyright © 1995, reprinted with permission of the University Press of Kentucky. And Amy Lawrence's "American Shame" was first published as "Jimmy Stewart Is Being Beaten: *Rope* and the Postwar Crisis in American Masculinity," in *Quarterly Review of Film and Video* 16:1 (1995): 41–58. We are most grateful for permission to reproduce all of this work here.

Photo stills were provided by the Film Stills Archive of the Museum of Modern Art in New York City; we are grateful to Terry Geesken and Mary Corliss for their gracious assistance.

Notes

1. For a valuable account of the history of middle-class ideology from 1940 to 1960, emphasizing a reemergent domesticity, see Elaine Tyler May, *Homeward Bound: American Families* ˙ *.old War Era* (New York: Basic Books, 1988), esp. chap. 1.

2. ˙inema and the Invention of Modern Life (Berkeley: University of California Press, 1995), 10.

3. See Miriam Hansen, *Babel and Babylon: Spectatorship in American Silent Film* (Cambridge: Harvard University Press, 1991); Tom Gunning, *D. W. Griffith and the Origins of American Narrative Film: The Early Years at Biograph* (Urbana: University of Illinois Press, 1991); Vivian Sobchack, ed., *The Persistence of History: Cinema, Television, and the Modern Event* (New York: Routledge, 1996); Lary May, *Screening Out the Past: The Birth of Mass Culture and the Motion Picture Industry* (Chicago: University of Chicago Press, 1983); Lizabeth Cohen, *Making a New Deal: Industrial Workers in Chicago, 1919–1939* (New York: Cambridge University Press, 1990); Michael Paul Rogin, " 'The Sword Became a Flashing Vision': D. W. Griffith's *The Birth of a Nation*," *Representations* 9 (1985): 150–95; Robert C. Allen, *Horrible Prettiness: Burlesque and American Culture* (Chapel Hill: University of North Carolina Press, 1991); Eric Lott, *Love and Theft: Blackface Minstrelsy and the American Working Class* (New York: Oxford University Press, 1993); Robert A. Rosenstone, ed., *Revisioning History: Film and the Construction of a New Past* (Princeton: Princeton University Press, 1995).

4. See Robin Wood, *Hitchcock's Films Revisited* (New York: Columbia University Press, 1989); Tania Modleski, *The Women Who Knew Too Much: Hitchcock and Feminist Theory* (New York: Metheun, 1988); Virginia Wexman, "The Critic as Consumer: Film Study in the University, *Vertigo*, and the Film Canon," *Film Quarterly* 39 (1986): 32–41; Leonard Leff, *Hitchcock and Selznick* (New York: Weidenfeld and Nicolson, 1987); Robert E. Kapsis, *Hitchcock: The Making of a Reputation* (Chicago: University of Chicago Press, 1992). This discussion is not intended as a survey of extant Hitchcock scholarship. For a rich and substantial introduction to Hitchcock criticism, see the superb anthology edited by Marshall Deutelbaum and Leland Poague, *A Hitchcock Reader* (Ames: Iowa State University Press, 1986).

5. We have in mind here the remarkable work of Raymond Bellour and that of his followers, and essays that have grown out of the influential account of film spectatorship advanced by Laura Mulvey. What might be called the "school" of Cavell is not numerous, but the subtlety and intellectual intensity of its members' work has made it influential; they include Marian Keane, William Rothman, and, of course, Cavell himself. The compulsion to quote Shakespeare in essays on Hitchcock seems to be an identifying trait. Rothman has produced the most work on Hitchcock, but the characteristic tone seems to derive from the philosopher.

6. See Fredric Jameson, "Allegorizing Hitchcock," in *Signatures of the Visible* (New York: Routledge, 1990), 99–127 (the citation appears on 110); and "Spatial Systems in *North by Northwest*," in Slavoj Žižek, ed., *Everything You Always Wanted to Know about Lacan (But Were Afraid to Ask Hitchcock)*, 47–72. See Žižek's introduction to the latter volume, "Alfred Hitchcock, or, The Form and its Historical Mediation," 1–12; his essay in that volume on *Psycho*, "In His Bold Gaze My Ruin Is Writ Large," 211–72 (citation, 262); and his "The Hitchcockian Blot," reprinted in James Naremore, ed., *North by Northwest* (New Brunswick, N.J.: Rutgers University Press, 1993), 221–27.

I

Love, American Style
Hitchcock's Hollywood

Debra Fried

Hitchcock responds to American culture in his use of the filmmaking institutions that were put at his disposal when he crossed the Atlantic in 1940. When they begin to be made in Hollywood, Hitchcock's films join a large body of major studio releases, with their constellation of conventions, techniques, and genres. By looking at how Hitchcock turns these devices to his own account, we can see not only how his American films inflect and enrich the possibilities of such conventions but also how such conventions become a shorthand in his commentary on American culture. This is not to deny that the British studios (Ealing, Gainsborough) had their own, often similar, conventions and procedures, which are to some degree reflected in Hitchcock's British films. But the power, scale, and rigidity of the institutions of movie-making were markedly greater in America than in Britain.

Once he starts working for independent producer David O. Selznick, Hitchcock's commentary on America is in some measure the product of the American studio machine that largely defines American culture for Americans and the world. As a director not quite fully expatriate but merely transplanted, Hitchcock might seem equipped to reveal features of American life no other director could see. But in Hollywood, directors may often be more cattle than auteurs. Both on and off the set, the director is subject to front office control and redefinition: A director's scripts are reviewed, his shooting schedule watched, his public image marketed. All this control might seem decidedly un-American, and this notion governs one strain of writing about directorial style in the classic studio system.

In his 1986 study of Frank Capra's films, *American Vision*, Raymond Carney reads in the Capra hero's attempts to escape the constricting social web a mirror of Capra the director's own chafing for self-expression against the claims of the studio system. In a passing note, Carney champions what he sees as Capra's improvisatory, actor-oriented directorial style over Hitchcock's meticulously planned cinematography, in which the actor is, in Carney's view, eclipsed and indeed turned into "cattle," as Hitchcock notoriously joked they were. Carney compares Capra's and Hitchcock's use of James Stewart in this respect: "Hitchcock's Stewart *is* cattle—weak, vulnerable, victimized, passive, reacting to events beyond his control. Capra's Stewart is a man threatened with being treated as cattle by everyone around him, whose very task is to resist what Hitchcock's Stewart is forced to accept by the visual tendentiousness and narrative coercions of Hitchcock's aesthetic."[1] For Carney, the Hitchcock aesthetic becomes identified with his directorial style both as evident onscreen and as we understand it to be offscreen, and on the sound stage during and before the filming; and this style of control over the actor, as over every other feature of production, translates into the plot's control over the hero, a control he is "forced to accept" by the very manner of Hitchcock's filmmaking.

It is not new, of course, to suggest that Hitchcock's rigid control over the production of his own films and over individual devices in them has something to do with the loss of control to which so many of his heroes fall victim. Robin Wood's 1977 formulation is perhaps the most balanced:

> As soon as one begins to contemplate Hitchcock's work thematically, it becomes evident that its technical elaborations, the manifest desire to control audiences, have a thematic extension. . . . The desire to control, the terror of losing control: such phrases describe not only Hitchcock's conscious relationship to technique and to his audiences, but also the thematic center of his films. The personal relationships that fascinate Hitchcock invariably involve the exercise of power, or its obverse, impotence.

In 1989 Wood returned to this earlier idea with somewhat different emphasis:

> Domination—power/impotence as two sides of the same coin—is clearly the central concern (one might say the driving obsession) of Hitchcock's work on all levels, methodological, stylistic, thematic; the distinction of that work—its importance for us today—lies in the ways in which that obsession is pursued to the point where its mechanisms, its motivations, its monstrousness, are thoroughly exposed.[2]

While issues of control and power pervade his career, Hitchcock's articulation of this "thematic center" takes on an American accent in Hollywood.

Carney's view poses an important question for the student of Hitchcock as interpreter of American culture. For Carney, when the beleaguered Capra hero rebels, we cheer because we see in his protest the same spirit of defiance of the big boss that continually animates Capra's work on the studio lot (a favorite Capra bad guy like Edward Arnold would cut a good figure behind a desk in the front office). When Hitchcock heroes (at least the ones played by Stewart) rebel, we wince because we see in their fruitless protest the iron grip of the filmmaker (and much has been written on how Hitchcock's villains can be seen as director-surrogates). What's wrong with this logic (aside from its assumption, which bears some scrutiny, that a director who portrays a successful protest against societal strictures is superior to one who portrays unsuccessful protests)?

Because he is working in a major studio, in the early 1940s, under the close surveillance of Selznick and others, Hitchcock too is in a state of defiance on the studio lot, but his defiance takes a different form from Capra's.[3] It is precisely by curtailing the improvisatory in the profilmic event that Hitchcock wrests control from the studio moguls—an act of self-assertion that in Carney's argument about Capra is necessarily good. Selznick was used to keeping his hand on the reins by requiring from his directors a large number of repeated takes in the dailies from which he could choose what to edit together into the final cut. Selznick's method of control is based on proliferation, selection, and discarding—the more footage left on the cutting room floor, the greater Selznick's control over the final product.

Leonard J. Leff, among others, has suggested that in the stocky, white-haired Raymond Burr of *Rear Window* Hitchcock presents a jokey double for Selznick (who would do to Hitchcock's films what the Burr character does to his wife's corpse), and in the empty "O." of "Roger O. Thornhill" he mocks David O. Selnick's pretensions.[4] While it is hard to be certain how illuminating such anecdotal surmises are for thinking about Hitchcock's relation to his first American producer, we might venture in this vein that the repeated, pointless, wearying burying and unburying and reburying of Harry all in one day in *The Trouble with Harry* may be a figure for the deadly rhythms of shooting a film Selznick-style, with many repeated takes.

One recalls in this regard Hitchcock's punning game of inventing an ideal film crew, starring "Dolly Shot" and "Ward Robe" and directed by "Manny Takes." Hitchcock was no Manny Takes. His meticulous diagramming of the film before the camera's roll enabled him to shoot less footage each day for the rushes than Selznick's other directors. According to this logic, Hitchcock thus gains control over Selznick by eliminating spontaneous choice throughout the filmmaking—from lighting man to star. He can shoot it once, and shoot it right, because it has all been envisioned in the storyboard. Now we could say that this makes Hitchcock the director more like his scheming villains, with their elaborately wrought plots, than like his heroes, who are unwittingly thrown into those plots and whose seemingly zigzag random itineraries (*Foreign Correspondent, Saboteur,* and *North by Northwest* come to mind) reflect the villain's careful planning. Bad guys plan, good guys act spontaneously: certainly there is some truth to the claim that this is a prevailing myth of Hollywood narratives. Yet against the studio system's

Hitchcock in Hollywood: lending his own shading to certain stock conventions

attempt to turn him into cattle, Hitchcock refines a cinematic style (already largely in place in his British work) that allows him to control the film.

This style of filming a minutely preconceived scenario, by making the work of the actor part of the mise-en-scène, places the actor as identifiable star in the limelight and makes casting a particularly telling interpretive act. If actors are mise-en-scène, then Cary Grant is there to be recognizably Cary Grant, as Mt. Rushmore is there to be recognizably Mt. Rushmore. Grant is Grant, as Robert Benchley is plainly himself in *Foreign Correspondent* and as Hitchcock is plainly Hitchcock in his cameo appearances, particularly in the American films. The practice that viewers like Carney see as reducing the actor to obedient puppet going through the motions, particularly in the American films, underlines and relies on the actor's status as star.[5]

The developing canon of Hitchcock's American films lends its own shading to certain stock conventions and techniques of classical editing, as well as the use of certain stars. Since the Hollywood industry turned out thousands of films in the classic continuity style, the capacity of any one of its arsenal of devices either to accumulate meaning, from reuse in movie after movie, or to grow meaningless with iteration is very great indeed. Just as a familiar star cast in a revisionary genre can take on new meanings, familiar devices of editing and composition and other "automatized elements can shed their familiarity and become intriguing."[6]

Take a device as simple as the cutaway (even the most hackneyed, like the cut to a ringing telephone) across Hitchcock's work. The famous cutaway in Hitchcock's *Suspicion*—the snapping shut of Joan Fontaine's purse as she refuses Cary Grant's first kiss—indicates Fontaine's fearful withholding less through the obvious symbol of the closing purse than in its contrast to the fluid camera traveling around the reciprocal kiss they share later, in her father's study (a similar camera movement glorifies the final Grant-Bergman embrace in *Notorious*). It is as if the unaccepted kiss is figured in the need for, or the reliance upon, editing. Yet such a cutaway can be predictive as well: The cutaway to Pamela's hand releasing her reading glasses when Robert Donat kisses her on the train, at their first meeting, predicts her eventual yielding to him. For it is hard to imagine a fully motivated use of the cutaway—to any detail hidden or muted or offscreen in the preceding shot—in the editing of a kiss that is accepted and returned; indeed, at least in Hitchcock's grammar of editing love scenes, the long take for the long reciprocal kiss seems to be a house rule. If an explanatory or emblematic detail is to be included in a sanctioned kiss, it is best incorporated via camera movement— as when Hitchcock tracks back to the long shot from the close-up of Olivier and Fontaine's kiss in *Rebecca*, to discover the huge fireplace with its dancing flames, in front of which they embrace. A straight cut from the close-up of the clinch to the leaping fire would be parodic, maladroit, snickering, as if a lover glanced at his watch midkiss. The cutaway to the fireworks behind Grace Kelly and Cary Grant in *To Catch a Thief* is one instance of the cutaway in a love scene used for parodic intent, in this case largely to mock the pretensions of the Grace Kelly character. One might then turn to the extension of this Hitchcockian house style for love scenes, in seeing the shower-murder in *Psycho* as a "kiss" so unreturned, so qualified in its motivations, that it is *all* cutaways, an embrace fragmented and decentered into a score of details of the scene, fragmented, ultimately, into its ever threatening cousin, murder.

Another instance: In the noticeably artificial shots involving rear-projected landscapes in such films as *Spellbound, Notorious,* and *Vertigo,* Hitchcock employs a shopworn device to the ends of psychological portrayal. In classic studio films, rear projection, sometimes called a process shot, is a way to save the time and expense of filming on location. It might be seen as merely a patent instance of the budgetary concerns of a film leaving their mark on its style of representation; and to some degree it is true that the entire style of continuity editing reminds us of the division of labor in film production and the practice of shooting a film "out of continuity" so that it may be edited into continuity later. But the student of Hitchcock's films as commentary on American culture may begin to think of this cliché—a mere convenience, really—as a convention: that is, as a meaningful device, a cinematic shorthand, not simply a shortcut.

In Hitchcock's American films, the flatness of such backgrounds reflect illusions or incompletely scrutinized passions in the characters performing in front of them. Rear projection is almost inevitable in filming the car chases and shared car rides that become more prominent in Hitchcock's American productions, and this method of filming them begins to accrue significance. The severe frontality of shots through the phantom windshields as drivers pretend to steer while a rear-projected landscape zooms behind them is remarkably stiff—"driving heads" dictate framings as unimaginative as Hitchcock's despised "talking heads." Yet such shots are often essential to the itineraries of the American films. Think of Olivier and Fontaine driving "into the camera" behind a projection of Monte Carlo in *Rebecca*, in which Maxim de Winter's inscrutability to his young passenger is most graphically established. Or Grant and Fontaine's several car trips in *Suspicion* (at the end of one she gets kissed, and at the end of the other, almost killed). Or Cummings and Lane driving handcuffed and fighting in a desert drive in *Saboteur*; or Stewart facing screen front, behind the wheel, negotiating San Francisco's hills in *Vertigo*; or Grant's escaping while intoxicated in *North by Northwest*, and, a bit earlier in that film, as he's wedged between his captors in the backseat of a cab, the row of three blank faces staring straight ahead predicting the stony stares of Mt. Rushmore. In *Notorious*, Grant is taken for a ride by loose woman Bergman; she speeds—and the rear-projected landscape accelerates behind the pair—as she says, to wipe that smile off Grant's face.

> Even the technique of back projection, generally used to reduce the costs of outdoor filming, serves a stylistic function here, bringing the characters closer to us and helping to preserve the intimacy of their relationship. The outside world is never allowed to intrude. They are always in sharp focus, and it does not matter that the world around them appears a bit fuzzy.[7]

There seems some connection in Hitchcock between these frontally staged but wholly conventional setups and the blankness of faces, of making faces unreadable. Frontally framed car rides tend to leave the film viewer staring at the staring, often impassive face concentrating on the road ahead (Grant's facial contortions in his drunken drive in *North by Northwest* are memorable because they represent an exception). Hitchcock's frontally shot scenes in moving cars—an absolutely standard-issue studio technique—begin to accrue meanings. Hitchcock can turn such standard framings into signature shots.[8]

The stationary camera directed at actors who sit in a stationary car while a movie landscape whizzes behind them on a screen results in framings that in Hitchcock's films reinforce the problem of the unknowability of the other: a concern that shows up early in the British films but takes on richer dimensions in the American ones, largely through Hitchcock's exploitation of a range of ordinary big-studio practices. The "profilmic event"—what is actually set up on the sound stage so that the camera will record it in the desired way, to achieve the desired illusion (here, that two people are driving in a car)—is part of that signification. The project of exploring such connections between studio conventions and Hitchcockian thematics has the novelty of paying attention to the ordinary workhorse shots of a Hitchcock picture, not just the spectacular daring sequences of Hitchcockian virtuosity.

Ubiquitous studio practices such as using process shots for driving scenes tend to unabashedly confess (once you stop thinking of them as simply natural) that the Hollywood institutions, in David Bordwell's words, create "the spectator as an invisible onlooker at the ideal vantage point."⁹ In some measure, shot-reverse-shot technique promotes the illusion that we are in the room with the interlocutors, invisible but privileged to switch from the vantage point of whichever speaker it is most important to be looking at during any moment in their exchange. But in process shots with cars, the camera, like a peculiar backward-facing hood-ornament, is placed where we could never be. This device, so patently directed solely at guaranteeing that the viewer can see and hear the performers in the scene, so that the performers are as legible to us as they could be, in Hitchcock's hands can become a figure for the illegibility of people, for the obstructing and unrevealing blank that a face, even a gorgeously eye-filling and familiar face, can be.

But the kinds of meaning that Hitchcock can make this device to bear are also deeply dependent on context. It makes sense to allow the categories of devices-in-context to proliferate in order to see what we learn from examining instances in the category side by side. I have just taken a brief survey of the category of scenes of driving filmed with rear projection in Hitchcock's American films. Some attention has already been paid to another such category: love scenes filmed with rear projection in Hitchcock's American films. The name of the technique, "rear projection," confesses part of the illusion that the technique is designed to conceal: The scene that is depicted as *behind* the actors is of course understood to represent a scene that is all around them; they are filmed in front of a screened view that is understood to surround them. David Bordwell notes that "re-recording sound effects was . . . compared to process photography: the sound 'background' of a restaurant crowd or a traffic-filled street was like the back-projection added to give realism and save money."¹⁰ One of the limits of rear projection technique is that it "does not create a very convincing set of depth cues. Foreground and background tend to look starkly separate, partly because of the absence of cast shadows from foreground to background, and partly because all background planes seem equally diffuse."¹¹ Flat and shallow to the eye, process backgrounds can come to remind viewers of, and hence to represent, the artificiality of filmic representation itself. Mary Ann Doane notes an ingenious instance of such usage in Hitchcock's *Spellbound* (1945). The first romantic encounter in that film, Doane writes,

> leans heavily upon one of the most clichéd scenarios of Hollywood film: the walk of two lovers through a beautiful country setting. The fake "Dr. Edwards" [Gregory Peck] . . . extends the following invitation [to Constance, played by Ingrid Bergman]: "We'll look at some sane trees, normal grass and clouds without complexes." In the scene itself, these "trees," "grass," and "clouds" are quite obviously the result of the technique of rear projection and it is thus the very artificiality of the "nature" background which is marked.

Doane's remarks depend on a viewer who is able to recognize a "clichéd scenario" and for whom that scenario can bear significance within the film precisely because it is recognized as such. The use of rear projection in this scene has a function not in spite of its familiarity but because of it. Strolling in this landscape, the two lovers discuss "the representation and the representability of love—a theme which is a recurrent obsession of the film."[12] This use of rear projection, then, must be read in the context of other uses of that device within other films from the studio years in Hollywood, as well as in the context of other uses of that device within the film itself. *Spellbound* also contains what are probably the most notoriously bogus-looking of Hitchcock's process shots, when Bergman and Peck are skiing their way to Peck's psychological breakthrough. The film's insistence that by remembering his past trauma Peck will learn his real identity is undercut by the flat unreality of the snowy slopes rushing by, against which the two are patently posing, not skiing, while it does all the moving for them. The avenue of outward-opening doors, representing Bergman's release from repression during her first kiss with Peck, associates screen depth with unharnessed feeling and release, but here the deeper Peck goes into his psyche, the shallower the frame looks.[13]

The uses of rear projection within a director's canon is another context that may be brought to bear on any one instance of the device. The "representability of love" is also a recurrent obsession of Hitchcock's *Vertigo*, a film in which rear projection becomes increasingly visible and in which it will eventually function like a flashback. In the first half of the film, when Scottie (James Stewart) is falling in love with a woman who calls herself Madeleine (Kim Novak), the rear-projected pounding surf in front of which Hitchcock poses the pathologically self-deceived lovers for their first big clinch underscores their delusions. Later the film embraces the full potential of process photography: After Scottie has dressed Judy so that she resembles the dead Madeleine, Hitchcock grants the couple one of his slow, fluid 360-degree circling movements, as if embracing them, but here, as the camera circles them, the background of Judy's apartment is replaced by the stables near the mission in which Scottie kissed Madeleine for the last time. Rear projection here clearly serves Scottie's illusion of being able to substitute one girl for the other, when they were the same girl all along. The use of rear projection to indicate Scottie's success at turning one girl into the other may allude to the association of the device with a film genre that is impossible without it—double role films. In films in which an actress plays two parts, she is able to have a conversation with herself by playing one role in front of rear-projected footage of herself in the other role (two 1946 films, for instance, *The Dark Mirror*, with Olivia de Havilland, and *A Stolen Life*, with Bette Davis, involve twin sisters vying for the same man). Hitchcock's use of process shots in love scenes are best read in the context of the multitude of instances where the footage (often of a landscape in motion) behind a pair of lovers bears a good deal of the burden of representing the passion within them. Richard Corliss, discussing the screenplays of Howard Koch, notes an affinity between his *Casablanca* (Michael Curtiz, 1942) and his *Letter from an Unknown Woman* (Max Ophuls, 1948) in the way both films link rear projection and romance: "The entire courtship sequence [in *Letter*] recalls the similarly forboding Parisian affair of Rick and Ilsa in *Casablanca*: the backdrop 'world tour' suggesting the lovers' ride through a back-projected Paris." This intertextual note reinforces our sense that the Prater "train ride" in *Letter* comments on the illusory nature of film and the illusory voyages on which it takes its characters, and viewers, simply by seating them in front of a screen on which pictures move. It is within this nexus of romantic scenarios that Hitchcock's stagings of romance must be placed.

ROBIN WOOD SAID THIRTY YEARS AGO that "'suspense' belongs more to the method of [Hitchcock's] films than to their themes. . . . Look carefully at almost any recent Hitchcock film and you will see that its core, the axis around which it is constructed, is invariably a man-woman relationship: it is never a matter of some arbitrary love-interest, but of essential subject matter."[14] Charles Affron asks in *Cinema and Sentiment*, "Is it not fruitful to read (as has in fact been done) Hitchcock's thrillers as love stories?" but then quickly concedes that Hitchcock has no real place in his study of affect in classic Hollywood film, since "the love scenes of *Notorious* and *Rear Window* punctuate what appear to be suspense films."[15] Hitchcock works with and within standard Hollywood genres. We miss a great deal that his 1930s and 1940s audiences experienced when we lean too much on the model of Hitchcock as auteur, as a master filmmaker who authors his own films more or less independently of the compromised hack work of the studio system. If we are to recuperate the response of Hitchcock's public when his films were released, we must recognize that their response was shaped in large part by their viewing and recollection of many films and many film genres. In order to look Hitchcock's films squarely in the face, we must look with equal scrutiny at a large body of other films, classic Hollywood films in particular, whose "essential subject matter" is also love between a man and a woman.

An important extension of Wood's observation can be found in Stanley Cavell's work in Hollywood romantic comedies. *The Thirty-Nine Steps* (1935) and *North
by Northwest* (1959) belong to a tradition of major Hollywood movies, including
such films as *His Girl Friday* (1940) and *It Happened One Night* (1934), which Cavell
dubs "comedies of remarriage."[16] In these films the question is not whether the
man and the woman will get together but whether they will get together again,
will remarry, whether literally (*The Philadelphia Story*) or more obliquely (*It Happened
One Night*). The subject of these comedies, according to Cavell, "is the legitimizing
of marriage, as if the pair's adventures are trials of their suitability for that condition."[17] Equally revealing affinities link Hitchcock's films and the Hollywood
melodramas, such as *Random Harvest* (1942), *To Each His Own* (1946), and *Letter from
an Unknown Woman* (1948), that Charles Affron classes as " 'recognition' fictions,"[18]
in which a man cannot recognize his own lover, wife, or mother until the end of
the last tearjerking reel. In order to understand how and why Hitchcock tells love
stories, we must trace a similar family resemblance between Hitchcock's films and
other Hollywood genres.

Hitchcock both won and lost the Oscar for Best Picture of 1940. His first
American film, *Rebecca*, garnered the award over another nominee, *Foreign Correspondent*, his second American film. There is little surprising in the Motion Picture
Academy's preference (and ours) for the elegant adaptation of DuMaurier's popular
Gothic romance over the clunkier "message" picture urging America to open its
eyes to the brewing European crisis. But the placement of these two films in
competition disguises the concerns they share, concerns that were already present
in Hitchcock's British films but that emerge more strongly in the Hollywood years,
through Hitchcock's adaptation of a spectrum of Hollywood conventions. These
concerns, in the broadest definition, are the status of the individual, and his or
her desires, vis-à-vis the large designs and fate of the nation.

In a narrower definition, more attuned to the filmmaker's options and to
matters of genre, these concerns are the status of the love story within the espionage plot. In Hitchcock, romance and suspense tend to be linked in a specific
way, with variations: The woman has to overcome her skepticism about the
man—to recognize him as *not* a murderer—in order to fall in love with him and
aid his cause, which often involves the tracking down of the real murderer, whose
crime may ultimately be against an entire nation. And until the woman comes to
this revelation, she threatens to obstruct the pursued man's quest to clear himself
and hence to save a larger cause than either of them, but one that cannot be
helped without this shift of individual emotions.

The Thirty-Nine Steps may be the paradigmatic case, but we can trace variations
of this scenario from *The Lodger* all the way through *North by Northwest*. In Hitchcock's psychological thrillers, such as *Spellbound* and *Marnie* (1964), a psychoanalyst
figure spends most of the film trying to help the disturbed patient and beloved
to bring to full recall the fitful hints of recognition that haunt him, in much the

same way that Mr. Memory's theme song dogs Hannay's memory but will not declare itself. Another group of Hitchcock films centers around the man's failure to recognize the woman, a group that includes *North by Northwest*, *Vertigo* (1958), and *Notorious* (1946); in the first two of these films the man mistakes the woman both for a murderer and for a loose woman, and in *Notorious* Grant mistakes Bergman for a loose woman whose very sexual laxity puts her political loyalty in question. There are, admittedly, crucial questions raised by the differences between the films in which the man fails to recognize the woman and the films in which the woman fails to recognize the man; is sexual looseness the female equivalent of murderousness? And can suspicion of sexual looseness or infidelity ever be dispelled, or dispelled as thoroughly, as suspicion of murder can be? Murder suspects can clear themselves by finding the true murderer, but the woman accused of infidelity cannot as readily point to another person who will take on herself the burden of sexual guilt. In the light of that difference, we can identify a third group of Hitchcock films, including *Murder!* (1931), *Rope* (1948), and *Strangers on a Train* (1951), involving a murderous conspiracy between two men that takes on overtones of a sexual bond. The stakes of recognition are equally high in those films in which the woman must come to recognize that the man is not a murderer—that is, must fall in love with him—before the man can recognize and apprehend the real murderer.

How does this scenario of a world saved by a lover's recognition translate into the Hollywood idiom? The British director who chooses particular American stars banks on audiences who will recognize and remember the stars' screen personae. Andrew Sarris recognized years ago that "Hitchcock gave Stewart and Grant meanings they could not have got from any other director."[19] We can sometimes learn as much from the casting decisions Hitchcock wished to make as from those he did make. Selznick orginally wished to cast Nova Pilbeam of *Young and Innocent* for the Joan Fontaine role in *Rebecca*, while "Hitchcock had urged Selznick to consider naming an *American* actress to play the heroine in order to stress her isolation at Manderley." Whereas Selznick's choice would have linked Hitchcock's British work with his American, Hitchcock thinks of casting as interpretive: Insofar as the audience knows the actress is American, they know she is (only an) actress. Later, Hitchcock wants Joseph Cotten to play what developed into the Leo G. Carroll role in *Spellbound* (1945), a bit of casting that would have linked *Spellbound* to the 1943 *Shadow of a Doubt*.[20] The meanings Hitchcock attaches to stars are not opposed to but contingent on the identities already given these stars by Cukor, Hawks, Capra, and others. Featuring in the thriller stars whose reputations are built on romantic leads creates a crucial link between the love and suspense stories of Hitchcock's American films of the 1940s and 1950s.

These films explore eros as the province in which skepticism is worked out. In these films a refusal to recognize the other as innocent is tantamount to disastrous political complacency; this refusal often takes the form of urging the man who claims he's innocent simply to "go to the police," to resort to public, institutional structures to clear his name. Once the woman believes the man, she also believes that the police would only adopt her earlier skepticism, and she at last understands the urgency of the man's search for the villain, the real murderer. The mistake, in Hitchcock's America, is to doubt the power of ordinariness, in its power both to harm and to sustain.

This is the mistake that Bosley Crowther makes in his tepid review of *Foreign Correspondent* at its first release. He found impossibly silly the story of reporter Joel McCrea uncovering a den of international espionage: "With the newshawk hopelessly entangled in a monstrous spy plot, beyond his control or even his comprehension . . . the patron is likely to suspect that his leg is being pulled." And although in his review of *Saboteur* Crowther acknowledges that in 1942 another Hitchcock film about "fifth columnists" is "virtually a social obligation," he criticizes the film's basic premise in virtually the same terms that the Priscilla Lane character in the film tries on the falsely accused Bob Cummings: "Actually, there is no reason for the hero undertaking his mad pursuit," Crowther says; Hitchcock and his writers show a "general disregard of authorized agents, and their slur on the [Brooklyn] Navy Yard police somewhat vitiates the patriotic implications which they have tried to emphasize in the film. One gathers that the nation's safety depends entirely on civilian amateurs."[21] Precisely, *Saboteur* implies; but, then, the dependence on the individual—his or her struggle as the arena of national struggle—is the meat and potatoes of Hollywood film plots.

As Nicholas Roddick argues in his book on Warner Brothers in the 1930s, "The classic Hollywood style rested on the individuality of social issues. Problems which appeared general at the outset would be resolved only at the level of the central character . . . but in a way which appeared to imply a more general resolution."[22] Hitchcock's "wrong man" plots almost guarantee that this formula will operate in some measure: The man who must find a nation-threatening spy in order to clear his own name of a murder rap will necessarily make an effort to save his country in the more immediately urgent pursuit to save his neck. And when he cannot spot the real murderer until the obstructing woman recognizes him and falls for him, he is embroiled in a scenario at odds with the antiisolationist rhetoric of *Casablanca* (1942), that "the feelings of three little people don't amount to a hill of beans in this crazy world." In Hitchcock's plots, politics and romance are so intertwined that casting Hollywood's romantic heroes to chase international spies seems entirely appropriate. From the edge of Mt. Rushmore to the marriage bed is a short trip.[23]

Notes

1. Raymond Carney, *American Vision* (New York: Cambridge, 1986), 275.

2. Robin Wood, *Hitchcock's Films Revisited* (New York: Columbia University Press, 1989), 217, 361.

3. Joel W. Finler points out that Leff and others have somewhat overstated this point. Selznick's hand is felt most heavily on a relatively marginal film like *The Paradine Case*, and Selznick lent Hitchcock to other studios more than he bent him to the yoke of his own: *Hitchcock in Hollywood* (New York: Continuum, 1992), chap. 1.

4. Leonard J. Leff, *Hitchcock and Selznick* (New York: Weidenfeld and Nicolson, 1987), 30, 277.

5. Stanley Cavell's reading of *North by Northwest* emphasizes the connection between the giant onscreen image of Cary Grant's face in close-up and the monumental faces of Mt. Rushmore. That Robert Benchley appears onscreen and Dorothy Parker writes dialogue for *Saboteur* suggests that the study of the function of the Algonquin Wits in Hitchcock has yet to be written.

6. Kristen Thompson, *Breaking the Glass Armor: Neoformalist Film Analysis* (Princeton: Princeton University Press, 1988), 11.

7. Stefan Sharff, *Alfred Hitchcock's High Vernacular: Theory and Practice* (New York: Columbia University Press, 1991), 67.

8. In a footnote in *The Murderous Gaze*, William Rothman begins to catalogue Hitchcock's shot-reverse-shot sequences with an eye to what overtones begin to seep into this perfectly ordinary shooting and editing of a conversation, when we see enough of them in Hitchcock's films.

The standard nature of the use of rear projection for scenes of two people talking and driving is seen in part by the very fact that the sturdy, reliable, all but mandatory shot-reverse-shot rhythms for a dialogue of two are generally not in force when two characters are shown talking in a moving car. Virtuoso variations such as the sequence of Lana Turner losing control of her car in *The Bad and the Beautiful* (there a car is moved, turned, and rocked on a platform while rain and lights are played on it from outside) also point to how very standard the standard format is.

9. David Bordwell, Janet Staiger, and Kristin Thompson, *The Classical Hollywood Cinema: Film Style and Mode of Production to 1960* (New York: Columbia University Press, 1985), 214.

10. Bordwell, *The Classical Hollywood Cinema*, 302.

11. David Bordwell and Kristin Thompson, *Film Art*, 2d ed. (New York: Knopf, 1986), 160.

12. Mary Ann Doane, "The Film's Time and the Spectator's 'Space'," in *Cinema and Language*, ed. Stephen Heath and Patricia Mellencamp (Lanham, Md.: University Publications of America, 1983), 43.

13. Cf. Robin Wood's suggestion that "the use of back-projection in *The Birds* is a matter of deliberate choice rather than of mere convenience," particularly in shots of Melanie, where posing her against a patently process background "has the effect of giving an air of unreality to her situation, of isolating her from the backgrounds, of stressing her artificiality by making it stand out obtrusively from natural scenery" (*Hitchcock's Films Revisited*, 157. This passage comes from the essay on *The Birds* in the original *Hitchcock's Films*.) Wood makes similar observations about rear projection in *Marnie* and *Torn Curtain* in *Hitchcock's Films Revisited* (174, 192, 203).

14. Wood, *Hitchcock's Films* 20–21.

15. Charles Affron, *Cinema and Sentiment* (Chicago: University of Chicago Press, 1982), 17.

16. Stanley Cavell, *Pursuits of Happiness: The Hollywood Comedy of Remarriage* (Cambridge: Harvard University Press, 1981).

17. Stanley Cavell "*North by Northwest*," in *Themes out of School: Effects and Causes* (San Fransciso: North Point Press, 1984), 154. Following Cavell's analysis, William Rothman's reading of *The Thirty-Nine Steps* stresses the film's "juxtaposition of a romantic relationship with ties to 1930's comedies like *Bringing Up Baby*, *The Awful Truth*, and *The Philadelphia Story* with the world of a Hitchcock film in which death, betrayal, mutilation, vengeance, madness and terror are real threats. The crystallization of the Hitchcock thriller format in *The Thirty-nine Steps*, the creation of a film in whose world the spirits of comedy and romance are so tardy in announcing themselves, and in which their power and efficacy are at issue, is an important development within the evolution of the genres of popular film" (*Hitchcock: The Murderous Gaze* [Cambridge: Harvard University Press, 1982], 134).

18. Affron, *Cinema and Sentiment*, 161.

19. Sarris, *The American Cinema*, (New York: Dutton, 1968), 60–61.

20. Leff, *Hitchcock and Selznick*, 51, 118; cf. Wood on the "miscasting" of Cotten in *Under Capricorn* in *Hitchcock's Films Revisited*, 334.

21. Bosley Crowther, Review of *Foreign Correspondent*, *New York Times*, March 29, 1940; Crowther, Review of *Saboteur*, *New York Times*, May 8, 1942.

22. Nicholas Roddick, *A New Deal in Entertainment* (London: British Film Institute, 1986), 6.

23. Cf. Lesley Brill, *The Hitchcock Romance: Love and Irony in Hitchcock's Films* (Princeton: Princeton University Press, 1988): "The transferences of guilt and the identifications of the innocent with the wicked occur not as final ironies but as ironic precursors of romantic configurations" (25). While I find misguided Brill's attempts to read Hitchcock's films as archetypal romance plots (in the Fryean sense), I am in agreement with his general thesis about the close link of the romantic and "thriller" plots.

2

Unveiling Maternal Desires
Hitchcock and American Domesticity

Elsie B. Michie

She already has her war job. Her patriotism consists in
not letting quite understandable desires to escape for a
few months from a household routine or to let a little
money of her own tempt her to quit it. *There must be no
absenteeism among mothers.*

—J. Edgar Hoover, "Mothers . . .
Our Only Hope" (1944)

Hoover's comments suggest the importance of the mother as a figure
who, in keeping the household going, maintains both the family and a patriotic
image of America. In this paper I analyze the way the mother is the vehicle for
but also resists such an idyllic image of the domestic sphere in two Hitchcock
films, one made in the era of Hoover's comments, *Shadow of a Doubt* (1943), the
other in the postwar period, the second version of *The Man Who Knew Too Much*
(1956). These two films differ from the rest of the Hitchcock canon because in
them the mother is represented not critically, as in films like *Psycho, Notorious, The
Birds,* and even *North by Northwest,* but positively. Ronnie Scheib's lyrical description of Emma Newton (Patricia Collinge), the mother in *Shadow of a Doubt,* could
equally well be applied to Jo McKenna (Doris Day), the mother in *The Man Who
Knew Too Much*: "She seems to move through a flow of energy which is both
feeling and action, identity and instinct, obeying an inner necessity of domestic
security."[1] However, in these two films, as in the passage from Hoover, celebrating
the delights and powers of motherhood is also a way of countering the mother's

"quite understandable desires" for something else—for money, a life, or even time of her own outside the home. While, for the bulk of their narratives, *Shadow of a Doubt* and *The Man Who Knew Too Much* idealize the mother's tenderness, altruism, and ability to merge with others, qualities associated with the kind of fluidity Scheib describes, at key moments in both films the fear suddenly surfaces that what the mother actually desires is not union with her family but separation from them. These two Hitchcock films show clearly how the domestic ideology that is invoked to counter the fear of the maternal desire for independence ends up evoking the thing it fears.

As Hoover's rhetoric and Scheib's use of the phrase "domestic security" in his encomium to Emma Newton imply, the figure of the "good" mother anchors a set of values associated not simply with home and family but also with an idealized image of the nation. The families central to both *Shadow of a Doubt* and *The Man Who Knew Too Much* are defined as emphatically American. In the earlier film, the government agents characterize the Newtons as a perfect example of the "average American family." In the later film, we learn, as the story opens, that we are about to hear how a single clash of cymbals rocked the lives of an *American* family.[2] Hitchcock intensified the American quality of *Shadow of a Doubt* by choosing Thornton Wilder—whose *Our Town* he had admired—to write the screenplay and by shooting the film in an actual small town, Santa Rosa, California, where he used members of the local community to advise his actors and play small parts in the film. Similarly, in selecting Doris Day for the female lead in *The Man Who Knew Too Much*, Hitchcock engaged an actress uncharacteristic of the type he usually preferred but one who had been defined in Hollywood as conveying a quintessential American quality. What Robin Wood says of *Shadow of a Doubt* could therefore also be applied to *The Man Who Knew Too Much*:

> What is in jeopardy is above all the Family—but, given the Family's central ideological significance, once that is in jeopardy, everything is. The small town (still rooted in the agrarian dream, in ideals of the virgin land as a garden of innocence) and the united happy family are regarded as the real sound heart of American civilization; the ideological project is to acknowledge the existence of sickness and evil but preserve the family from their contamination.[3]

In this passage, however, in order to define the home (and, by extension, family and nation) as a locus of peace and security in which one would feel immune to foreign intrusion, Wood must inevitably evoke the forces that threaten to invade that sanctuary. The same process occurs in both Hitchcock films, where the family can be defined as a haven only by being represented as open to and besieged by the kind of external threats Wood describes.

In *Shadow of a Doubt*, as the title suggests, doubt enters the domestic sphere in the form of the mother's brother, Charles Oakley (Joseph Cotten), a murderer of widows who attempts to hide his criminal identity by becoming part of the Newton family. In *The Man Who Knew Too Much*, terror intrudes on the McKenna family when their only child is kidnapped by political assassins who threaten to murder him. The differing ways in which the family is beleaguered in the two films reflect the differences in America's foreign policy during the two periods (the threat of external invasion of America during wartime, the threat of something being taken away from America during the period of the cold war) and also the differences in Hitchcock's relation to his adoptive country when he made the two films. At the time of *Shadow of a Doubt*, Hitchcock was just beginning to become part of American society. (During the making of the film, he put down roots by buying a house near Santa Rosa, the town in which the film was made.) More than ten years later, during the making of *The Man Who Knew Too Much*, he finally became an American citizen. Appropriately, at the party celebrating his changed national affiliation he announced his return to England to scout locations for the only one of his British films he was to remake in an American version. It is thus from his own marginalized position as an outsider who chose to become identified with a new "mother" country that Hitchcock represents the American family as a locus of idealized fantasies but also fears about merging and safety.

Despite differences between the two films, the positioning of the family in the narrative follows virtually the same pattern in *Shadow of a Doubt* and *The Man Who Knew Too Much*. In both, the family is initially, very briefly, represented as a harmonious unit that is then broken: in the first film, by the intrusion of a foreigner; in the second, by the loss of a family member. Because the family remains disrupted for the bulk of the story and reemerges as whole only at its end, the scenes at the very beginning and end of both films, before and after the disruption, show most vividly the kinds of fantasies that can be articulated around idealized images of the mother and the domestic sphere. But from my point of view, the most interesting moments in both films occur right after the opening and right before the ending, the moments when the family is about to be disrupted and when it is about to be made whole again. Those "liminal" moments foreground the boundary between the idealized domestic sphere and what is external to it and, in the process, reveal the ambiguities inherent in the figure of the "good" mother. Particularly in the penultimate scenes of both films, as the family is about to be returned to wholeness, there is a moment when the mother lingers on the threshold of the home and holds onto a vision of another kind of life before she returns to her traditional domestic role. In that scene the central maternal figure of the film refuses, very briefly, to be a vehicle for idealized fantasies about the family and instead articulates her own desires, desires that threaten the domestic ideals she is supposed to embody.

Occurring right before the conclusion of each film, these scenes convey an uncanny sense of disruption which is perfectly captured in a vignette that takes place during the opening sequence of *The Man Who Knew Too Much*, when the

McKenna family is riding a Moroccan bus to Marrakesh. The film's action begins when Hank, the McKennas' young son, is standing in the aisle and loses his balance, "accidentally" pulling the veil off a Muslim wife who is sitting near him, thereby exposing her face in public. Though this moment of exposure is represented as shocking in terms of Muslim culture, in both *Shadow of a Doubt* and *The Man Who Knew Too Much*, the moment when the veiled desires of the "typical" American wife and mother are exposed turns out to be equally shocking. The terror of the two films ultimately lies less in the hostile figures or actions that threaten the family from the outside (the intrusion of a murderer, the kidnapping of a son) than in the unheard desire that lies hidden at the heart of the domestic realm, what Slavoj Žižek describes as "the *desire of the other* . . . the mother's desire with its fathomless 'Che vuoi?' "[4] But while Žižek characterizes the mother's desire as terrifying because it is unknowable, both these films suggest that the mother articulates her desires quite clearly if one can learn to listen carefully enough to what she says.

What would be disrupted by hearing the mother speak her own desires is the fantasy of being able to merge completely with her. In *Shadow of a Doubt*, Uncle Charlie fantasizes a return to and reunion with Emma Newton, the older sister who helped bring him up as a child. In *The Man Who Knew Too Much*, the mother, Jo McKenna, is represented as being in complete harmony with her son, Hank. I use the word "harmony" advisedly, since in both films the fantasy of union with the mother is associated with what Kaja Silverman describes as the "fantasy of the maternal-voice-as-sonorous-envelope . . . the image of the infant held within the environment or sphere of the mother's voice is an emblem of infantile plentitude and bliss."[5] I can think of few clearer filmic evocations of this fantasy than Doris Day singing "Que sera" to her son in both the opening and closing sections of *The Man Who Knew Too Much*. There is no such dramatic exercise of the maternal voice in *Shadow of a Doubt* (though both mother and daughter hum the waltz that identifies Uncle Charlie as the Merry Widow Murderer). Incorporating women's voices was, however, important to Hitchcock in the making of the film. As John Russell Taylor explains, Hitchcock originally hired Thornton Wilder to write the screenplay, but Wilder had already signed on to do military duty in the Department of Psychological Warfare and could not complete the work. Though Wilder suggested another male writer to finish the script, Hitchcock chose

> Sally Benson, author of *Meet Me in St. Louis*, who had a particularly attractive light touch in handling the domestic scenes and those involving children. The finishing touches were put to the script in the course of shooting, by Patricia Collinge, who plays the mother in the film and wrote the scene between the girl Charlie and the detective when they speak of love and marriage.[6]

The fact that Hitchcock used a woman writer to convey the closeness of the ties among the Newton family members and that he asked the actress who plays the mother to write the dialogue for the clearest love scene in the film suggests that he was interested not just in women's voices but specifically in the maternal voice, whose power is more dramatically bodied forth in the later film *The Man Who Knew Too Much*.

In that film, the mother's voice marks the lack of differentiation between herself and her son, a confusion that is repeatedly emphasized as the story begins. In the opening scenes of the film set on the bus, the French agent Louis Bernard engineers a meeting with the McKenna family and is introduced first to the mother, Mrs. McKenna, and then to the son, Hank. When he later hears the name Jo (the mother's first name), he assumes it to be masculine and thinks that Hank is called by two names.[7] In the scene soon after, when Bernard comes to the McKennas' hotel room in Marrakesh, the bond between mother and son is dramatized once again when Hank and Jo sing "Que sera" together. While Bernard is in a separate room of the suite and can only listen to the two as they sing, the film's audience witnesses the intimate interaction between mother and son as they transform what might be a tedious everyday routine of getting ready for bed into a virtual dance. The singing of "Que sera" marks the domestic union of mother and son not just at the opening but also at the close of the film, when Jo Conway/ McKenna performs at the embassy. In that second scene, when mother and son are physically separated, her voice becomes the medium that unites them, as the camera emphasizes by moving away from Doris Day's face as she sings to track the path of her song as it travels through the embassy and finally reaches Hank. As Žižek notes, "Here, Hitchcock makes use of a formal procedure whose audacity has not yet been fully perceived: the camera directly 'tracks' the voice, 'shows' its resonance on the staircase and its climb to the attic room where the son is locked up."[8] This filming technique is as close as Hitchcock can come to finding a visual equivalent for what Silverman has described as the ability of the maternal voice to "spill over from subject to object and object to subject, violating the bodily limits upon which classic subjectivity depends."[9]

To understand all that is at stake in the final reunion between mother and son in *The Man Who Knew Too Much*, it helps to read the whole sequence of Doris Day's final performance in terms of the argument Silverman makes, using the work of Guy Rosolato, about the fantasy of the "good" mother.[10] When Jo Conway/ McKenna performs at the embassy, she is shown continuing to sing "Que sera" until she hears her son whistling the same tune in response, a perfect instance of

Rosolato's fantasy of the maternal voice [which] also revolves around a second sonorous image: the image of the child harmonizing with the mother, and making its emissions "adequate" to hers. However, he is quick to point out that sounds can be placed in unison only after they have been differentiated from each other, and he makes that observation the basis for a simultaneous reading of musical, psychic, and corporeal separation and restoration.[11]

In *The Man Who Knew Too Much*, once Jo hears her son harmonize with her, she shifts from "Que sera" to a second song whose words are difficult for the viewer to distinguish because, at that point, the film no longer focuses directly on Jo's singing. All we can make out in the background, as the song echoes through the halls of the embassy, is its chorus, which contains the phrase "We'll kiss again and again and again." (In the credits, this song is identified as "We'll Love Again.") This almost incantatory refrain emphasizes the way the pleasure of uniting with the mother involves a fantasy of repetition or, as Silverman argues, "an after-the-fact construction or reading of a situation that is fundamentally irrecoverable."[12]

One can most clearly see Doris Day's singing as evoking a nostalgic desire to recover past bliss not in the film itself but in Robin Wood's response to it in *Hitchcock's Films Revisited*. Toward the end of his discussion of *The Man Who Knew Too Much*, Wood breaks from his analytical tone to make the following confession: "I want to conclude by celebrating the real climax of the American version, Jo's song at the embassy. Middle-aged academics are not supposed to admit that they burst into tears every time Doris Day begins 'Que sera, sera,' but in my case it is a fact. What makes this moment so moving is its magical resolution of apparent oppositions."[13] What happens to Wood at this moment is that the pull of the film's domestic ideology is so strong that he is drawn into participating in fantasies about the "good" mother. We will see a similar collapse of critical distance in the works of a number of critics as they approach *Shadow of a Doubt*.

In that earlier film the desire to return to and merge with the "good" mother is enacted by a particular character, Charles Oakley, whose thoughts reveal the way that, as Tania Modleski has explained, in Hitchcock's films, "misogyny and . . . sympathy actually entail one another," as in *Psycho*, where "Norman Bates's close relationship with his mother provokes his lethal aggression towards other women."[14] Similarly, in *Shadow of a Doubt* Uncle Charlie's impulse to idealize women who, as he says of his sister Emma, are "busy about their homes and families" cannot be separated from his desire to punish women who do not main-tain those domestic ideals—the widows he defines as "fat, wheezing animals" suitable for killing. Uncle Charlie's splitting of women into two categories is characteristic of his generally Manichean vision of the world as a "foul sty" saved only by the values preserved in the sanctuary of the domestic realm. The opening sequence of the film presents the viewer with a split vision of the world, moving from the urban decay of the first scenes of trash heaps, derelicts, and abandoned buildings to the pastoral beauty of Santa Rosa, which is shot as if, as its name suggests, it is a paradise filled with light and flowers.[15] In *Shadow of a Doubt*, the abrupt initial shift from the urban world of the East to the garden world of the West occurs at the moment when Uncle Charlie, having decided to seek refuge from the police by hiding in the bosom of his sister's family, sends them a telegram that closes with their address. As he articulates the words "Santa Rosa," the film's music and lighting are suddenly transformed and we see the ideal American small town.[16] For a brief moment early in the film it is as if Uncle Charlie is able to impose his vision of Santa Rosa as he will describe it when he is on the verge of leaving it at the very end of the film, as a place of "hospitality and kindness and homes."[17]

The fantasy of a perfect small town and an ideal domestic realm is embodied for Charles Oakley in his older sister, Emma Newton, who helped to take care of him when he was a child and who also runs her own family as a "true" wife and "good" mother. Uncle Charlie's sense of completion at the moment of his reunion with Emma is emphasized by the filming of his arrival at the Newton house, the liminal moment just before the solidarity of the family is disrupted by his entry into their home. In that scene the two figures, brother and sister, initially stand at two ends of a pathway, Emma in the doorway of her house and Charles at the point where the sidewalk meets the walkway of the house, she on the threshold of the home and he on the border where the domestic meets the public. (In *Shadow of a Doubt*, the domestic realm seems to extend from the house into the garden, ending only where the lot touches the street.) She begins to run down the pathway toward him, but he stops her, telling her not to move.[18] He then meets her midway and, in the moment when the two are poised, about to embrace, tells his sister that she does not look like Emma Newton (he has already used the name Mrs. Joseph Newton to address his telegram to her) but like "Emma Spencer Oakley of 46 Vernon St., St. Paul, Minnesota, the prettiest girl on the block." In calling Emma by the name she bore as a child and referring to their childhood home, Uncle Charlie makes it clear that his returning to Emma is a way for him to recover the past. His articulation of Emma's full maiden name is particularly revealing, since, in the first spoken lines of the film, uttered by the landlady who enters Charles's room in the boarding house in Philadelphia, he is addressed not as Mr. Oakley but as Mr. Spencer. His choice of a pseudonym marks Uncle Charlie's desire to merge his identity with Emma's so that they would be confused in much the same way that mother and son are confused at the opening of *The Man Who Knew Too Much* because their names cannot be distinguished.[19]

I call attention to Uncle Charles's use of Spencer as his pseudonym not just because that name reveals his unspoken fantasies about his sister but also because it proves to be a stumbling block for critics, whose mistakes about the use of names in the film reveal the way they become caught up in Uncle Charles's fantasies. In two of the best-known articles about the film, James McLaughlin's "All in the Family: Alfred Hitchcock's *Shadow of a Doubt*" and Robin Wood's "Ideology, Genre, Auteur," both critics use the name Spencer, the pseudonym Charles

Oakley has chosen for himself, as if it were his actual name and even as if it were the name of his sister's entire family. McLaughlin misquotes the film when he reports Mrs. Potter, the widowed friend of Mrs. Green, the wife of the bank president, as saying, " 'One good thing about being a widow, *Mr. Spencer* . . . is that you don't have to ask your husband for money.' "[20] (In that scene, Uncle Charles has specifically been introduced as Mr. Oakley.)[21] Robin Wood makes a similar mistake when, in criticizing Emma's family (the Newtons) for not conforming to his conception of the ideal family, he asserts that "the most striking characteristic of the *Spencers* is the separateness of each member; the recurring point of the celebrated overlapping dialogue is that no one ever listens to what anyone else is saying. Each is locked in a separate fantasy world."[22] While Ronnie Scheib does not make a similar mistake about Uncle Charles's pseudonym, he does mistakenly describe Uncle Charlie as carrying the Newton's youngest daughter Ann (Edna May Wonnacott) up the stairs, when in fact it is her father who carries her. (Ann is the member of the Newton family who most clearly sees through Uncle Charlie and rejects him. She will not even sit next to him at dinner). Scheib's mistake suggests that, like the other critics, he has become so caught up in Uncle Charlie's fantasies—in this case, the fantasy of becoming a full-fledged member of the Newton family—that he reads the scene as if that fantasy has been fulfilled. For all these critics, the domestic ideology Uncle Charlie espouses is so compelling that they are unable to distance themselves fully from it and are drawn to read, even to misread, the film from his perspective.[23]

In his chapter on *Shadow of a Doubt* in *Hitchcock—The Murderous Gaze*, William Rothman solves the problem of inadvertently slipping into Uncle Charlie's point of view by defining that point of view as Hitchcock's. For Rothman, as Fredric Jameson notes, "the Outsider around whom so many of these films turn—the lodger, Fane, Uncle Charles, Norman himself—proves to have been not merely the expression of a particular interest to Hitchcock, but the very inscription of Hitchcock himself (and his demiurgic function) *within* the film."[24] Reading Uncle Charlie's point of view and Hitchcock's as one and the same leads Rothman to choose self-consciously to identify with Uncle Charlie in order to try to understand and explain what motivates his killing of widows:

> In his conversation with Truffaut, Hitchcock speaks of Charles as a killer with a mission. One way of understanding that mission is to think of it as ridding the world of "fat, wheezing animals" that incarnate lost beauty and grace. But we can also understand Charles's mission as a commitment to listening for and responding to these lonely women's heartfelt calls. (Of course, Charles may be read as believing he hears such calls.) It is fundamental to *Shadow of a Doubt*, as I read it, that Charles's killing can be viewed as expressing either contempt for his victims or compassion,

indeed love, for them. Failure to acknowledge this ambiguity, and to *appreciate* its implication, is a failure to comprehend the film.[25]

While Jameson suggests that such totalizing positions as Rothman's can be avoided by "de-centering the subject" or ceasing to view Hitchcock as the master controlling the film text, Tania Modleski critiques Jameson's position, arging that

> in calling into question Rothman's "organicist" author aesthetics, Jameson counterposes a notion of artistic and filmic fragmentation, which he puts into a "dialectical" theory of the fragmentation and discontinuity of American daily life. What is made possible by this move . . . is a replacement of the older notion of artist as master with one of the theorist as master: the man who is able to situate the fragmented, partial, decentered aspects of art and daily life into a historical totality.[26]

Modleski advocates a different kind of critical positioning, one that "implicitly challenge[s] and decenter[s] directorial authority by considering Hitchcock's work as the expression of cultural attitudes and practices existing to some extent outside the artist's control."[27] Using this kind of approach with *Shadow of a Doubt* allows us to distance ourselves from Uncle Charlie's Manichean splitting of the world into idealized homes or foul sties and women into true wives or disgusting widows by viewing it not as a transhistorical absolute, a vision of good and evil that must be justified or explained, but as a cultural construction that has a particular history and comes into Hitchcock's film from specific sources.

The moment when *Shadow of a Doubt* was made, the early 1940s, was a time when there was a shift away from independent roles for women, which had been advocated in the 1930s. As Elaine Tyler May explains, "For young single working women in the 1930s, the experience of some form of economic independence . . . offered an alternative to the role of dependent housewife,"[28] a change in women's status that was echoed in the films of the period. However, as May goes on to point out, "Hollywood's professed advocacy of gender equality evaporated during the forties,"[29] when there was an increased emphasis on "wifely" duties[30] and motherhood, an emphasis that was, if anything, intensified in films of the 1950s. One can see how gender roles changed from the 1930s to the 1940s and 1950s by looking at *Shadow of a Doubt* and *The Man Who Knew Too Much* in relation to their filmic precursors. Such a precursor is easy to identify in the case of *The Man Who Knew Too Much*, a remake of Hitchcock's 1930s version of the same film. *Shadow of a Doubt* also involves remaking an earlier film, William Wyler's 1941 film version of Lillian Hellman's 1939 play *The Little Foxes*, which was made a year before Hitchcock's film. Hitchcock appears to have had Wyler's film in mind when he was casting his own film, because the actresses he chose to play the Newton mother and daughter have a strikingly similar relation in the film version of Hellman's play. As Rothman notes, "Collinge's performance, like Teresa Wright's, is technically all but indistinguishable from her performance in William Wyler's *The Little Foxes.*"[31]

Hellman's play allows us to identify a historical source for the domestic ideology that, I have been arguing, permeates both *Shadow of a Doubt* and contemporary critical responses to it. The title of Hellman's play comes from John Ruskin's "Of Queens' Gardens,"[32] the classic Victorian celebration of women's domestic power which was so popular in America that it continued to be used as a textbook in both public and private school systems right up through the time Hellman was writing in the 1930s.[33] Given the fact that the 1930s was a time when women resisted typical domestic roles, it is not surprising that Hellman's play invokes Ruskin's celebration of the power women can and should exercise in their own homes, in order to criticize that domestic ideology through the figures of two sisters-in-law, played by in the film by Patricia Collinge and Bette Davis. The Patricia Collinge character, Aunt Birdie, embodies the tenderness, harmony, and culture that hark back to the domestic realm of a bygone era. With her love of music and knowledge of art, she incarnates the domestic graces Ruskin praises in a woman, but she is also a helpless alcoholic who has no defense against the husband who abuses her. In contrast, the Bette Davis character seizes what power she can in the home, but that power makes her abusive. She tyrannizes the members of her own household, manipulates her brothers, and is ultimately so ambitious that she kills her husband, or at least allows him to die, in order to become a rich widow. That the Bette Davis character should be read as a gloss on Ruskin's essay is suggested by her name, Regina, which, ironically, given her behavior, echoes the passage where Ruskin characterizes the ideal woman as a queen, the ideal husband and wife as: "Rex et Regina—Roi et Reine—'Right-doers'; they differ but from Lady and Lord, in that their power is supreme over the mind as over the person—that they not only feed and clothe, but direct and teach."[34] In direct contrast to this vision of domestic bliss, Hellman's play shows women in the home either losing all power or learning to use what they have destructively.

In *The Little Foxes* the solution to the problem of women's relation to the domestic sphere lies not in the choices made by the two women of the older generation but in the eventual actions of a woman of the younger generation, Regina's daughter Alexandra ("Zandy"), played by Teresa Wright, who is also raised by her Aunt Birdie. Brought up to believe in traditional domestic values, Zandy is initially incapable of dealing with the world outside the home. She is particularly shocked by her first meeting with a woman who has a career, a newspaper reporter, whom Alexandra finds it impossible even to address. Over the course of the play, however, as Alexandra learns to understand the behavior of her cold but domineering mother and her lovable but helpless aunt, she comes to the decision that the only way she will be able to discover and exercise her own powers is by using them outside the domestic sphere. The play ends with her running out of the door of her home to meet her future elsewhere. It was this possibility—that women might desire to take action outside the home—which the idealization of the figure of the wife and mother was designed to counter in "Of Queens' Gardens." Ruskin acknowledges that "we hear of the 'mission' and 'rights' of Woman, as if these could ever be separate from the mission and the rights of Man;—as if she and her lord were creatures of independent kind and of irreconcilable claim. This, at least, is wrong."[35] In *The Little Foxes*, it is precisely the idea that women might have a separate and independent mission that saves them from domestic stagnation.

While Hellman's 1930s play presents a critical picture of Ruskin's idealized domestic sphere, in Hitchcock's 1943 remake of Wyler's film those domestic values return, though in a slightly distorted form, since they are, as we have seen, initially associated with the figure of Uncle Charlie. The split between the Regina and Birdie characters in *The Little Foxes*—between the adult woman who takes pleasure in her financial independence and the woman who is tender and altruistic and cares primarily for others—represents precisely what the Joseph Cotten character in Hitchcock's film defines as a split between bad widows and good mothers. The Bette Davis character, Regina, displays exactly the characteristics that make Uncle Charlie loathe the women he kills. In contrast, the Aunt Birdie character, with her faded gentility and her nostalgic recollections of her mother and their ideal life on the plantation Lionnet, represents the kind of values Uncle Charlie wants to bring back to the home. As he rhapsodizes when he gives Emma a picture of their parents, his mother's era—1888—was wonderful because it was a time when the world was "sweet and pretty. . . . Not like the world now."[36] The crucial difference, however, between Wyler's film version of Hellman's play and Hitchcock's film is that in the latter Patricia Collinge plays a character who is not a helpless alcoholic but an idealized maternal figure who is in her own way powerful, because she holds her family together in the midst of a series of crises of which she is blithely unaware. *Shadow of a Doubt* reinscribes Ruskin's vision of home as

> the place of Peace; the shelter, not only from all injury, but from all terror, doubt and division. In so far as it is not this, it is not home; so far as the anxieties of the outer life penetrate into it, and the inconsistently minded, unknown, unloved, or hostile society of the outer world is allowed by either husband or wife to cross the threshold, it ceases to be home; it is then only a part of that outer world which you have roofed over, and lighted fire in.[37]

This is precisely the position Wood describes when he asserts that the "ideological project" of Hitchcock's film is "to acknowledge the existence of sickness and evil but preserve the family from their contamination."[38]

It is only peripheral details in the film, particularly associated with the Newton daughter played by Teresa Wright, which suggest that it is set at a historical moment when women were beginning to have increasing freedom or mobility, a freedom which, in this film, is connected with their ability to drive. We hear repeatedly about women drivers in *Shadow of a Doubt*. When the Newtons first learn that they have received the telegram which subsequently turns out to be from Uncle Charlie, Joseph Newton immediately assumes that it has come from his sister, who has, as we subsequently learn, just obtained her driver's license and who must, as a result, have been in an automobile accident. A few scenes later an observant viewer may notice that it is Charlie who drives her family to the train station to meet her uncle. In case one overlooks that marginal detail, the film later calls attention to the fact that Charlie can drive, though her parents cannot, in the scene where the family is setting out to attend Uncle Charles's speech at Emma's women's club and Emma exclaims, "Oh Joe, I wish you could drive a car." Given Uncle Charlie's belief that women should be sweet and pretty, good wives and mothers confined to the domestic sphere, it is appropriate that he twice attacks Charlie in the garage. (The garage seems to mark the margin of the Newtons' apparently safe and pastoral domestic realm.) The first time he shuts the door on her when she is talking to the detective, Jack Graham, about marriage and then tells her that in his youth couples did not behave in that way. The second time, he uses the fact that Charlie is the family driver to send her to the garage to get the car, and then he shuts her in once again, this time attempting to asphyxiate her.

The tension between women's independence and domestic duties, which remains marginalized in *Shadow of a Doubt*, is brought center stage in Hitchcock's later film, the 1956 *The Man Who Knew Too Much*, as becomes evident when one contrasts the later version of the film with its 1934 precursor. The British version of *The Man Who Knew Too Much* was made at a time when, as May argues, "popular culture bolstered the side of the 1930s that challenged traditional gender roles."[39] In that version the heroine is extremely active, a crack shot who competes with men and, in the end, takes a gun from a policeman and uses her superior marksmanship to kill the man who has kidnapped her daughter. Initially she is shown dancing with Louis Bernard, the stranger her family has just met, and joking about the idea of taking a lover other than her husband. In contrast, in the later version of *The Man Who Knew Too Much*, Jo McKenna is completely devoted to protecting her family; is extremely suspicious when the stranger, Louis Bernard, approaches them; and shows no desire to flirt with him. Moreover, in the second version, the skill that enables the mother to recover her lost child is no longer marksmanship but music, a power traditionally associated with women, specifically, as we have seen, with the maternal voice.

These differences make it easy to dismiss the second film as less interesting than the first, as Philip French does when he describes Doris Day as "a querulous pouting homemaker who pops pills and saves her son by sitting down at the piano to play and sing a doleful pop tune ('Que sera, sera')" and who is no match for the international crack shot played by Edna Best, who "saves her daughter with a well-aimed bullet in the 1934 version."[40] Similarly, Ina Rae Hark argues that in the second version of the film the husband is given a more active role, and the "central female characters have been rewritten to stress their womanliness and the power of motherhood to overcome their usual deference to male authority."[41] In other words, "Hitchcock has revised the film so that men and women do not stray from their assigned roles in patriarchy."[42] What arguments such as French's and Hark's overlook is the tension inherent in the representation of an apparently idealized domestic figure like Jo McKenna, a tension that, as I will argue, is also present in Hitchcock's representation of Emma Newton as the "good" mother. In the case of Jo McKenna, the "domestic" qualities that are so emphasized in the second version of *The Man Who Knew Too Much* clearly function as a counterweight to a possibility that is never even addressed in the case of the heroine of the 1934 version of the film: the possibility of women having a successful career outside marriage. Indeed, Jo McKenna's career has made her so much more famous than her husband that, in one scene, the Jimmy Stewart character, Dr. McKenna, is addressed as Dr. Conway, as if he has taken on Jo's maiden name.[43] The differences between the first and the second versions of *The Man Who Knew Too Much* perfectly illustrate the way the threatening possibility of a woman having a mission separate from the home leads almost automatically to what feels like a heavy-handed invocation of "domestic" virtues.

In the 1956 version of *The Man Who Knew Too Much*, the tensions at the heart of domestic ideology are revealed most clearly in the two scenes I initially characterized as liminal: the one where the family has just been first disrupted, and the one where it is about to be made whole again. In the first of these two scenes, when Dr. McKenna tells his wife that their son has been kidnapped, we see a sinister side to domestic relations. As soon as the couple enters their hotel room, the husband begins to order his wife around, and she responds by asking if they are going to have one of their "monthly" fights, a phrase that simultaneously tells us that their marriage is not as happy as it appears to be and suggests that one explanation for such "periodic" disruptions would be Jo's biology. This is the first of a series of gestures that work to define Jo's unhappiness as a sign not of her frustration with marriage but of her hysteria. Jo's doctor husband proceeds to tell his wife that she should take a pill in order to calm her overexcitable nature. (In fact, she has not been behaving hysterically; he is medicating her before he gives her the news of their son's kidnapping in order to control her reaction.) At this point, we learn that he has already diagnosed her as having a problem with taking too many pills.[44] The whole scene between Jo and her husband begins to feel as if he is enforcing domestic "tranquillity" on her. First he compels her to take a pill, which she later discovers to be a sedative, before he will give her any information. Then he practically forces her down on the bed. (At one point we see his hands at her throat. At another he is confining her arms at her sides so that she can't move around.) By the end of the scene, Jo looks and behaves as if she were a helpless hysteric, though we see no evidence of that behavior elsewhere in the film.

In the second of the two liminal scenes we see not the husband defining his wife as a hysteric but the wife expressing, at least indirectly, her frustration with marriage. Appropriately, Jo voices her desire for something other than the home in the only scene in the film in which she resumes the professional role she had before marriage, when she performs at the embassy as Jo Conway. By listening carefully to the differences between her early, intimate, domestic performance of "Que sera" and her later public or professional performance of that same song, we can hear Jo comment on her own life. Slavoj Žižek also finds it essential that we to pay attention to the specific words of the song; " 'Che sara, sara,' [sic] what will be, will be—how could one avoid noticing, in this answer to the child's question as to what will become of him when he grows up, the malevolent in-difference that pertains to the very nature of the superego."[45] Interestingly, he associates Day's performance of the song not with bliss, as Wood does, but with malevolence, with feelings, as his earlier comments make clear, that threaten to engulf the male subject:

> This incestuous song which links the subject to the Thing (the maternal body), i.e. by means of which the Thing catches him with its tentacles, is, of course, none other than the notorious "Che sara, sara" [sic] sung by Doris Day in the embassy where her son is kept prisoner. It is, as said above, a song through which *the mother reaches, 'catches,' her son*, that is to say a song which expressly establishes the incestuous umbilical link.[46]

Žižek's fascination with the mother as a locus not of fantasies but of fears leads him, however, to make the same kind of mistake as those we saw in the various critical readings of *Shadow of a Doubt*. Žižek's position means that he fails to notice that when Doris Day sings "Que sera" at the embassy, she is singing *to* her son, but she is no longer singing *about* him. The wording of the second rendition of the song makes it clear that in it she is no longer singing about a male child but about a female one; she is singing the daughter's relation to the mother.

The final singing of "Que sera" thus opens up the kind of space Tania Mod-leski has argued one frequently finds in Hitchcock's films, the space for a narrative of female maturation.[47] But in the case of Jo McKenna at the end of *The Man Who Knew Too Much* and, as we shall see, of Emma Newton in the penultimate scene of *Shadow of a Doubt*, this implicit narrative of female development is presented from the position of its end point: The mother looks back over her life and marks the juncture where she felt a sense of loss or resistance when she was pulled into the next stage of her development. In her first rendition of "Que sera" in the bedroom of her hotel, Jo functions only as a respondent. She sings nothing but the refrain, "Que sera," allowing her son to sing two verses, one where he asks his mother, the other his teacher, about the future. In the second rendition of the song, Jo begins by singing the verse Hank first sang but identifies herself as a little girl who asks her mother whether she will be pretty. Day then sings two middle verses where she asks first her teacher, then her sweetheart, what will become of her. The wording of these middle verses is the same as when Hank sang them; it does not identify the gender of the singer. The growing child simply asks, "Will I paint pictures? Will I sing songs?" then, "Will we have rainbows?" These verses suggest that at this point in the child's development masculinity and femininity have not yet been fully differentiated. When Jo performs "Que sera" at the embassy, she repeats these androgynous middle verses until she hears Hank whistling in response. Then she moves on to a verse that she sings from the position of being a mother who has children of her own to advise. (While in the earlier rendition of the song, to be the mother means simply to be an echo, or in Žižek's terms to be the superego, in the second rendition, the mother is given a verse to sing from her own perspective.) What I find most interesting here is the moment when Jo appears to get stuck in the middle of "Que sera," almost like a record caught in a groove. In that moment, she resists the movement of the song and of her own maturation by holding onto the verses that describe the period before the girl child gets married. This moment of performative stasis suggests what has run through the film like a subtext: that Jo Conway McKenna had a life and desires of her own before she became a wife and mother, desires she remembers and whose loss she mourns despite the apparent bliss of her union with her son.

The mininarrative of women's development that Jo McKenna articulates briefly when she sings "Que sera" at the end of The Man Who Knew Too Much is represented in Shadow of a Doubt both in the penultimate scene, where Emma responds to her brother's departure, and in the relative positioning of the film's three central female figures: the youngest Newton daughter, Ann, who is still presumably in the early, androgynous phase of development; the older daughter, Charlie, who is poised on the brink of adulthood and the possibility of marriage; and the mother, Emma, who has long been married and taken care of her family. The female figure most in the foreground of the story, Charlie, is positioned between her mother and her younger sister, both of whom are represented as powerful within their quite different respective spheres. As has been suggested, in Shadow of a Doubt Emma is portrayed as having a kind of Ruskinian power to rule the domestic realm, a power we see, for example, in the scene where she brings Uncle Charlie breakfast in bed on his first morning in the Newton household. When she puts the tray on his lap, thereby preventing him from getting up, she is serving her brother but also confining or limiting him. She also brings out his baby picture and tells the story of the childhood accident that "changed" him, gestures that remind Charles of his infancy and of Emma's power. In the end of that scene Emma refuses to obey Uncle Charlie when he tells her not to let

Stuck in the middle of "Que sera": voicing the tension at the heart of the domestic ideal

reporters into her house, clearly demonstrating her sense that she has full power to make decisions about who should be allowed entry into the domestic sphere.[48] When the reporter and photographer (actually two agents pursuing the Merry Widow murderer) enter her home, Emma again exercises her control by refusing to allow them to take pictures of objects that do not have the appropriate appearance, refusing to break the eggs for the cake until she is ready for them, and refusing to make a cake for no reason when the photographer misses the shot. Blithely unaware of the complicated set of power plays taking place between Uncle Charles and his pursuers in these scenes, throughout the film Emma simply refuses to allow the domestic routine to be disrupted. Despite the building melodrama surrounding Uncle Charlie's identity as a murderer and his eventual murderous attacks on Charlie, Emma continues to serve perfectly planned three-course dinners and carefully prepared plates of hors d'oeuvres. Indeed, the tension of the film depends on its alternation between organized domestic occasions produced by Emma and the scenes that reveal the disruption or disorder of the evolving murder plot.

Ann's power is different. From the opening scenes of the film she is characterized as having an overwhelming interest in reading and the written word. The first time the camera enters the Newton household, we see Charlie upstairs lying on her back in bed, thinking, we later learn, about her mother and the family. This scene is traditionally read as paralleling the earlier scene where Uncle Charlie is shown lying on his bed in a similar position in the rooming house in Philadelphia. But the scene with Charlie daydreaming is also contrasted to the one that immediately follows it, where Ann is shown lying not on her back but on her stomach, actively reading a book that absorbs her so much that she takes it with her and goes on reading as she answers the phone. Late in the film, when Saunders (Wallace Ford), one of the government agents in pursuit of Uncle Charlie, says that he cannot tell what Ann knows and what she makes up, she replies that she never makes anything up but gets everything from books, and that it's all true. The film confirms Ann's assertion of the "truth" of what she reads: The literary material she cites functions as an accurate commentary on the problems faced by her older sister. Ann refers by name to both *Ivanhoe* and *Dracula*, two texts particularly applicable to Charlie, who initially conceives of her Uncle Charles as a kind of Ivanhoe, a white knight come to "save" the Newton family but discovers over the course of the film that he is instead, as McLaughlin has noted, a kind of Dracula, come to drain the family of its vitality.[49] Ann also knows a series of proverbs or maxims, most of which have to do with women. At one point, she tells Charlie not to sing at the table because if she does she will marry a crazy husband. This is an apt comment, since Charlie has just accepted a ring from her Uncle Charlie, thereby entering into what amounts to a figurative marriage with a man who turns out to be an insane murderer of widows. Later, while stepping on the cracks on her way home from church, Ann talks about breaking her mother's back, an image that harks back to Charlie's initial perception of her own mother and, presumably, of mothers in general as performing back-breaking labor. (It is this perception that makes Charlie wish for her Uncle Charles in the first place; she wants to do something to make her mother's life better, different, more than the domestic routine of "dinner, dishes, bed.") It is easy to dismiss Ann as either a reader of romances or an unimaginative literalist. Yet her reading contains precisely the kind of knowledge Charlie needs as she is about to enter into her adult life, stories and sayings about the kinds of things that can happen to women.

Charlie is shown most clearly caught between Ann's realm of book learning and Emma's realm of domestic duties in the sequence of events that leads her to discover the truth about her Uncle Charlie's identity as the Merry Widow Murderer. On his first night in the Newton household, Uncle Charlie appropriates Joseph Newton's newspaper, ostensibly to make it into a playhouse for Ann (a perfect image of Uncle Charles's desire to turn the written word into an emblem of domesticity for the girl child).[50] Charles's ulterior motive in playing this game is, however, to destroy the section of the paper that contains an article referring to himself. It is this paper that, when she steals it back, becomes the means for

Charlie to discover her uncle's secret. As she attempts to piece the paper back together, Charlie pretends to Ann that she is looking for a recipe, an aim that would be consonant with her preparation to become a wife and mother like Emma. What Charlie needs at that moment, however, are not her mother's domestic skills but the literary or information-gathering skills of her younger sister. It is Ann who suggests that Charlie go to the library to find a copy of the newspaper that Uncle Charlie has mutilated, Ann who knows the library hours, and Ann who points out that Charlie would know them too if she used the library more, thereby suggesting that as Charlie is becoming an adult woman—she has just graduated from high school—she is turning away from reading. (Ann's fantasies of growing up are to have a house full of sharpened pencils and marry a librarian.) From the beginning it is the skill of reading that has allowed Charlie to resist Uncle Charlie. When he first arrives at the Newton household and gives Charlie an emerald ring, she puts it on her finger without looking at it. When he finally persuades her to examine it, she is interested not in the stone but in the faint inscription on the inside of the band: "To TS from BM." Her lack of interest is contrasted, later in the film, with the response of her classmate from high school, Louise Finch (Janet Shaw), who works as a waitress in the Til-Two Bar, an environment which presumably suggests that she should be read as more sexually experienced than Charlie. Louise takes one look at the ring, immediately recognizes that the stone is a real emerald and exclaims, "I would just die for a ring like that," a comment that links her to the women who have died because they possessed such rings—the widows who have been murdered by Uncle Charlie. It is in the library that Charlie will learn how to interpret the meaning of the inscription on the ring.

In the library scene the camera is positioned so that, as Rothman notes, "our knowledge and Charlie's for the first time coincide."[51] We see the text of the newspaper article displayed on the screen, read the information contained within it, and understand the inscription on the ring at the same moment that Charlie does. As Mladen Dolar explains, "The ring provides the moment of recognition. This is underlined in a beautiful backwards tracking shot when the camera recedes higher and higher under the ceiling, losing sight of the ring, and we see Charlie small and alone in the dark library."[52] Presumably the scene is horrifying because in it Charlie finally learns, without a shadow of a doubt, that her uncle is the Merry Widow Murderer. For us as viewers, his identity has long been apparent, yet the scene in the library still feels horrifying. I would argue that, for Charlie, as for us, the final horror of the newspaper article lies less in the discovery of Uncle Charlie's identity than in the story of his victims. We might think here about the end of *Psycho*, where the psychiatrist asserts that matricide is a crime "most unbearable to the son who commits it," ignoring, as Tania Modleski has noted, the fact that it is actually "most unbearable to the victim who suffers it."[53] So, too, in the case of *Shadow of a Doubt*, it is the suffering of the widows, ironically described as merry, rather than of Uncle Charlie that becomes visible in the library scene.

The newspaper article Charlie reads begins dramatically with a banner head-line about the Merry Widow Murderer but ends with a paragraph about the woman he has just killed: "His latest victim, on January 12th in Gloucester, Mass. was Mrs. Bruce Matthewson, the former musical comedy star, known to audiences at the beginning of the century as 'the beautiful Thelma Schenley.'" After Charlie reads the paper, she takes the ring out and looks at it once again, this time with the information that enables her to read the inscription "To TS from BM." Those initials mark the moment when a woman was about to move from single life into marriage, to change her name from Thelma Schenley to Mrs. Bruce Masterson.[54] (The narrative of a woman's life that is embedded in the newspaper article in the middle of *Shadow of a Doubt* therefore contains in outline the story that underlies *The Man Who Knew Too Much*, the story Jo Conway enacts by leaving her singing career on the stage and becoming Mrs. Jo McKenna.) This newspaper article reminds the reader that the ring, which has been read as "an emblem of Charles's mystery,"[55] was also an emblem *in* and is still an emblem *of* the life of the woman he murdered. The scene in the library is thus finally horrifying because inscribed on the ring and in the newspaper article is the story not just of Uncle Charlie's crimes or even of the suffering of his victims but of the path Charlie must follow if she is to become a wife and mother.

The horror implicit in the moment in the library makes itself felt once again toward the end of *Shadow of a Doubt* in the scene that I have argued parallels the one in *The Man Who Knew Too Much* where Jo McKenna sings "Che sera" at the embassy. This is the scene where the family, which has been disrupted over the course of much of the film, is about to be made whole again through the exorcism of the figure who threatens to disrupt it. Like Jo Conway's performance of "Che sera" at the end of *The Man Who Knew Too Much*, Emma's response to Uncle Charles's sudden and, from her point of view, inexplicable announcement that he is leaving Santa Rosa can, on the surface, be read as confirming all the fantasies about union with a maternal figure that have been evoked over the course of the film. However, if we listen carefully to what Emma says in that moment, as we have listened to what Jo sings at the end of *The Man Who Knew Too Much*, we can begin to hear ways in which she resists the domestic ideology Uncle Charles espouses. Indeed, the entire scene that precedes Emma's final speech can be read as undermining Uncle Charlie's Manichean division of women into "good" wives and "bad" widows. In that scene Emma Newton and the wealthy widow Mrs. Potter (presumably Uncle Charlie's "next" victim) are brought together on screen for the first time in the film, and they turn out to be not different but similar; they belong to the same women's club, share the same taste in food, and in some sense understand one another. As Rothman notes, when Emma verges on hysteria in speaking of what the loss of her brother means to her, Mrs. Potter is the only one of her listeners who looks back at her, a response which suggests that the widow understands and sympathizes with the desires Emma articulates.

At first when Emma starts talking, almost tearfully, about the pleasure of having her brother Charles at home and how desperately she will miss him when he leaves, she sounds as if she feels exactly the same way that he does, as if his return to her home had completed her and his leaving will destroy her: "But I can't bear it if you go. It's just that we were so close growing up. Then Charles went away and I got married." As she goes on talking and the camera moves away from her face to focus on her daughter Charlie's response and then the scene fades to black, the tenor of her comments begins to shift. In the end we hear her explain what happens when a woman gets married, "And, you know how it is, you sort of forget you're you. You're your husband's wife." The film viewer can now understand the power of Uncle Charlie's early identification of her as Emma Spencer Oakley. If that name allowed *him* to articulate the fantasy of recovering a childhood sense of union with her, it allowed *her* to fantasize about returning to the period before she was married, before she had to merge with her husband and family and lose not only her name but also her sense of having a self. As in the moment at the end of the second version of *The Man Who Knew Too Much* when Jo Conway sings "Que sera" and for a brief moment holds onto the verses that tell the story of a woman's life before marriage, in this moment at the end of *Shadow of a Doubt* the desires of the figure who has been idealized as the "good" mother throughout the film are momentarily unveiled, and she turns out to want not the fantasy of blissful union that underlies the image of home as a haven but her own separate identity.

The penultimate scenes of both *Shadow of a Doubt* and *The Man Who Knew Too Much* allow the film viewer to catch a glimpse of a tension that lies at the heart of the ideal domestic realm, which is itself supposed to embody, in the words of Robin Wood, "the real sound heart of American civilization."[56] As Wood's comment implies and as we have seen, critics who approach these two films tend to have an investment in the kind of domestic ideology that is articulated in texts like Ruskin's "Of Queens' Gardens." They will therefore find it difficult to acknowledge the maternal desires that threaten to disrupt the idealized image of home and family. Such domestically inclined critics will look at the mother in the penultimate scenes of both films, expect her to articulate her desire for merging with the rest of her family, and hear just what they expect. The reason for such critical expectations is that, in these scenes, the mother *does* feel most intensely her separation from those who love her (Emma feels the pain of her brother Charles's imminent departure, Jo is acutely aware of her son Hank's absence). As a result, there is great pressure for her to function as an emblem or voice of family unity. In these two Hitchcock films, however, this extreme pressure is shown to elicit not the reinforcement of domestic ideals but the expression of the maternal desires those ideals are meant to suppress. The brilliance of these penultimate scenes, and of the two films in general, is that they show the idealized images of mother, home, and family not to be based on absolute, permanent, or fixed values but to be articulated as part of a system of fears and desires that work to counter one another. This representation of the domestic realm as subject to and part of an interplay of diverse discursive forces is of immense use, particularly to feminist critics. Among other things, it allows us, as I have shown in the cases of Emma Newton and Jo McKenna, to locate a site of female resistance in a figure who has traditionally been read as *the* embodiment of conservative feminine values; it has allowed us to hear the contradictory impulses at war within the breast of the "true" wife and "good" mother.

Notes

1. Ronnie Scheib, "Charlie's Uncle," *Film Comment* (March–April 1976): 56. Interestingly, while Scheib celebrates Emma as a maternal ideal, he does not see similar figures in the rest of Hitchcock's work: "Emma and her Eden will disappear in late Hitchcock. In her and in her only is reflected the state of natural grace from which all subsequent Hitchcockian mothers are so disastrously fallen" (62). By contrast, Robin Wood, in his comments on the second version of *The Man Who Knew Too Much* in *Hitchcock's Films Revisited*, asserts that among the extensive gallery of negative maternal figures in Hitchcock's American films, "the one unambiguously and actively positive mother . . . is Jo McKenna" (*Hitchcock's Films Revisited* [New York: Columbia University Press, 1989], 361). Both critics' insistence that the "good" mother is a lone instance in the Hitchcock canon prevents them from considering what Emma Newton and Jo McKenna have in common. It thereby prevents them from addressing these maternal figures as cultural or ideological constructs.

2. Day was so American that she had never been outside the United States before the making of *The Man Who Knew Too Much* and found shooting in Morocco extremely unsettling.

3. Robin Wood, "Ideology, Genre, Auteur," *Film Comment* (January–February 1977): 49.

4. Slavoj Žižek, *The Sublime Object of Ideology* (New York: Verso, 1988), 121.

5. Kaja Silverman, *The Acoustic Mirror: The Female Voice in Psychoanalysis and Cinema* (Bloomington: University of Indiana Press, 1988), 73.

6. John Russell Taylor, *Hitch: The Life and Times of Alfred Hitchcock* (New York: Pantheon, 1978), 185.

7. Interestingly, Dr. McKenna (Jimmy Stewart) goes on to explain that he has called his wife Jo for so long that he can't think of any other name for her, an interesting assertion given that, as we later discover, Jo Conway was the stage name the Doris Day character made famous before she married and changed her name. Hank then pipes up and says he calls her by another name; he calls her Mommy.

8. Slavoj Žižek, *Enjoy Your Symptom!: Jacques Lacan in Hollywood and Out* (New York: Verso, 1992), 118.

9. Silverman, *The Acoustic Mirror*, 80.

10. Silverman emphasizes that the blissful image of union with the mother, as described by Rosolato, is only one side of the coin. As she explains, "The fantasy in question turns upon the image of infantile containment—upon the image of a child held within the

environment or sphere of the mother's voice. I have described this image as neutrally as possible, but in fact its 'appearances' are always charged with either intensely positive or intensely negative affect" (ibid., 72).

11. Ibid., 85.

12. Ibid., 73.

13. Wood, *Hitchcock's Films Revisited*, 370.

14. Tania Modleski, *The Women Who Knew Too Much: Hitchcock and Feminist Theory* (New York: Methuen, 1988), 5.

15. The film frequently makes the connection between Santa Rosa and its floral namesakes. When Uncle Charlie first finds himself in young Charlie's bedroom, safe in the domestic realm, he immediately takes a rose from the bouquet and puts it in his buttonhole. Charlie's younger sister Ann is associated with flowers throughout the film. She is constantly putting them behind her ear, and, when asked to pick flowers for the Sunday dinner table, asserts that simple ones are the best.

16. The shift from the urban world of the East in *Shadow of a Doubt* to the garden world of Santa Rosa is like the shift from black and white to color—from Kansas to Oz—in *The Wizard of Oz*. But in Hitchcock's film, made four years after Fleming's, the fantasy is not of escaping *from* the drudgery of home but of escaping *to* a home that is itself perceived as a kind of fantasy land.

17. That Uncle Charlie has the controlling visual perspective, at least in the early parts of the film, is suggested by the initial scenes where the detectives are attempting to pursue him and he mysteriously disappears. The camera then shoots the detectives from a great distance and height, pulls back, and we see Uncle Charlie sitting on the top of a building looking down at his pursuers. At that moment, Uncle Charlie's point of view is defined as both extremely powerful and equated with the film audience's. As Ann Cvetkovich has argued, "Hitchcock proposes an analogy between libidinal and visual forces" ("Postmodern *Vertigo*: The Sexual Politics of Allusion in De Palma's *Body Double*," in *Hitchcock's Rereleased Films*, ed. Walter Raubicheck and Walter Srebnick [Detroit: Wayne State University Press, 1991], 151). It is not surprising that the scene in which Uncle Charlie assumes visual control is immediately followed by the scene in which he sends a telegram to his sister in Santa Rosa, a gesture that reveals, as I will argue, his libidinal desires.

18. In analyzing the way this sequence is shot, William Rothman comments, "On his line, 'Emma, don't move,' we might expect a continuity cut to a shot that again frames Charles at mid-range and has Emma join him in the frame; or a shot from Charles's point of view which frames Emma like a picture. . . . Instead, Hitchcock gives us another frontal shot, this one dominated by trees and devoid of human presence. Again, the human figures enter this 'empty' frame simultaneously from opposite sides. . . . Charles and Emma are viewed from a great distance, and when they pause they are very far apart. Only when Charles says, 'You look like Emma Spencer Oakley . . . ' do they run towards each other and embrace, upon which Hitchcock cuts to a closer shot" (*Hitchcock—The Murderous Gaze* [Cambridge: Harvard University Press, 1982], 189).

19. In *The Man Who Knew Too Much*, as in *Shadow of a Doubt*, the stranger who eventually disrupts the family is also the initial witness to its harmony and cohesion. In *The Man Who Knew Too Much*, it is Louis Bernard, the spy whose death leads to Hank's kidnap-

ping, who first confuses mother and son and later testifies to the beauty of their singing together.

20. James McLaughlin, "All in the Family: Alfred Hitchcock's *Shadow of a Doubt*," *Wide Angle* 4 (1980): 16, emphasis added.

21. Interestingly, McLaughlin also misquotes the scene where Uncle Charles embraces his sister on the walkway outside her house, reporting that he says "You're Emma Spencer" (ibid., 15). In fact, he says, "You look like Emma Spencer Oakley."

22. Wood, "Ideology, Genre, Auteur," 50, emphasis added.

23. The fact that both McLaughlin and Wood adopt Uncle Charlie's perspective is suggested by other details of their argument. McLaughlin cites Uncle Charlie as an authority in setting up the overall argument of his article when he states, "The facade of the Newton family house in *Shadow of a Doubt* is composed of sweetness and sunshine; behind it, however, lies, in the words of Uncle Charlie, 'a foul sty' " ("All in the Family," 13). In "Ideology, Genre, Auteur," Wood consistently refers to the mother of the Newton family not by her given name Emma but as Emmy, the nickname Uncle Charles adopted for his sister when they were children and continues to use as an adult.

24. Fredric Jameson, *Signatures of the Visible* (New York: Routledge, 1990), 121.

25. Rothman, *Hitchcock—The Murderous Gaze*, 234–35.

26. Modleski, *The Women Who Knew Too Much*, 120.

27. Ibid., 3.

28. Elaine Tyler May, *Homeward Bound: American Families in the Cold War Era* (New York: Basic Books, 1988), 40.

29. Ibid., 67.

30. Ibid., 65.

31. Rothman, *Hitchcock—The Murderous Gaze*, 359, n. 6.

32. The title *The Little Foxes* comes from a long paragraph at the end of Ruskin's essay in which he quotes the Bible in order to exhort women to act as queens in their own homes: "You shall see the troops of the angel keepers, that, with their wings, wave away the hungry birds from the pathsides where He has sown and call to each other between the vineyard rows, 'Take us the foxes, the little foxes, that spoil the vines, for our vines have tender grapes.' Oh—you queens—you queens; among the hills and happy greenwood of this land of yours, shall the foxes have holes, and the birds of the air have nests; and in your cities, shall the stones cry out against you, that they are the only pillows where the Son of Man can lay his head?" (*Sesame and Lilies* [London: Atheneum, 1905], 103–4).

33. Robert B. Stein notes that "there were many more reprintings of Ruskin's work in America than in England" (*John Ruskin and Aesthetic Thought in America, 1840–1900* [Cambridge: Harvard University Press, 1967], 264–65). Elizabeth K. Helsinger, Robin Lauterbach Sheets, and William Veeder comment that "in America, where the *Critic* in 1898 called Ruskin one of the four most famous living authors (together with Twain, Tolstoy and Zola), *Sesame and Lilies* was his most popular book. It was reprinted more than thirty-five times in the nineteenth century. In the early 1900s it was still a popular text" *The Woman Question: Defining Voices, 1831–1883* [New York: Garland, 1983], 96). The Louisiana State University Library, for example, has a Standard English Classics edition of *Sesame and Lilies*, with in-

troduction and notes by Mrs. Lois G. Huffner, head of the Department of English in the Teachers College of Indianapolis (Boston: Ginn and Co., 1927).

34. Ruskin, *Sesame and Lilies*, 98.

35. Ibid., 71.

36. In Hellman's play this domestic bliss of the past is immediately criticized by being linked to the plantation and the institution of slavery.

37. Ruskin, *Sesame and Lilies*, 82.

38. Wood, "Ideology, Genre, Auteur," 49.

39. May, *Homeward Bound*, 41.

40. Cited in Robert E. Kapsis, *Hitchcock: The Making of a Reputation* (Chicago: University of Chicago Press, 1992), 153.

41. Ina Rae Hark, "Revalidating Patriarchy: Why Hitchcock Remade *The Man Who Knew Too Much*," in Raubicheck and Srebnick, *Hitchcock's Rereleased Films*, 217.

42. Ibid., 118. In his chapter "The Men Who Knew Too Much (and the Women Who Knew Much Better)," Robin Wood makes a similar point when he discusses the differences between the two versions of *The Man Who Knew Too Much*. Unlike Hark, he reads the differing representation of the mother in the second version of the film positively, as proof that "the strength of family ideology could scarcely be more eloquently confirmed" (*Hitchcock's Films Revisited*, 368).

43. Wendy Lesser argues that "*Vertigo* refers back to the 1956 remake of *The Man Who knew Too Much*, which is in turn a movie about a man's 'remake' of his wife" (*His Other Half: Men Looking at Women through Art* [Cambridge: Harvard University Press, 1991], 132). If *The Man Who Knew Too Much* is a prelude to *Vertigo*, I would argue that it is also a postscript to *Rear Window*. That earlier film ends with a career woman, played by Grace Kelly, pre-sumably about to get her wish and marry the Jimmy Stewart character. *The Man Who Knew Too Much* shows us what it would be like for a woman who had a successful professional life of her own to become a wife and mother. The three films that have Jimmy Stewart as hero—*Rear Window*, *The Man Who Knew Too Much*, and *Vertigo*—would then function as a trilogy in which Hitchcock comments on women's victimization in marriage.

44. In this scene, the McKennas' marriage is increasingly being shown to follow the classic pattern of the kind of 1950s marriages discussed in Betty Friedan's *The Feminine Mystique*, where the wife attempts to live a purely domestic life but finally seeks various unsatisfactory means of escape from what she experiences as imprisonment.

45. Žižek, *Enjoy Your Symptom!*, 118.

46. Ibid.

47. In discussing her article on *Rebecca*, Modleski notes that "some films do allow for the (limited) expression of a specifically female desire. . . . Such films instead of following the male oedipal journey, which film theorists like Raymond Bellour see as the trajectory of *all* Hollywood narrative, trace a female oedipal trajectory, and in the process reveal some of the difficulties for women in becoming socialized in patriarchy" (*The Women Who Knew Too Much*, 2).

48. Ronnie Scheib describes how the camera work in this scene makes Emma curiously powerful and mobile: "In the scene where she defends her decision to dedicate her family's image to the service of its country, her constant motion contrasts vividly with the repressed energy of Uncle Charlie's lying propped up in bed, disturbed both by the news and by

the apparent unpredictability and firmness of Emma's movements, comments and actions. Emma is seen in a variety of positions, intercut with reaction shots of Uncle Charlie, between the dresser, closet, and bed (unpacking his bags). Yet each time she moves it seems to be towards a new and unexpected off-space, not exactly violating spatial logic, but in excess of it, implying a greater freedom of movement than the actual trajectory would impose" ("Charlie's Uncle," 56).

49. McLaughlin discusses Uncle Charlie as a Dracula figure throughout his article "All in the Family: Alfred Hitchcock's *Shadow of a Doubt*," but especially on pages 13–14.

50. Interestingly, when Ann's brother Roger enters the room, Uncle Charlie refers to the newspaper building he has constructed not as a house but as a farm. With his belief in the domestic values of the past, Uncle Charlie is relentlessly interested in enforcing traditional conceptions of gender difference, as is clear in the gifts he brings the Newton family. He gives the males, Roger and Joe, a gun and a watch, and he gives the females, Ann, Emma, and Charlie, a stuffed animal, a fur, and an engagement ring. The film is quite clear about Ann's response to traditional definitions of femininity in her disgusted refusal to "play house" and her disappointment with her gift.

51. Rothman, *Hitchcock—The Murderous Gaze*, 210.

52. Mladen Dolar, "Hitchcock's Objects," in *Everything You Always Wanted to Know about Lacan (But Were Afraid to Ask Hitchcock)*, ed. Slavoj Žižek (New York: Verso, 1992), 35. Appropriately, given Žižek's own emphasis on the mother as "thing," the critics he anthologizes in *Everything You Wanted to Know about Lacan (But Were Afraid to Ask Hitchcock)* discuss the ring in *Shadow of a Doubt* as a significant "object" but are uninterested in the inscription on it. This is, of course, the mistake Uncle Charlie makes when he gives the ring to Charlie. He sees the ring as an object, a valuable and beautiful emerald; she effectively gives the object a "voice" by reading what is written on it.

53. Modleski, *The Women Who Knew Too Much*, 9.

54. Appropriately, the newspaper account never refers directly to the husband but lets us know his identity (the referent for BM) by noting Thelma Schenley's married name.

55. Rothman, *Hitchcock—The Murderous Gaze*, 193.

56. Wood, "Ideology, Genre, Auteur," 49.

3

American Shame
Rope, *James Stewart, and the*
Postwar Crisis in
American Masculinity

Amy Lawrence

Of all Hitchcock's American films, the one that has benefited the most from the shifting tides of theory is *Rope* (1948). Upon its rerelease in the mid-1980s, *Rope* emerged from decades of critical and popular obscurity into the powerful embrace of "high theory" exemplified by the endless play of language à la Derrida in Thomas Hemmeter's "Twisted Writing" and the bracing heights of "queer theory" in D. A. Miller's "Anal *Rope*."[1]

While I admire Miller's essay as much for its elegance and logic as for its daring, several of his key points turn on a reading of the film's climactic image that needs to be reopened. Rupert Cadell (James Stewart), former housemaster to roommates Brandon (John Dall) and Philip (Farley Granger), has finally decided to resolve his suspicions and open the chest around which Brandon and Philip have staged their party and in which they've placed the body of their former schoolmate and victim, David Kentley. As Rupert flings open the lid, the back of the lid blacks out the image, disguising a cut. Of all the "hidden" cuts in the film, Miller argues that only this one "is 'completely successful' in feigning a continuity from which nothing can appear to have been omitted."[2] However, the cut, it seems to me, does *not* work, if by "working" one means it erases our awareness of a cut. As the camera tilts up from blackness to reveal Cadell's face, he is suddenly much closer than we'd expected. The camera has in fact moved during the cut, producing the effect of a jump cut.

Miller argues that we are led to expect a point-of-view shot (Rupert's view of the body), but there is no need to see what's in the chest—we already know.[3] The suspense throughout the film has been structured around the question "When

Publicity still from Rope (*1949*)

will Rupert look in the chest?" When he does, the point is not *what* he sees but how he looks seeing it. What we finally see in the film's dramatic, penultimate cut, what the whole film, I shall argue, has been leading up to, is a close-up of Jimmy Stewart.

The importance of stars in Hitchcock's American films can hardly be over-estimated. Hitchcock's work throughout the 1940s and 1950s is deeply embedded in the star system. In *Rope*, as in their collaborations in the 1950s, it is Stewart who serves as Hitchcock's icon of American manhood. In this essay I would like to examine how Stewart's first film with Hitchcock highlights one of the recurrent themes of Stewart's star image: the exploration of an American masculine subjectivity threatened at all times by a frequently undefined but inescapable sense of shame. While key elements of Stewart's persona (a propensity for physical and spiritual suffering, lingering fears of inadequacy) were established in the 1930s, particularly in his work with Capra, these would intensify and deepen in his postwar work with Hitchcock and Anthony Mann. The importance of the war in terms of Stewart's performances in this period and the public's perception of Stewart's own war record add new dimensions to the already troubled Stewart persona, dimensions *Rope* addresses in unsettling ways. In order to see what issues are raised

by Stewart's presence in *Rope* (and what that presence precludes), it will be necessary first to answer the questions, "Who is 'James Stewart' and what is he doing
in *Rope?*"

It is clear that Hitchcock's need for a "James Stewart" type stems from the
persistence of unresolved issues in Hitchcock's work at this time. The film *Rope*
most resembles and to which it is most often compared is *Lifeboat* (1944). Companion pieces of formal experimentation, both films are predominantly films of
ideas where romance is subordinated to talk and overt action precluded by the
physically restricted settings. For both, the "excesses" of technical experiment have
been seen as an attempt to make up for narrative/cinematic problems, while dis-
tracting the audience from problematic thematic issues.[4]

Both *Rope* and *Lifeboat* begin with sudden violence (the murder of David, the
sinking of the ship). A group of "types" comes together in a confined space. In
Lifeboat they are (literally) without direction; in *Rope* they don't realize they need
one. In neither film do they properly recognize the evildoer(s) in their midst. But
Rope supplies what *Lifeboat* lacks, and we've almost forgotten it when James Stewart
is casually discovered "already there" in a decidedly antistar entrance. A "natural"
leader, "superior" to the others, the one who watches and who catches every slip,
Rupert's late entrance puts him in the position of *Lifeboat's* Willy (the U-boat
commander played by Walter Slezak). As with Willy, the film revolves around
Rupert from the moment he enters. Rupert, like Willy, is the one we and the
other characters watch the most closely. You have to watch Rupert because, like
Willy, much of the time "you cannot really be sure whether Rupert is essentially
good or essentially evil."[5] Rupert serves simultaneously as the text's original fascist
and its ultimate American, the charmingly glib nihilist who asserts that "murder
is a privilege for the few" and the righteous defender of the American way ("Did
you think you were God, Brandon?"). In *Lifeboat* the bestiality of those who kill
the beast is something neither the characters nor the text has the strength to face.
Through Stewart, Hitchcock can consolidate the contradictions of *Rope* within a
star persona that is one of the most sympathetic, troubled, disturbing, and American in Hollywood at this time. The payoff to the prolonged suspense in *Rope* is
what *Lifeboat* shirks, a moment of revelation condensed into a close-up of a star,
the dawning self-awareness of a specifically American shame: Jimmy Stewart with
blood on his hands.

Who Is James Stewart?

Rope is one of the transitional films that form part of the long postwar
phase of Stewart's career, when he spent five years trying to reestablish his prewar
popularity. This crucial transitional period saw Stewart make a decisive shift from
comedy to drama. In his first flush of success between 1936 and 1940, most of

his films were comedies, with a few "women's films" thrown in.[6] By the time he regained his stride after the war with the first Mann western (*Winchester 73* in 1950) until *The Man Who Shot Liberty Valance* in 1962, the dramas vastly outnumbered the comedies. In the transition period from 1946 to 1950, the films are evenly split: six comedies, six dramas.[7] Many of these either were only moderately successful at the box office or were outright flops. All of them show Stewart quite consciously trying to reestablish his prewar popularity.

Offhand, James Stewart seems the most transparent of American actors. According to Andrew Britton, "as far as James Stewart is concerned—he is, as we all know, an embodiment of homely, middle-American integrity and moral earnestness."[8] James Naremore, in his study of acting, lists among Stewart's attributes "a lanky, awkward diffidence suggestive of Lincolnesque virtue; a drawling wit accompanied by a wise glint in the eye; a clod-kicking shyness and innocence concealing 'natural' intelligence and passionate idealism."[9] Stewart's image had been formed through his work with directors specializing in comedy, like W. S. Van Dyke, George Stevens, Ernst Lubitsch, and most of all Frank Capra. Frank Capra in particular stresses the sense that with Stewart's performances, "you were looking at the man, not an actor. You could see this man's soul."[10]

But what Capra prized most about Stewart was his intelligence. "When you're dealing in the world of *ideas* and you want your character to be on a higher intellectual plane . . . you turn to persons like Jimmy Stewart because he has a look of the intellectual about him."[11] From Capra's *Mr. Smith Goes to Washington* (1939) to John Ford's *The Man Who Shot Liberty Valance* (1962), we find Stewart cast as the character who upholds the written word, the law, *ideas*. Throughout *Rope* we watch Stewart think.

Rupert's (and Stewart's) brand of intelligence is essentially a critical one that combines equal parts charm and danger. Like Brandon, Rupert uses a private humor that often puts others at a disadvantage. When he first enters, he undercuts social niceties with unexpected twists. Kenneth says, "It's nice to see you again," and Rupert shoots back, "Why?" When Janet hopes David's descriptions of her have done her justice, he responds, "Do you deserve justice?" Mrs. Wilson tells him she has his favorite paté, he says, "I don't like it anymore." When she wilts with disappointment, he whispers, "Just teasing." Any rudeness is softened by after-the-fact disclaimers and the judicious employment of charm.

According to the description of Rupert in the play, "he has a very disarming habit, every now and again, of retrieving the whole thing with an extraordinarily frank, open and genial smile."[12] In his performance, Stewart prefers a suppressed smile and a sparkle in his eyes directed toward the recipient, a reaction that creates a "shared moment." For instance, when he kids Mrs. Wilson about the paté, she tells him, "You're awful," and he answers, "Thank you"; and he kids the forgetful dowager Mrs. Atwater about the title of a Mary Pickford movie he saw once, telling her, "It was the 'something something.' Or was it just 'something.' " On the last line he shares a look with Janet as his smile widens, giving away the joke. Where the popular image of Jimmy Stewart stresses an unaffected spontaneity and humility, the awareness of his own performance that characterizes Rupert in these comic moments provides a glimpse of Stewart's "actorliness," a display of his pleasure in performance as such.

Often the gentle tone of mockery Rupert uses with the women (signified by a soft voice, even murmuring) is replaced by a harder, biting style when he puts someone on the spot. Because Rupert's "faintly mocking, cynical air" vacillates between spoofing and embarrassing directness, all the characters are kept on their toes and at a distance. Acerbic wit in 1940s Hollywood is often a sign of a desexualized or sexually subversive character. Clifton Webb's Waldo Lydecker in *Laura* (1944) is a classic example; George Sanders's Addison DeWitt in *All about Eve* (1950) is another. (As the gay subtext associated with these characters suggests, there are more complex sexual issues accumulating around Rupert that shall be discussed later.) Consequently, there is never a hint at a possible romantic interest between Rupert and Janet (this is probably the first time a younger leading man [Kenneth] was brought in to supply the "love interest" in a Stewart film). Rupert's teasing that he might marry the fastidiously fussy Mrs. Wilson signals his lack of seriousness.

Discussing Stewart's performance in 1954's *Rear Window*, Naremore discounts "Hitchcock's simplistic account of the Kuleshov effect or his glib descriptions of how the 'best' acting in movies is achieved" (by "doing nothing extremely well").[13] Naremore's comments on *Rear Window* apply equally to *Rope*: "As much a *tour de force* for the star as for the director," each film "heighten[s] the cleverness of Stewart's performance by severely constraining him."[14]

Stewart's acting is "the type most often associated with the medium: concentrated on the face and upper body, it emphasizes flesh tones, expressions in the eyes, and the grain of a voice."[15] If the impression of intelligence is created between the dialogue and the glint in his eyes, emotional and physical vulnerability are located in Stewart's voice, a smooth baritone alternately cracking, shaky, hoarse, or hesitant with fear. Stewart's control of his voice, its variations in intensity, volume, and color, not only adds variety to line readings but through the grain of the voice calls attention to his body, a body upon which a struggle between traditional definitions of feminine and masculine is being waged.[16]

Sexuality

For Richard Dyer, the function of the star-as-social-phenomenon is to cover over the impossibility of constructing and maintaining a clear-cut subject position.

> How they [do this] may be predominantly in terms of reaffirming the
> reality of people as individuals or subjects over against ideology and
> history, or else in terms of *exposing precisely the uncertainty and anxiety con-*
> *cerning the definition of what a person is.*[17]

Substitute "man" for "person" and you have James Stewart. The display of anxiety
and uncertainty that shoots through Stewart's career like electricity through a
wire converges on masculinity and heterosexuality.

As a leading man in the 1930s, Stewart's loose, unhurried sexiness ideally
suited the romantic roles in screwball comedies such as *You Can't Take It with You*
(1938) and *Vivacious Lady* (1938). A lanky 6'4", Stewart, who weighed only 130
pounds when he went into the army in 1940, carried clothes well without having
the fashion status of Gary Cooper or the muscular build of Cary Grant. Throughout his career Stewart's long hair is almost always worn straight back without a
part, a stray lock falling into his eyes at moments of stress. Although seldom
"packaged" as a model of masculine beauty, Stewart is very good-looking. Naremore singles out his "unusually beautiful and expressive eyes."[18] He also has strikingly nice hands, which he uses to good effect in film after film. (As early as *After*
the Thin Man in 1936 he can be found stealing a scene by flexing his long, well-
shaped fingers against the black velvet sleeve of a woman he's comforting for
having left him.) He often plays scenes in full profile rather than three-quarter
shots, a position that makes the most of his relaxed posture and, in close-up, his
sensual lower lip and long lashes.

Once his persona crystallized in the late 1930s, the particular kind of sexiness
enacted by Stewart could be put into play for specific ideological functions. Stewart's style of masculinity, attractive to women because of its friendly interest, free
of pressure or threat and demonstrated by a kind of unhurried ease with his body,
complemented the assertive angularity of actresses who challenged limiting definitions of femininity. In discussing the careers of Katharine Hepburn and Marlene
Dietrich, Andrew Britton attributes each actress's newfound popularity to the
switch to comedy. What he fails to note is the crucial presence of Stewart. In
Destry Rides Again (1939), Stewart plays a character whose strength lies in the
apparent rejection of any of the affectations of traditional masculinity. In *The*
Philadelphia Story (1940), his status as an agent of patriarchy selling domesticity
door to door ("you have hearth fires banked within you") stands out by contrast
to Cary Grant's openly vicious attacks on Hepburn's character's independence.[19]

There is a ten-year gap between the one-night stand with Stewart that sends
Hepburn back to Grant and matrimony and the characters Stewart played in his
first real postwar hits: the completely unsexed Elwood P. Dowd of *Harvey* (Stewart's successful attempt to revive *his* career with an adaptation of a Broadway hit)
and the obsessive neurotic fratricide in *Winchester 73* (both 1950). *Harvey* is the
last of Stewart's screwball comedies, *Winchester 73* the first western. The change

in genre, with its possibilities of reinvention, brings with it a distinct change in Stewart's portrayal of heterosexuality. As is typical in the western, male-male relationships predominate. In *The Far Country* (1955), for example, Walter Brennan plays Stewart's sidekick, who uproots himself to follow Stewart around the frontier and plans to live with him for the rest of his life in a small house on a ranch in Utah. It is Brennan's death that shatters Stewart's illusions of self-containment and makes him recognize his need for other people. When it comes to women, a skittish negotiation with bad girl Ruth Roman is more his speed than the devotion of French tomboy Corinne Calvet.

Not all the changes in Stewart's troubled depiction of heterosexuality are due to genre. After the war, many of his films reveal a crisis centered on romance. His relationships are most painful when they are most sexual, the romantic scenes riddled with what a contemporary account termed a "tense urgency" and "romantic anguish."[20] When he succumbs to the perfume of Donna Reed's freshly washed hair in the 1946 *It's a Wonderful Life*, it is staged like a breakdown. The violence of his resistance to marriage and small-town business opportunities ("I don't want any plastics, I don't want any ground floor, and I don't want to get married—ever—to anyone") as he shakes her, his voice breaking, tears in his eyes (what Silverman calls "his protest against the imperatives of capital and the family"),[21] is remarkable primarily because we are seeing a man being torn apart. Heterosexual attraction as the thing that prevents him from realizing his ambitions appears again in *Magic Town* (1947), where he plays a Gallup-type poll-taker who thinks he has found the perfect microcosm of American values.[22] Love for the local newspaper editor (Jane Wyman) again threatens to tear him in two, and when he finally kisses her, the expression on his face can best be described as one of exquisite pain. In the remarkable western *The Naked Spur* (1953), Stewart is literally reduced to tears every time he grabs Janet Leigh, the very act of acknowledging desire forcing him to confront a crisis of masculine identity that is almost unbearable. Little wonder that in the sweetly gentle *Harvey*, Stewart has given up women entirely and thrown in his lot with a six-foot-tall invisible male rabbit. It was love at first sight.

The psychic cost of postwar heterosexual desire, the searing pain of it in Stewart's films, cannot be attributed to the usual scapegoat, the newly independent postwar woman. Stewart's prewar films had proved he was especially adept at partnering challenging women. The problem was masculinity itself. According to Britton, "The meaning of the Stewart persona might be said to be—'if you are the perfect, middle-class, heterosexual American male you go mad.' "[23] Britton maintains that a "significant amnesia" is necessary for fans devoted to an untroubled image of Jimmy Stewart; for them "his performances, for Mann and Hitchcock, as obsessional neurotics and 'action-heroes' trembling on the brink of psychosis, simply do not exist."[24] I would counter that what makes the positive qualities of Stewart so precious (precious in the sense of something one is loathe to give up or part with) are their hard-won status. Stewart's gentleness, integrity, stability, and happiness are qualities *shown to be* under enormous threat from both inside and out.

Jimmy Stewart Is Being Beaten

Stewart's "crisis of masculinity" is made visible most prominently through the spectacle of his suffering. Film after film requires Stewart to "exhibit unusual degrees of neurotic suffering, moral anguish, and physical pain."[25]

In discussing the suicidal hero of *It's a Wonderful Life*, played by Jimmy Stewart, Kaja Silverman argues that George Bailey is defined by a series of injuries or castrations, "splittings" from himself, "upon which his subjectivity is shown to depend."[26] Masculinity (as a form of subjectivity built on the splitting of the subject in accession to language, submission to the law of the father, and the necessary cutting off of symbolic castration) is built upon a lie: "Our dominant fiction calls upon the male subject to see himself, and the female subject to recognize and desire him, only through the mediation of images of unimpaired masculinity."[27] Bailey is a striking demonstration of the way the traditional male subject "not only accepts these 'wounds' as the necessary condition of cultural identity, but [is taught to take] pleasure in the pain they induce in him."[28]

For Silverman (who does not discuss Stewart-as-star or his performance), the unending series of humiliations, losses, and sufferings Bailey goes through are remarkable because "so open a display of wounds would normally be totally incompatible with an affirmation of the dominant fiction and its phallic representations."[29] However, this "display of wounds" is in fact typical of Stewart throughout his career. Not only is he emotionally vulnerable (Naremore calls him "the most intensely emotional leading man to emerge from the studio system"),[30] but he frequently carries physical wounds as a signifier of emotional distress. He bears prominent leg wounds: in *Magic Town* a war buddy identifies Stewart by pulling up his trouser leg to find the large scar he got in the war; in *The Stratton Story* (1949) he plays a baseball player whose leg has been amputated; in *Naked Spur* he's shot in the leg, and the wound plagues him throughout the film: He grows delirious from the pain, falls off his horse, and cannot climb back up a hill. In *Rope*, Rupert has a limp from another war wound, and in *Rear Window*, of course, Stewart spends the film in a full leg cast (by the end he has two). Even more disturbing is the damage done to his hands, as I discuss below.

Stewart's performances are frequently built around the display of these wounds, often dwelling on the scenes in which they're inflicted to such an extent that the issue of masochism becomes unavoidable. Silverman discusses the relationship between masochism and a conflicted or subversive masculinity, pointing out that for Theodor Reik in *Masochism in Sex and Society*, "what is . . . rendered visible" in masochism "is the subject's 'suffering,' 'discomfort,' 'humiliation,' and 'disgrace' rather than its grandeur or its triumph."[31] Stewart's performances epitomize the actorly display of these traits. Think of the filibuster scene in *Mr. Smith Goes to Washington*, where the naive idealistic junior senator, falsely accused and in disgrace, argues himself hoarse defending "lost causes" until he collapses. Or the inquest scene in *Vertigo* (1958), where there is an almost sadistic glee in the public humiliation of Stewart's traumatized, disgraced Scottie as the coroner recites with great relish Scottie's failures, weaknesses, and overwhelming inadequacy.

The "neurotic suffering" and spiritual agony of these performances is joined by physical pain in such Mann films as *The Naked Spur*, *Bend of the River* and—the most extreme example—*The Man from Laramie* (1955). In the latter, he is backed toward the camera, a small figure surrounded by men on horseback, lassoed, and dragged through a fire (a stunt Stewart not only performed but suggested). In another scene he is ambushed by Dave, the arrogant rancher's son. In the shootout preceding Stewart's capture, a ricochet wounds Dave in the hand. Dave has two of his men hold Stewart so he can take his revenge. "You're not gonna kill him?" one asks. Stewart's character shows extreme fear, twice kicking out the full length of his legs trying to keep Dave away. As the two men hold Stewart by the throat, in a close-up they take the glove off his shaking hand. Dave puts the barrel of the gun directly against Stewart's palm. The camera pans quickly to Stewart when we hear the shot. In the Cinemascope close-up, Stewart's head rolls back, his eyes screwed up tight, the lack of music emphasizing the strangled animal-like cry deep in his throat. After a long moment of suffering, he opens his eyes, looks up at Dave and rasps, "Why you *scum!*"[32]

In these scenes of violation, Stewart's expression classically "alternates between grotesquely distorted pain and a soft, almost erotic yielding."[33] The staging of scenes of forcible restraint, suspense, and prolonged suffering whose enactment is itself the peak of "masochistic ecstasy"[34] make Stewart's "wounding" "a loss which the film overtly thematizes both as a castration and an erotic event."[35]

The eroticization of Stewart's "weakness" results from depicting it as feminine. In his "feminine" vein, he breaks down in tears (*It's a Wonderful Life*, *Naked Spur*, and others too numerous to mention),[36] threatens to lose consciousness as his body falls limp after a beating (*Winchester 73*, *Bend of the River*, *Man from Laramie*), or faints outright (*Made for Each Other*, *Mr. Smith Goes to Washington*).[37] The 1950s westerns attempt to recuperate this weakness for masculinity through violent outbursts and revenge narratives. *The Far Country*, for instance, is described as the story of "a peaceful cowpoke who gets trampled on at every turn until he just explodes."[38] The fervent hope that castration isn't permanent, that lost manhood can be regained, is literalized in *Winchester 73*, once humorously described as "man gets gun, man loses gun, man gets gun."[39]

It is important to note that these attempts to restore Stewart's "manhood" through a climactic act of violence as often as not fail to eradicate the disturbing effects of the scenes of suffering. In *Laramie*, for instance, the aftermath of the violence is unexpectedly prolonged. After Stewart is shot, Mann cuts to the men on horseback watching like witnesses to a gang rape (an audience being essential to a masochistic scene). Over the shot (which lasts forever) we hear Stewart making a tortured gurgling sound in his throat, half crying, half panting. When we cut back to Stewart he is standing unsteady, his legs too far apart, trying to wrap his hand in a bandanna (a gesture used in *Rope*, where he is also shot in the hand). As he turns to walk away, a man calls to him. He stops. Someone brings up a horse, while another gently helps him up. Slowly riding away, Stewart never turns around, and we never see his face; shame is inscribed in his posture.

Shame, like masochism, needs a real or imagined audience to witness its finely honed sense of suffering. Stewart's suffering is usually an index of his fear of the shame that would result from the public exposure of his failings (real or imagined). Fear of the exposure of his masculine insufficiency (failing to protect his Native American wife from racist murderers in *Broken Arrow* [1950], failing to save Madeleine in *Vertigo*); of his personal misconduct (betraying all of his friends and the woman he loves in *Magic Town*, having been an outlaw who narrowly escaped hanging in *Bend of the River*); his forbidden desires (a bounty hunter who is willing to sell a corpse for the reward in *Naked Spur*, tracking down his brother in revenge for their father's death in *Winchester 73*); his historical guilt (when he is tricked into massacring Native Americans by a criminal ex-cavalry officer in *Naked Spur*); and his hiding the fact that masculinity itself is built on illusion (*The Man Who Shot Liberty Valance*).

While Silverman links masochism to homosexuality as two potentially utopian means of subverting dominant definitions of masculinity, Stewart's masochism focuses on heterosexuality and traditional masculinity as sites of psychic crises, revealing their complexity. Unlike the actors with whom he was most often compared in the 1930s (Grant and Cooper in particular), Stewart's sexuality was not the subject of rumor. However, when he married in August 1949 at age forty-one, a year after *Rope*'s release, the headline in *Life* magazine showed a keen sense of relief: "Jimmy Stewart is married *at last*."[40] D. A. Miller's description of Rupert as "if not a gay bachelor . . . a confirmed one" is thus given extra resonance by Stewart's presence.[41] (*Life* calls him "the Great American bachelor.") Miller argues that Rupert's sexuality is "nothing but a *non-homosexuality* . . . engaged in rejecting a determination that thus can't fail to determine it."[42] While this may be true of Rupert as a character, I would argue that Stewart's star persona ultimately leads us and Hitchcock elsewhere. Stewart's career adds up to one of the most conflicted representations of masculine subjectivity in Hollywood film; for this deconstructive project, heterosexuality is essential.

"Something queer? What's that?"

Patrick Hamilton's play *Rope* was first produced in England in March 1929 and played London's West End that April. In the introduction to the published version, Hamilton goes out of his way to disavow any connection to the Leopold and Loeb case in America, which the play was widely thought to parallel.[43] Hume Cronyn worked on a treatment of the play with Hitchcock in 1947; Arthur Laurents is credited with the screenplay.[44]

The first thing one notices in reading the play is how the structure has been tightened up for the film. In the play, except for victim David Kentley's father and widowed aunt, none of the guests knows or is associated with the victim. In fact, we never see David. In the film, of course, his murder is the film's first shocking cut. In the Cronyn/Laurents adaptation, all of the guests are closely connected to David. Janet is David's fiancée and has recently broken up with Kenneth, her former fiancé and David's best friend. This increases every character's stake in the events of the drama. Simple techniques for generating suspense have also been added to the film, most notably when we watch Mrs. Wilson clearing the chest after supper as party chitchat goes on just offscreen.

There are also changes in slang, language, and style, and these are not incidental. What dates the play is its arch British drawing room quality. For instance, there is a grab bag of ethnic stereotypes, including a "comic" French valet (in place of the faithful Mrs. Wilson), and Philip's character (called Granillo or Granno in the play)[45] becomes a "rather ornately dressed" "Spaniard."

But the most striking difference between play and screen can be seen in the Anglicized Rupert.

> He is of medium height and about twenty-nine. He is a little foppish in dress and appearance, and this impression is increased by the very exquisite walking-stick which he carries indoors as well as out. He is lame in the right leg. He is enormously affected in speech and carriage. He brings his words out not only as though he is infinitely weary of all things. . . . His affectation almost verges on effeminacy, and can be very irritating. (31)

A character straight out of Oscar Wilde, Rupert's "enormously affected" world-weariness, especially when combined with the other traits, has defined "foppishness" since the Restoration. (At one point he opines, "Oh, dear Heaven! What unmentionable fatigue" [75].) Miller also invokes Wilde when discussing whether or not it can be "proved" that Brandon and Philip in the film are homosexual. If the film depends exclusively on connotation to establish homosexuality (what can be inferred from things like "standing too close," the *perception* of affectation, "manner"), then "one straightforward thematic consequence" of connotation's tendency "to recruit every signifier of the text . . . would be the implicit homosexualization of almost all the other male characters," including "the bachelor pedagogue Rupert himself."[46]

In Hamilton's play, Rupert's sexuality is hardly a question; at every point it is as flagrantly closeted as Brandon's. In place of the older philosopher/publisher/schoolmaster of the film, the play gives us a young poet, forever marked by the trauma of the first World War à la Siegfried Sassoon, A. E. Housman, Wilfred Owen, and Rupert Brooke (from whom the character probably got his name). Rupert is even recognized by Sir Kentley: "Are you the great Cadell, then? . . . Oh—I've read your poems" (33). (In the film, Brandon and Philip are the "artistic" ones; Mr. Kentley recognizes Rupert through his relationship with his son.)

The play repeatedly raises issues of manhood and masculine identity, though they are almost always clouded by double meanings or outright ambiguity. The privileged signifier of double meaning in the play is precisely the repeated use of the term "queer." As with all signifiers of the closet, it can be read as "innocent," unintended, as if the viewer is reading "too much" into it.[47] Structurally, the term is privileged by its exclusivity; Brandon, Granillo/Philip, and Rupert say it only to each other and only when they are alone. When Rupert first uses the freighted term, in fact, it collapses murder and homosexuality and brings down the first act curtain.

> Rupert: I have just thought of something rather queer.
> Brandon: Something queer. What's that?
> Rupert: All this talk about rotting bones in chests . . . (47–48, ellipsis in original)

Alone with Brandon at the beginning of act II, Rupert reminds him of his tendency "as an infant" to tell stories about hidden corpses. Brandon again presses for definition.

> Brandon: What about it, though?
> Rupert (lightly): Oh, nothing. Just queer, that's all. (49)

Brandon insists a second time on Rupert's saying the unsayable, but Rupert sidesteps him with a tautology, as if the word itself says everything without ever being defined.[48]

> Brandon (pouring out whisky. Quietly): How queer—exactly?
> Rupert: Oh, just queer. (50)

Earlier Rupert had added, "You were a morbid child."

"Queer" also defines the relationship between Brandon and Granillo, especially its problems. When Rupert walks in on a fight between them, Brandon says, "Rupert. This is nothing to do with you. Granno and I have a certain trouble between us which concerns no one else" (81). Earlier he had confronted Rupert,

"You didn't know that Granno and I behaved like that, did you, Rupert?" Rupert notes that their argument was "a queer thing to quarrel about," and Brandon defiantly responds: "Yes. But we do quarrel about queer things nowadays, don't we, Granno?" (56).

When Brandon is not being put on the spot, attention turns to Rupert himself. After Rupert has left, Granno/Philip says he thought Rupert had "got on to it." Brandon muses wistfully, "I sometimes rather wish he had. God. Rupert. Queer lad. I wonder . . . I wonder if he had been with us he wouldn't have got drunk" (73). The suggestion that his excessive drinking is a sign of repression (or self-hatred) is not foreign to Rupert's self-assessment. Having already had four drinks by the time he arrived and several more in the course of acts I and II, he returns for another at the beginning of act III. One of the first things he says is "Must we have all this light? . . . I am a creature of half-lights" (75–76). When Brandon tries to get him to leave, he responds with the evanescence of things left undefined: "Surely you're not going to spoil my mood?" (78). Brandon specifies, "You're in a queer mood, to-night, Rupert, too" (linking them all with "too"). But Rupert quickly denies it: "No—not a queer mood. An inspired mood, rather" (79), at which he pins the evidence of their guilt (a music-hall ticket) on his lapel, at a stroke disassociating himself from them. "Not a queer mood."

Although all these lines have been eliminated or changed in the film, their trace remains. For instance, in the play when Rupert has to acknowledge his role in Brandon's crime, he says, "This is a very queer, dark and incomprehensible universe, and I understand it very little" (88). In the film the world is still "dark and incomprehensible," if not quite so queer—or at least more securely closeted. The film substitutes code words for the original code and mise-en-scène for the unspeakable.

Rope can easily be seen as a saga of the closet where action equals identity (where what you do in private becomes who you "are") and where the evidence of what Brandon and Philip have done is smack in the middle of the room for all to see—but no one thinks to look. The chest literalizes the closet, a signifier of hiddenness bearing witness to what is inside, again calling to mind Miller on connotation and Sedgwick's "epistomology of the closet" and questions of how we think we "know" what we can never "see."[49]

If we take into account Miller's assertion that "a-man-standing-too-close-to-another" acts as one of the text's signifiers of "gay sex," then it is notable that Brandon often stands very close to Rupert, who makes no attempt to move. (Look at Stewart's casual body language when he points out that there is a gun in Brandon's pocket.) When Brandon asks Rupert how he would have gotten rid of David "if you were I," Brandon is so close to Rupert it is impossible to tell whether they're touching or not. When Rupert, with the fervor of a sinner saving his soul,[50] refuses to be part of Brandon and Philip's "we" ("we've always said, you and I"), it isn't their gay identity that unhinges him. That certainly predated the murder.

Rupert objects to Brandon as a killer; his is repugnance located in the recognition of his own guilt.

War Wounds: James Stewart in *Rope*

Shame is a painful feeling caused by the consciousness or exposure of unworthy or indecent conduct. . . . It is similar to guilt.

—*Random House College Dictionary*, rev. ed. (1974), s.v. "shame"

James Stewart would never play a killer.

—Alfred Hitchcock, as recalled by François Truffaut[51]

"Good Americans usually die young on the battlefield, don't they?" Brandon asks disingenuously, smirking at the absurdity of David's recent death. Guaranteed to irk patriotic postwar audiences, this question positions the film in a specifically postwar context, raising several thorny issues that coalesce in the character of Rupert and the figure of James Stewart.

In *Lifeboat*, Hitchcock refuses to make the distinction between war and murder. The effect is a political paralysis where the characters and the plot are wracked with contradictions that cannot be resolved, only restated in an even starker form. In the film's last scene, when a second German sailor pulls himself on board, the others instantly suggest killing him and just as quickly react with disbelieving horror when he asks "Aren't you going to kill me?" ("What are you going to do with people like that," asks one of the Americans, eager to kill him only seconds before.) The only positions available when the film ends are a smug self-righteousness or a self-serving amnesia, breathtaking in the speed with which it represses the characters' awareness of the base acts of which they are capable.

In *Rope*, it is in trying to maintain the distinction between war and murder that the screenwriters most fundamentally alter Rupert's character. Rupert is the first character in Hamilton's play to publicly confess to murder. He tells the other guests, "It would be positively disingenuous to say that I don't approve of murder. Furthermore, I have already committed murder myself" (64). He points out that when one person kills another,

> they call that murder. But when the entire youth and manhood of a whole nation rises up to slaughter the entire youth and manhood of another . . . then society condones and applauds the outrage, and calls it war. How, then, can I say that I disapprove of murder, seeing that I have, in the last Great War, acted on these assumptions myself?

When Janet insists he "must have *some* moral standards," he retorts, "Must I?"

Janet: Don't be absurd. You wouldn't hurt a fly.
Rupert: Wouldn't I? I've hurt thousands in my time. (65)

The play's disillusionment with war and heroism is a typical product of Hitch-cock's generation in the aftermath of the First World War. (We can see Hitch-cock's personal inability to contribute wholeheartedly to the war effort reflected in the failed propaganda of a film like *Lifeboat* and in the two unreleased shorts he made in 1944, *Bon Voyage* and *Adventure Malgache*.) However, such a stance is not only unlikely in 1948 but must be actively censored and/or repressed, especially in relation to Stewart.

In the film Rupert is the soldier who stands in opposition to Brandon and Philip, his status reenforced by the well-publicized biography of World War II pilot James Stewart. Yet Stewart's war work is as repressed as it is celebrated. He is often called a war hero (the 1946 *Newsweek* article cites his rank as "a full colonel with the DFC and cluster, the Croix de Guerre with palm, and seven battle stars"[52]), but no one says what particular missions he flew or what the medals were for.

One of the most popular ways of reading Stewart's refusal to talk about his experiences as wing commander for a bomber squadron was to see it as "charac-teristic" modesty. According to *Newsweek*, Stewart had a clause in his contract specifying that he would not act in war films. *Newsweek* finds it necessary to explain this refusal, using it to reiterate his humility and heroism:

> [It] might have been easier if Stewart had made his return to civilian life in a war film, where he wouldn't have been acting so much as remem-bering. But he insisted that his contract specify no war roles, for two excellent reasons: He logged 2,000 hours flying B-24s overseas and had enough war to last him a lifetime, and he wants to avoid even the slightest suspicion that he is attempting to cash in on his war record. He just wants to forget the whole thing and be an actor.[53]

Frank Capra tells another story about Stewart's desire to "forget the whole thing and just be an actor." During the filming of *It's a Wonderful Life*,

> Capra sensed that Stewart still had doubts about whether acting was an important enough profession for someone who had experienced what he had in the war, so the director asked the old pro, Lionel Barrymore, to give the star a pep talk. . . . When Stewart told Barrymore he didn't think acting was "decent," Barrymore asked him "if he thought it was more 'decent' to drop bombs on people than to bring rays of sunshine into their lives with his acting talent." Stewart told [Capra] that Lionel's barbs had knocked him flat on his ass, and that now acting was going to be his life's work.[54]

Whether Stewart's postwar films, with their tormented, neurotic, suicidal he-roes, bring "rays of sunshine" into people's lives is a moot point. After years of newsreel and fictional footage of the Blitz, focusing on the consequences of aerial bombardment for the people on the ground, it was a public relations challenge to make Allied bomber pilots heroes, especially if their targets were not exclusively military. For instance, it isn't likely that the trench warfare of World War I would have enabled Hamilton's Rupert to have "hurt thousands" in his time; but given the military "improvements" made in the following twenty years, the situation of a bomber pilot like Stewart was a different matter. As Barrymore's comment makes clear, there was a lingering ambivalence about the massive destruction it had taken to win the war. However, there was (and remains) a great fear that questioning the morality of war itself is tantamount to attacking veterans—despite the fact that this ambivalence (as Stewart's reaction shows) was perhaps most keenly felt by the veterans themselves. As a combat veteran Stewart was trapped by a contradiction which, in the wake of the officially sanctioned postwar euphoria, produced psychological turmoil veterans were left to negotiate alone. Consequently, nearly all of Stewart's postwar roles are haunted by an undercurrent of confusion, guilt, and shame that is historically specific but can never be articulated.

Despite Stewart's reticence, his war experience was immediately recognized as having left a visible trace. If Stewart was never wounded in the war, its effects were nevertheless written on his body. "The boyishness Stewart projected as a personality before the war, *Newsweek* notes, has 'vanished with his return from the B-24s, which left him with a few unboyish gray hairs' " (emphasized in Hitchcock's film).[55] Contemporary critics like Bosley Crowther thought they could see more substantial changes in Stewart: "He has grown in spiritual stature as well as in talent during the years he was in the war."[56] This urge to read physical changes in a positive light is carried over in the film when Mrs. Wilson tells us "Mr. Cadell got a bad leg in the war for his courage," putting a positive "masculine" reading on what might otherwise be seen as a sign of castration or impotence.

In *Rope* Hitchcock leans on James Stewart to do what stars do, to bring about what Dyer calls "a 'magic' reconciliation of . . . apparently incompatible terms."[57] This is done by "throwing [political issues] onto the realm of personal experience and feelings."[58] Stars depoliticize "consciousness by individualizing it, rendering the social personal," and converting "the opinion expressed in the film to an expression of [their] being."[59] Stewart's performance of Rupert's final speech substitutes emotion for analysis, selling access to the star, who through bravura acting exposes his deepest guilt, showing us his raw nerves, his desperate *need* to believe, in exchange for our not pressing actor or character with "cold hard logic."

After Rupert opens the chest, we are treated to a climactic outburst of the kind we have come to expect in a James Stewart movie. As early as *After the Thin Man* in 1936 (where he broke down and confessed to murder), key Stewart films climax with an emotional speech that allows the actor to pull out all the stops. The same structure recurs in *Mr. Smith Goes to Washington* (1939), *Naked Spur* (1953), and *Vertigo* (1957). In the play Rupert's denunciation scene was a privileged moment, the hero "suddenly letting himself go—a thing he has not done all the evening, and which he now does with tremendous force, and clear, angry articulation" (89). Yet Hitchcock's Rupert, as a former teacher, war hero, and star, is in a far more complicated position morally. Unlike Jefferson Smith, who renounces the fallen authority figure, Rupert *is* the discredited father-figure who must renounce himself while remaining the hero. "You make me ashamed of every concept I ever had of superior or inferior beings. And I *thank* you for that shame."

The passion with which Stewart invests this speech locates it firmly within the tradition of Stewart-style masochism. After a catalogue of denial ("I couldn't believe it was true"), Rupert/Stewart really "finds" himself by embracing shame. But far from providing the underpinnings for a utopian masochism that exposes and renounces the crucible of traditional heterosexual masculinity, this ecstatic shame becomes a force for repression. His momentary acknowledgment of complicity is merely the price Stewart's Rupert pays to establish his "difference" from Brandon and Philip—and it's cheap at the cost.

The great lie of the outburst ("There's something deep inside me that would *never* let me do it") is the pivot on which the tension of the denunciation rests. The distinction between Brandon's murderer and Stewart's soldier is society: One acts on his own, the other is shielded by society's authority. Whatever he has done (or is about to do) is out of his hands.

> It's not what *I'm* going to do, Brandon, it's what *society's* going to do. I don't know what that'll be . . . (suddenly louder) But I can guess! And I can help! (much louder) You're going to *die*, Brandon! (swings around to face Philip)—Both of you! You're going to die!

What Miller calls Rupert's "immunity" is "decisively established by the synergism of two tactics, of which the first is a manifest stupidity ['you've given my words a meaning I never *dreamed* of'] and the second an equally unconcealed violence."[60] At first the gun wrested from Philip hangs limply from Rupert's wounded hand, as if he doesn't know what to do with it; and now its aim is ambiguous, *almost* pointing at Brandon, as if its direction were a by-product of Rupert's gesture and not quite conscious.[61] The violence in Stewart's voice, however, is unmistakable ("Did you think you were *God*, Brandon?" "You're gonna *die*!").[62]

The vehemence with which Stewart denounces Brandon and Philip indicates the importance of projecting the bloody guilt outward, his inquisitorial zeal necessitated by the fear that the guilt lies within. However, as Stewart begins to pace, Hitchcock places Brandon directly in the center of the frame, the obstacle around which Rupert must maneuver, pacing desperately back and forth, but which he cannot escape.[63] To save himself he has to sell them out.

The lynch-mob mentality that demands blood in place of justice and is blind to its own trespass requires a scapegoat. A 1922 U.S. Department of Labor report on juvenile delinquency stated in flawless homophobic logic that "a young man, easily ascertainable to be unusually fine in other characteristics, is probably 'queer' in sex tendency."[64] The American fear of "unusually fine" young men is what enables Rupert to project onto Brandon and Philip everything that unnerves him in himself. Rupert may not fear their homosexuality, but it is Brandon and Philip's "otherness" as gay men that makes it possible to project onto them the things Rupert wants to fix as "other" than himself: his incipient fascism, the "perversity" of his disdain for propriety, his careless playfulness with what others hold sacred—in other words, all the traits Brandon, Philip, and Rupert share.[65] That, and having killed. The resounding bad faith of Rupert's attempt to deny his resemblance to Brandon and Philip is underscored by Hitchcock and Stewart's final "touch."

Rupert goes to the window, slaps open the latch with the gun barrel, and fires three shots. Turning away as voices rise from the street, he looks hesitantly at Brandon, then turns a long troubled look toward Philip. With great difficulty he lifts his bad leg off the windowseat, having to steady himself against the piano for a moment before he can stand. Once again Stewart slowly looks back and forth between Brandon and Philip. Finally, he limps across the room toward the chest. At the last moment he uses his bad leg to pull a chair closer and sits heavily, worn out, his gun hand resting protectively on the chest's firmly closed lid. The illusion that we can read the thoughts of actors on their faces and in their bodies is insisted upon in this moment of "pure cinema," the "victory" transformed into guilt, shame, and utter defeat.

To paraphrase Britton, if you are Jimmy Stewart, the perfect, middle-class, heterosexual American male, you learn to live with it. Like Rupert Cadell, "James Stewart, war hero," did what he was supposed to do to be a good American. When Hitchcock cuts to Stewart looking in the chest, we see him brought face to face with the unthinkable: that James Stewart is a killer.

Notes

I would like to thank Al LaValley and Rick Millington for their invaluable comments on earlier drafts of this essay.

1. Thomas Hemmeter, "Twisted Writing," in *Hitchcock's Rereleased Films: From Rope to Vertigo*, ed. Walter Raubicheck and Walter Srebnick (Detroit: Wayne State University Press, 1991); D. A. Miller, "Anal *Rope*," in *Inside/Out: Lesbian Theories, Gay Theories*, ed. Diana Fuss (New York: Routledge, 1991). For a Lacanian view on the "Law of the Father," see Robert G. Goulet's "Life with(out) Father: The Ideological Masculine in *Rope* and Other Hitchcock Films," in Raubicheck and Srebnick, *Hitchcock's Rereleased Films*.

2. Miller suggests that all of the attempts to mask the five hidden cuts are somehow " 'spoiled' " because they fail to remain invisible (quoting V. F. Perkins, *"Rope," Movie* 7 [February–March 1963]: 11; "Anal *Rope*," 138).

3. *Rope's* promotional material (posters, trailer, publicity stills) tease the audience with scenes not in the film; see the oft-reproduced still used with Miller's article that shows the

chest facing the camera, promising us that if we see the film we'll see what's in it. The trailer promises to tell us all about Janet and David. Once the film starts, both promises are left in the dust.

4. Miller argues that the emphasis on "pure" technique perpetuates the "phobic dehomosexualization that is sedimented in such abstraction" ("Anal *Rope*," 140, n. 13).

5. Arthur Laurents, *Rope* screenplay, based on a treatment by Hume Cronyn, December 16, 1947. Laurents expands on Rupert's appeal: "He is completely self-possessed and elegantly detached. His manners are beautiful, his speech is eloquent."

6. For our purposes, Stewart's career breaks into four periods, each featuring particular genres: 1936–41, with musicals, comedies, romances (*You Can't Take It with You*, 1938; *Mr. Smith Goes to Washington*, 1939; *Destry Rides Again*, 1939; *The Shop around the Corner*, 1940; *The Philadelphia Story*, 1940); the mixed postwar period, 1946–50 (*It's a Wonderful Life*, 1946; *Call Northside 777*, 1948; *Harvey*, 1950); and 1950–62, where dramas and westerns predominate (the Hitchcock films; five Anthony Mann westerns; *Anatomy of a Murder*, 1959; and *The Man Who Shot Liberty Valance*, 1962). The last period, as elder icon, spans from 1962 to the present and features comic westerns or roles as the grizzled patriarch (*Shenandoah*, 1965; *The Shootist*, 1976; *Flight of the Phoenix*, 1966). I will concentrate on the first three.

7. The comedies include *Magic Town*, *On Our Merry Way*, *You Gotta Stay Happy*, *The Jackpot*, and *Harvey*; *Call Northside 777*, *Rope*, *The Stratton Story*, *Malaya*, *Winchester 73*, and *Broken Arrow* are the dramas. *It's a Wonderful Life* fits both categories, though most of it is played for comedy.

8. Andrew Britton, *Katharine Hepburn: The Thirties and After* (Newcastle upon Tyne: Tyneside Cinema Publications, 1984), 6.

9. James Naremore, *Acting in the Cinema* (Berkeley: University of California Press, 1988), 253–54.

10. Joseph McBride, *Frank Capra: The Catastrophe of Success* (New York: Simon and Schuster, 1992), 385.

11. Ibid.

12. Patrick Hamilton, *Rope's End* (New York: Richard R. Smith Inc., 1930), 31.

13. Naremore, *Acting in the Cinema*, 240.

14. Ibid., 241.

15. Ibid., 253.

16. Roland Barthes, "The Grain of the Voice," in *Image-Music-Text*, selected and translated by Stephen Heath (New York: Hill and Wang, 1977).

17. Richard Dyer, *Stars* (London: BFI Publishing, 1982), 183.

18. Naremore, *Acting in the Cinema*, 258.

19. Grant and Stewart's scenes together in *Philadelphia Story* are particularly interesting given their contrasting, complementary styles and the different ways they're used by directors like Capra and Hitchcock. It was Grant whom Hitchcock originally wanted for the role of Rupert Cadell (Donald Spoto, *The Dark Side of Genius: The Life of Alfred Hitchcock* [Boston: Little, Brown and Co., 1983], 305). Naremore suggests that Hepburn can resemble Stewart ("crossing her legs, she leans forward and props her elbow on her knee . . . , making her look as lanky and appealing as the young Stewart or Fonda" [Acting in the Cinema, 188]). Naremore also describes Stewart in *Destry* and *Philadelphia Story* in sexual terms, saying

that Stewart "performed the same 'service' for Hepburn as he had for Dietrich" in *Destry* (ibid., 176).

20. Jeanine Basinger, *The It's a Wonderful Life Book* (New York: Knopf, 1990), quoting press releases (38, 39). Members of the press were impressed that the famous telephone scene was shot in one take, with no rehearsals.

21. Kaja Silverman, *Male Subjectivity at the Margins* (New York: Routledge, 1992), 99.

22. Director-screenwriter Robert Riskin seems to have based the character on George Gallup, who pioneered the "quota sampling" method in 1936 (*Village Voice*, July 14, 1992, 90). The Stewart character's method fails when the town starts taking (and selling) its own polls and makes itself a national laughingstock by announcing that 76 percent of the population would vote for a woman for president.

23. Britton, *Katharine Hepburn*, 6.

24. Ibid., 6. He continues: "The image, in these cases, evacuates the ideological tensions embodied in the dramatic person by suppressing contradictory terms or representing them as something else. Thus, for example, in Stewart's case, 'moral earnestness and integrity' are repeatedly defined by his post-war films as at once the expression and progenitor of an intense repressive violence, barely contained and constantly threatening to erupt" (6).

25. Naremore, *Acting in the Cinema*, 255.

26. Silverman, *Male Subjectivity*, 102.

27. Ibid., 42.

28. Ibid., 102.

29. Ibid., 102.

30. Naremore, *Acting in the Cinema*, 254.

31. Silverman, *Male Subjectivity*, 198.

32. Interestingly, when Rupert opens the chest in the play, his reaction echoes Stewart in this and other films. He says, "Oh—you swine," then "wipes his hand across his mouth, his lips at once contemptuous and horror-struck," and "gives a shuddering sob" (Hamilton, *Rope's End*, 86). All these gestures are characteristic of James Stewart. ("Inevitably, at the point of his greatest trauma, he will raise a trembling hand to his open mouth, sometimes biting at the flesh" [Naremore, *Acting in the Cinema*, 65]).

33. These quotes describe the climax of *Rear Window*, when Stewart's character is being strangled (Naremore, *Acting in the Cinema*, 259).

34. Silverman also discusses the term "shattering" (*Male Subjectivity*, 200). Silverman acknowledges that hers is a " 'utopian' rereading of masochism" as working "insistently to negate paternal power and privilege" and sees "an obvious danger that it be taken literally, as designating the standard form of that perversion, rather than its visionary reconfiguration" (ibid., 211).

35. Silverman, discussing Franz Biberkopf's loss of his arm in Fassbinder's *Berlin Alexanderplatz* (ibid., 236).

36. Naremore calls Stewart the only studio system actor "who could regularly cry on the screen without losing the sympathy of his audience" (*Acting in the Cinema*, 254).

37. At the end of *Rear Window* alone, Naremore notes Stewart's "eyes fluttering up in a swoon . . . [his] eyes closed and mouth lax, as if he were about to faint" (ibid., 259).

38. Steven H. Scheuer, ed., *Movies on TV and Videocassette, 1989–1990* (New York: Bantom Books, 1989), 251. Fellow actors have noticed the feminine/masculine polarities in

Stewart. In a documentary on Stewart's career called *James Stewart: A Wonderful Life*, Richard Dreyfuss says, "He was a very feminine hero . . . very vulnerable," while on the other end of the spectrum Clint Eastwood counters, "He had a great way with violence. When he showed anger it was much more intense than most actors. He could be extremely volatile. When he snapped, the danger would come on very strong."

39. Clive Hirschhorn, *The Universal Story* (London: Octopus Books, 1983), 193.

40. *Life*, August 22, 1949, 22–23, my emphasis.

41. Miller, "Anal *Rope*," 128.

42. Ibid., 128.

43. In the introduction to the play, published under the title *Rope's End*, Hamilton claims, "It has been said that I have founded 'Rope' on a murder which was committed in America some years ago. But this is not so, since I cannot recall this crime having ever properly reached my consciousness until after 'Rope' was written and people began to tell me of it. But then I am not interested in crime" (ix).

44. Hume Cronyn, *A Terrible Liar: A Memoir* (New York: William Morrow and Co., 1991), 205–8.

45. Most of the names in the play differ from the film, except for Brandon, Rupert, and the older Kentley. David Kentley is Ronald in the play, Janet is Leila, etc. For clarity, I refer to everyone except Philip/Granillo by their film names.

46. Miller, "Anal *Rope*," 125–26.

47. The *Oxford English Dictionary* cites 1932 as the first time the word "queer" appears in print in England (in W. H. Auden), though slang often exists years before it can be written. The first traceable American use occurred in 1922.

48. Hemmeter argues that the film's "transcendental signifier" is the word "something," the great undefinable "whatzit" that prevents Rupert from committing the murders he talks about ("Twisted Writing," 258–60). Miller also sees that "something" as *"la raison du plus fort"* for the text, hiding behind a linguistic "sleight of hand"—only for Miller that "something" is an unnamed "quasi-intuitive opposition" to homosexuality ("Anal *Rope*," 127).

49. Eve Kosofsky Sedgwick, *Epistemology of the Closet* (Berkeley: University of California Press, 1990).

50. In the play Rupert calls the crime "a sin and a blasphemy" (89).

51. When musing on a different ending for *Suspicion* where the husband poisons his wife, François Truffaut suggests the more obsessive and neurotic Stewart for the role of the husband in place of Cary Grant, and Hitchcock counters with this line (Truffaut, *Hitchcock* [New York: Simon &Schuster, 1967]). Stewart played murderers early in his career, most notably in *After the Thin Man* (1936) and *Rose Marie* (1935).

52. Charles Wolfe, "The Return of Jimmy Stewart," in *Stardom: Industry of Desire*, ed. Christine Gledhill (New York: Routledge, 1991), 96.

53. He does, however, play ex-soldiers, something it would have been hard to avoid in films of the late 1940s and early 1950s.

54. McBride, *Frank Capra*, 525–26.

55. Wolfe, in "The Return of Jimmy Stewart," 104. In *James Stewart: A Wonderful Life*, a pair of newsreels feature Stewart near the beginning and the end of his war service. In the first he's neat and pressed, standing tall, looking down at the camera and smiling. In the second he's seated in a chair so low his legs look awkward sticking out in front of him.

His voice is not only softer but a little hoarse and shaky as he repeats, "We are going to do our best to be useful as soldiers in the United States Army." Older, more thoughtful, infinitely more vulnerable, he looks like he's had a hard time. Shellshock, tears, or a nervous breakdown do not seem unthinkable at this point. Seeming glimpses of the actual person are highly privileged moments in acting; the even thinner line between biography and scripted performance make these appearances especially touching.

56. Quoted in Basinger, The It's a Wonderful Life Book, 58.

57. Dyer, Stars, 30.

58. Ibid., 31, quoting Barry King, "The Social Significance of Stardom" (unpublished manuscript, 1974).

59. Ibid., 31, quoting King, "The Social Significance."

60. Miller, "Anal Rope," 127.

61. Miller argues that for the film "the only way to establish the integrity of a truly other subject position is performative; by simply declaring that one occupies such a position and supporting the declaration with a strong arm" (ibid., 127). An American display of force requires a change of weapons. In the play Rupert pulls out the sword concealed in his walking stick and summons the police with "a little silver whistle" (ibid., 83).

62. "In an especially tense situation, [Stewart's] normally earnest behavior . . . become[s] harsh, shrill, and manic" (Naremore, Acting in the Cinema, 254).

63. According to Silverman, "perversion" is not only sexual but subverts "many of the binary oppositions upon which the social order rests: it crosses the boundary separating food from excrement (coprophilia); human from animal (bestiality); life from death (necrophilia); adult from child (pederasty); and pleasure from pain (masochism)" (Male Subjectivity, 187). In Rope the greatest scandal is the proximity of food and a corpse, when Rupert asks, "Did you think you were God, Brandon? . . . Is that what you thought when you served food from his grave?"

64. Oxford English Dictionary. According to the OED, the British felt the term "queer" was imported from America.

65. I am indebted to Rick Millington for this insight.

4

From *Spellbound* to *Vertigo*
Alfred Hitchcock and Therapeutic
Culture in America

Jonathan Freedman

Now that depth psychology, with the help of films, soap-
opera, and Horney, has delved into the deepest recesses,
people's last possibility of experiencing themselves has
been cut off by organized culture. Ready-made enlightenment turns not only spontaneous reflection but also analytical insights—whose power equals the energy and suffering that it cost to gain them—into mass-produced
articles, and the painful secrets of individual history,
which the orthodox method is already inclined to reduce
to formulae, into commonplace conventions. Dispelling
rationalizations becomes itself rationalization. Instead of
working to gain self-awareness, the initiates become adept
at subsuming all instinctual conflicts under such concepts
as inferiority-complex, mother-fixation, extroversion, and
introversion, to which they are in reality inaccessible. Terror before the abyss of the self is removed by the consciousness of being concerned with nothing so very different from arthritis or sinus trouble.

—Theodor Adorno, *Minima Moralia*

The austere cultural critic Theodor Adorno wrote these angry and
passionate words in 1944, while living in Los Angeles and working with Max
Horkheimer on the essays that were to be published fifteen years later as *The
Dialectic of Enlightenment*. In June of that year, Alfred Hitchcock returned to Hol-

lywood from an extended vacation in England to prepare his second film for the brilliant but domineering producer David Selznick—*Spellbound*. One would like to imagine a meeting between these two—over brunch at Arnold Schoenberg's, perhaps, or sipping drinks with the Thomas Manns. Despite their obvious differences, they would have had much to discuss. Each man was, in his own way, at that moment attempting to reconcile himself to that bounteous but alienating land to which he found himself exiled by war and persecution; each responded to America with a volatile admixture of fascination and repulsion. Adorno's powerfully ambivalent response, which informs some of the most lyrical passages in his marvelously melancholic memoir, *Minima Moralia*, reaches its fullest articulation in the critical analysis of the "culture industry" offered in the *Dialectic of Enlightenment*—an industry of which American mass culture was the exemplar and Hollywood the apotheosis. Hitchcock's was manifested in a sustained and satirical account of American social institutions and cultural practices, ranging from his ironizing and subversive deployment of the icons of American public life (the Statue of Liberty, Mt. Rushmore) to his even more ironical (and undeniably prescient) investigation of such social formations as the advertising industry (*North by Northwest*), the suburb (*Shadow of a Doubt*), motel culture (*Psycho*), and, last but certainly not least, psychoanalysis—the principal subject of *Spellbound*, and a topic to which Hitchcock would repeatedly return thereafter.

My pairing of these two figures might strike the reader as somewhat fanciful; it would certainly have struck both men as highly problematic. Indeed, each might profitably be viewed as the precise embodiment of qualities the other particularly distrusted. For Adorno, Hitchcock would have provided a vivid emblem of the "culture industry" itself, and Adorno would have seen the popularity of his films as yet another sign of the insidious power of that industry to organize, influence, and control the mass audience it helped to call into being. For Hitchcock, a high-culture intellectual of Adorno's transcendent severity would have doubtless proved equally vexing. Although Hitchcock was a voracious reader, his formal education ended with secondary school, and his attitudes toward those who display their education and refinement never lost the angry suspicion of the self-made man. Indeed, possession of an excessive amount of cultural sophistication is precisely the sign of a Hitchcock villain: Witness the aptly named Vandamm (played with exquisite unctuousness by James Mason) in *North by Northwest*, whose connoisseurship and villainy are equated with one another—he hides microfilm in a hollowed-out objet d'art, and strokes his mistress at an art auction as if she were a pretty object to be added to his collection. Or think of the murderous aesthetes of *Rope*, who put into practice the Nietzschean doctrines of their favorite college professor, to that professor's slightly disingenuous but undeniably genuine consternation.

But these two anomalous figures might be united powerfully and persuasively by one quality: their common critical response to the American enthusiasm for—and transformation of—psychoanalysis. To be sure, as we shall see in more detail below, Hitchcock played a crucial role in the popular vogue for psychoanalysis registered in, and indeed largely wrought by, the Hollywood cinema of the 1940s and early 1950s. But we oughtn't underestimate Hitchcock's skeptical take on psychoanalysis, on the psychiatric profession, and, most important, on their cultural ramifications. Clearly, one reason for this interest in the American reworking of psychoanalysis was the appositeness to the experience of both Hitchcock and Adorno of this particular transaction between the Old World and the New—and between an aspect of European high culture threatened with extinction by the forces that Hitchcock and Adorno both sought to escape in America and the society that somewhat ambivalently gave a home to the likes of European leftist intellectuals and emigré filmmakers. The increasingly fervent adoption of Freud by the Hollywood film industry provided a sobering example of the power of the American cultural apparatus to remake even the most corrosive of discourses into affirmative fudge, and it would be easy to imagine that neither Hitchcock nor Adorno could help but wonder whether the same fate awaited their work there as well.

But there was more at stake for the two men in this New World remaking of psychoanalysis: Both saw this phenomenon as an essential part of the remaking of American culture itself. The postwar American vogue for what had earlier seemed to be the obscure, if not sinister, tenets of Freudian psychoanalysis led to that phenomenon Philip Rieff was later to label "the triumph of the therapeutic": the rise of a new social ethos that replaced religious or moral sanctions with considerations of mental hygiene, psychic balance, and above all personal "growth."[1] And for Hitchcock and Adorno alike, the results of this new ethos were dire indeed. From the perspectives of Adorno's dark post-Marxist Marxism and Hitchcock's equally gloomy post-Catholic Catholicism, the tenets of therapeutic culture contributed to the processes of human immiseration: in Adorno's case, by offering a mass-produced, "ready-made enlightenment" that, as we have seen, simultaneously prevents any real self-awareness and falsely reconciles men and women to their own social exploitation; in Hitchcock's, by adding one more snare to the ensemble of illusions by which human beings trick each other and are gulled in turn.

Indeed, I want to suggest in what follows that Hitchcock's response to the American reception of psychoanalysis and its role in the establishment of a distinctively therapeutic culture is even more acerbic than Adorno's and is certainly worthy of equally serious consideration. For to give it such attention would not only be to pay tribute to Hitchcock's powers as a critic of American culture—a critic of perhaps less gravitas but equal ambition as Adorno; it would also be to place him more precisely in the context in which he belongs, a context that not only sets him next to Adorno and Horkheimer but also places him alongside a figure whose work haunted most high-culture intellectuals of their day as he does our own: ironically enough, none other than Sigmund Freud. Indeed, it will be my suggestion here that Hitchcock as observer and critic of postwar American therapeutic culture may be most accurately compared with and judged against not only the writers of the Frankfurt School dispensation, nor against the American radical/conservative social critics following in their wake (critics like Rieff and Christopher Lasch), but rather with the determinedly despairing Freud of the late metapsychological writings: the Freud, that is, for whom the vicissitudes of the psyche and hence of culture itself are governed by the indominability of the death-drive, the inevitability of repetition-compulsion, the interminability of anal-ysis, and the impossibility of cure. And he may be so judged most fully, I would argue, in his responses to his fascinating and troubling new home—in his re-sponses to America itself.

JUST AFTER THE CREDITS of *Spellbound*, just before the film proper begins, the following words scroll down the screen:

> This movie deals with psychoanalysis, the method by which modern science treats the emotional problems of the sane.
> The psychoanalyst seeks only to induce the patient to talk about his hidden problems, to open the hidden doors of his mind.
> Once the complexes that have been disturbing the patient are uncov-ered and interpreted, the illness and confusion disappear . . . and the evils of unreason are driven from the human soul.

This prelude—added at the insistence of the film's producer, David Selznick; penned by psychoanalysis buff Ben Hecht; approved by the "psychoanalytic con-sultant" to the film, prominent Los Angeles psychotherapist May Romm (whose roster of patients included Selznick and his wife, Irene Mayer); and vetted by no less august a figure than Karl Menninger—never fails to elicit hoots from a con-temporary audience, but it may also serve to remind us of the cultural situation *Spellbound* responds to and of the social gesture it performs. The addition of these introductory words reminds us that the film that follows was both the product of and a participant in a specific historical event: the full integration of psychoanal-ysis into American cultural life. Americans had long provided Freud with one of his most attentive audiences, and the 1920s saw a notorious surge of interest in psychoanalysis among American writers and intellectuals. But until the 1940s, psychoanalysis remained largely a coterie concern, finding its most energetic prac-titioners and participants among eastern intellectuals—and more than a few ad-herents in the Hollywood film community, though these souls only rarely made psychoanalysis the explicit or implicit subject of their films.[2] With the end of World War II—a war whose inception brought a flood of European therapists to

American shores and whose conclusion brought a flood of veterans struggling with the aftereffects of shell shock—psychoanalysis moved into the American cultural mainstream. "During the war," reported *Life* in 1947, "millions of service personnel had direct contact with psychiatry for the first time and large numbers of them received more or less elaborate psychiatric treatment." Meanwhile, *Life* continues,

> a whole new literary genre became popular, with the learned Freudian and the analytic couch as its symbols. Novels about mental illness (*Private Worlds, The Crack-Up, Brainstorm, Snake-Pit* etc.) were frequent. Hollywood quickly followed suit, and numbers of "big" pictures of late have had psychiatric overtones. Indeed, it is rare to find a Hollywood musical these days without some kind of pseudo-Freudian "dream sequence." . . . [As a result] a boom has overtaken the once obscure and much maligned profession of psychoanalysis. It is part of the larger boom which has simultaneously engulfed the whole science of psychiatry, in which psychoanalysis is a special therapeutic technique, and which has made the 4,011 accredited psychiatrists about the most sought-after members of the entire medical profession. . . . In part this reflects the alarming prevalence of mental and emotional disorders in the population today; in part, it merely reflects the popular knowledge and acceptance of psychoanalysis, as a cure.[3]

The increasing "popular knowledge and acceptance of psychoanalysis" was not exclusively a mass cultural phenomenon, to be sure. Indeed, beginning in this period and continuing through the 1950s and 1960s, it was carefully fostered by American psychoanalysts themselves, of both the orthodox and, perhaps more important, "revisionist" tendencies. Karen Horney edited a popular guide to psychotherapy, a text that was summarized and favorably reviewed in such influential opinion-forming journals as *Time* and *Newsweek*, and *Self-Analysis*, a book that, as we shall see, is not irrelevant to *Vertigo*. (Horney is in favor of the practice, but within limits.) And psychoanalytic dogma—or, more frequently, the tenets of American revisionists like Horney, who ultimately rejected Freud altogether, or Karl Menninger, Erik Erikson, Erich Fromm, who modified Freud's teachings— were expounded to the general public either in these figures' own works (Menninger's *Love against Hate* was a middlebrow bestseller in the late 1930s, as was Fromm's *The Art of Loving* in the 1950s) or in those of a set of popularizers of psychoanalysis: Lucy Freeman's *Hope for the Troubled* (1953), Louis Bisch's *Be Glad You're Neurotic* (1949), and—to underscore the emphasis on self-improvement that characterized this profusion of popular writing—S. Pickworth Farrow's *Psychoanalyze Yourself* (1942).

The result was a blend of American pragmatism and European pessimism, of naive injunctions to self-help and a sustained grappling with the most fearsome aspects of the psyche (aggression, sexuality) and of society itself (crime, poverty, war). Peter Biskind has labeled this blend "therapeutic imperialism"—the claim that in psychoanalytic understanding and treatment could be found the solution to the complicated problems confronting both the individual and the world.[4] But perhaps a better term for it would be "therapeutic hygenics"—the claim that mental difficulties on a social scale could be best understood on the model of public health campaigns and hence were susceptible to a process of amelioration via social engineering. For, many of these American revisionists argued, not only career problems or marital difficulties but also juvenile delinquency and criminality could be traced to unresolved neurotic conflict and overcome with proper treatment. To cite but one of many examples, it was in this spirit that Harry Stack Sullivan called for a "world-wide mobilization of psychiatry against social problems": In mental hygiene, rather than social reform or political struggle, lay the hope of a world in which social or political conflict itself was the disease, not the cure

But this popular acceptance of an Americanized psychoanalysis inflected by practical, self-help, social engineering ideologies was enhanced by the Hollywood films of the postwar period. Until the 1940s, Hollywood films had turned to psychoanalysis rather nervously, if at all. Films on analytic themes were widely perceived as box-office poison, particularly in the small towns upon whom steady studio grosses depended, because references to psychoanalysis demanded higher degrees of both cultural knowledge and cultural tolerance than could be assumed. (As late as 1945, when *Spellbound* was released, *Variety* predicted that any film whose comprehension required "knowledge of the scientific words" of psychoanalysis would be "over the head" of its viewers.[5]) In such a climate, it is only natural that Hollywood films would portray psychiatrists as sinister or satirized figures. As Krin and Glen Gabbard have persuasively argued, Hollywood psychiatrists in the 1930s are usually eccentric, heavily accented villains (as in *Mr. Deeds Goes to Town*) or eccentric, heavily accented buffoons (like the spectacularly bumbling "alienist," Dr. Eggelhoffer, in *The Front Page* and *His Girl Friday*).[6] More important, in both of these cases, as in a number of 1930s thrillers, the psychoanalyst is associated not only with foreignness and fraudulence, as the Gabbards suggest, but with criminality itself. Psychoanalysts, that is to say, are positioned in these films as authors of a crime or as unwitting abettors, and the art they practice is thus represented as a self-mystifying practice under whose crooked cover criminal acts take place. To be sure, some films of the 1930s and early 1940s moved toward more sympathetic representations of psychoanalysis and its practitioners; interestingly and significantly, they are largely to be found in two specialized genres: the woman's picture (*Private Worlds* [1935] and *Now Voyager* [1942]) and the musical (Fred Astaire's dancing psychiatrist in Moss Hart's *Lady in the Dark*). But these were the exception. It was not until *Spellbound* that psychoanalysis was most fully purified of its aura of fraudulence and criminality; for it was in *Spellbound* that psychoanalysis first became, for the Hollywood cinema, the means of solving a crime, not a means of committing one.

This analogy between the art of psychoanalytic interpretation and the act of crime detection is, by now, a familiar critical gesture, canonized alike in scholarship and in popular fiction: In theoretical tomes and mass-market fiction alike, Freud routinely consults with Sherlock Holmes, and vice-versa. The linkage between the two has become so familiar, in fact, that we might forget the full ramifications of that juncture's first appearance in the Hollywood cinema and the work this linkage performs. Mary Ann Doane writes, "The psychoanalysis which the Hollywood cinema takes as its model is easily conformable to the structure of classical narrative. It provides an enigma (what is wrong with the character? What event caused him or her to be like this?), a justification for the classical device of repetition (the compulsion to reenact the trauma, the recurrence of symbols) and a final solution (the cure, the recovery through the memory of the early scene)."[7] But the entry of psychoanalysis into the "classic narrative" Doane describes did not occur until the former was processed through the Hollywood mystery plot. The process of psychoanalytic cure, that is to say, was made fully available as a narrative resource for the Hollywood cinema only when its central activity—the discovery or recovery of the meaning of a past event—was translated into the homologous narrative of the detective plot. And the result of this conjuncture was clear (and clearly akin to other reprocessings of psychoanalytic doctrines under way throughout American popular culture): Both the institution of psychoanalysis and the notion of the mysteries of the mind upon which it is founded were thoroughly defanged, neutralized.

But this work was not merely formal in nature. It was also part of a larger cultural work, one in which Hitchcock played a pivotal role in that his skepticism and his pragmatism intersected with the real-life agendas of both Selznick and the American psychoanalytic establishment. Hitchcock initially bought the property that was to become *Spellbound* knowing that Selznick was fascinated by psychoanalysis: Suffering from depression, deep into analysis with May Romm (so much so that he claimed to know more about analysis than Romm herself did),[8] the producer also aspired to an esteem from the American psychoanalytic establishment. And this establishment, in turn, was at that very moment interested in establishing its own credibility with a skeptical public via Hollywood. These efforts were led by astute, public-relations-minded Karl Menninger—founder of the Menninger clinics, a leading voice in public debates about crime and deviance, and head of the American Psychoanalytic Association, as well as best-selling author of popularizing tomes—who spent a good deal of time nurturing this conjunction. Menninger supervised the nascent Los Angeles Psychoanalytic Association; on his many trips to Los Angeles he met his second wife and consciously cultivated Hollywood connections. Menninger thought the Hollywood film could provide psychoanalysis with a kind of cultural respectability that it had hitherto failed to enjoy, and he seems to have seen Selznick as a key to this project. Selznick consulted Menninger on the making of one of his more earnest efforts, *Since You Went Away;* and when Selznick got interested in therapy itself, it was Menninger who recommended May Romm. But when Menninger got wind of the *Spellbound* project, he was not amused. He heard of the script courtesy of the director Joseph Mankiewicz, who—having received permission from his own analyst, Otto Fenichel—wrote Menninger to warn him of the script's less than reverent attitude toward psychoanalysis. "The psychoanalysts at the sanitarium are without exception maladjusted men [who] take turns in making passes at Bergman, whom they constantly tease as being emotionally and sexually frigid," he breathlessly reports, then *really* turns up the heat:

> I am convinced that the next period of years will bring psychiatry in general, and psychoanalysis in particular, into great prominence as a source of literary, dramatic, and motion picture material. The word "Psycho-neurotic" has already become a catchword (and catch-all) and in time will pass even "inferiority complex" in popularity. Remember that while books and plays reach limited audiences, the customers of the cinema are without number. I suggest to you, then, that both the American Psychiatric Association and the American Psychoanalytic Association consider *now* what can be done, in some way, to control—or at least temper—the presentation of their respective sciences that will be sent out to the far corners of the globe on millions of feet of film—and to prevent, if possible, the resultant disrespect and distrust that may be generated in the minds of millions of people.[9]

Menninger promptly wrote Selznick a letter of protest, adding a characteristically self-promotional invitation to the Menninger Clinic to see an example of a real facility in action. Selznick responded with an unctuous letter detailing his previous contribution to public knowledge about psychoanalysis, namely, *Since You Went Away;* it contained, he informed Menninger, "a sequence I personally conceived and wrote in the hope that it would have a value in making the American public aware of the work being done by psychiatrists to rebuild men who have been shaken by their war experiences" (405). Menninger responded by wryly reminding Selznick that the latter had evidently forgotten that he had consulted Menninger while making the earlier film, then he corrected numerous slips in the prologue to *Spellbound.* He also spoke with friends in Los Angeles, who contacted May Romm with news of the professionally powerful Kansan's reservations; Romm responded with a wry, if somewhat defensive, letter of her own:

> Naturally, the question arises, why should I should have anything to do with a film a picture which many have interpreted as casting aspersions

on psychiatry. Simply because had I not done so it would have been produced in a much more undesirable form than it is now.

To give you an example, I wanted to take out the word psychoanalyst and substitute psychiatrist in regard to the leading female character, but it was impossible to accomplish this. For even what I considered improvement, I had to chew carpet. (407)

Judging from a letter from Menninger's friend, Leon Bartemeier—the head of the American Psychoanalytic Association—Menninger was not mollified by Romm's "chewing carpet" with *him*. When Menninger learned "that the psychoanalysts in this picture are represented as maladjusted persons, that an actual treatment situation is depicted incorrectly, and that there are some effects which would place psychoanalysis in an unfavorable light," he prevailed upon Bartemeier to withdraw the promised endorsement, leaving the film to make its way on its own (409). As, it might be added, it quite successfully did: Although, as *Variety* had predicted, the film did poorly in rural venues, it was an enormous hit in urban ones, and an international success as well. And the combination of Selznickian gloss and Hitchcockian cunning seemed to appeal to the critics as well: The film was nominated for six Oscars, including Best Picture (a nod to Selznick) and Best Director (a nod to Hitchcock). I detail this conjunction (and, unfortunately, must gloss over some of its more lurid aspects—like the facts that Irene Selznick's analysis with Romm precipitated her decision to leave the philandering Selznick; or that the practical-minded Romm herself was soon to pursue Irene's father, Louis Mayer)[10] to suggest how fully Hitchcock's film participated in even as it commented upon the American professionalization of psychoanalysis. With his usual prescience, Hitchcock managed simultaneously to intuit the increasing power of a professionalized analytic establishment in the American cultural imaginary, to enhance the patina of cultural authority that psychoanalysis carried with it in its march into institutionalized respectability, and to poke fun at it in the process.

Spellbound enacts these roles with extraordinary vividness. Both the analytic process and the mystery—psychic and otherwise—that it probes are understood as being simple in determination and finite in duration. Neither psychological nor epistemological depths are evident in *Spellbound*; the symptoms of mental distress— the amnesia that afflicts the film's hero, John Ballantine (Gregory Peck), accompanied by a tendency to hear eerie music and faint at the sight of dark lines on a white background—disappear with the greatest of ease as soon as the traumatic event occasioning these manifestations is brought to consciousness. Thus, in this film, "mental illness" is represented as being something like physical illness: Once a psychoanalytic solution has been proposed by Dr. Ingrid Bergman—the film's "epistemological hero," to quote Doane's resonant description of the Hollywood analyst figure (47)—insight immediately replaces obsession, ego swiftly supplants id, and a state of absolute psychic normalcy is instantly, magically restored.[11]

But what makes *Spellbound* a particularly interesting case of the normalization of psychoanalysis that Menninger and Selznick were both seeking is the way that a second implication in that text supplements, and partially subverts, the first. The initial effect of psychoanalytic success is to cure Ballantine of his psychic imprisonment at the price of accomplishing his physical one. Although thanks to Constance Peterson he is able to remember the repressed event, the death of Dr. Edwards, he is nevertheless immediately arrested when this memory leads in turn to the discovery of the corpse of Edwards with a bullet in its back. Here again, in other words, psychoanalysis is understood to be, however ironically, a species of victimization, not one of liberation. In the final turn of the film, however, this aura of criminality is fully dispelled by one more act of analytic explication. Dr. Peterson is finally able to fully read the real-life referents of the events veiled within Ballantine's dream—the quarrel between the murderous Dr. Murchison and his victim, Dr. Edwards, at the 21 Club refracted into the playing of vingt-et-un at a casino, the shooting on a ski slope of the former by the latter represented by a mysterious figure lurking behind a chimney—and so is able to identify Murchison as the true murderer. Interestingly enough, this final act of interpretation is accomplished with the aid of her mentor, Murchison, who shows himself to be committed to the epistemological project of psychoanalysis even as he is undone by it. And after consulting one last time with his protégé, he takes out a gun and turns it on himself, in a famous close-up of an enlarged prop gun which then turns to the audience and fires. The epistemological project of psychoanalysis, the murder mystery, and our own experience of the film as spectators, in other words, are at this final suicidal moment made indissolubly one.

The film thus effects a rather complex intervention in the Hollywood response to psychoanalysis.[12] Although *Spellbound* defangs the psychoanalytic project, it does not disavow the criminality that thoroughly infects the early Hollywood notion of psychoanalysis. Rather, criminality is simultaneously severed from and projected back onto the analyst himself. Indeed, in this film, one psychiatrist is absolved of criminality precisely by discovering the criminality of another. And the implications of this maneuver are multiple, leading simultaneously in two completely different directions. On the one hand, Peterson's successful reading of Ballantine's dream, her deduction of Murchison's guilt, and Murchison's subsequent suicide would seem to purify the psychoanalytic act itself of any lingering taint of criminality or transgressiveness. By taking on the burden of criminality left over from earlier Hollywood psychoanalysis films, Murchison frees Dr. Peterson and the analytic arts she practices from any disturbing implications, with only Ingrid Bergman's foreign accent left as the residue of the earlier archetype. And by conflating the act of analytic interpretation and the solution of the film's mystery, psychoanalysis itself is thereby similarly freed to propose itself as the solution to its own criminality. Indeed, this is the path that most post-*Spellbound* psychoanalysis films of the 1940s and 1950s pursue: In films like *Home of the Brave,*

The Three Faces of Eve, and, my favorite example, *The Dark Past* (1947), in which a gangster who takes over a psychiatrist's home is cured of his recurring nightmares by the analyst and gratefully sets him free, the psychoanalyst is narratively merged with the detective in discovering a single repressed trauma whose unveiling— usually accomplished through the successful decoding of a dream—simultaneously frees the patient of neurotic symptoms and brings a crime to an end.

But Hitchcock's insistence on incriminating at least one psychiatrist has another effect: It also continues to ascribe to psychoanalysis itself a faint afterimage of its earlier sinister, criminal, transgressive identity, and indeed extends it in such a way as to inculpate the spectator, or at least make that figure feel potentially complicit in criminality. But as the psychoanalytic profession further established itself in the 1950s and early 1960s, Hitchcock strikes this note of mockery with increasing frequency. If, to leap ahead to the most famous example, *Psycho* is a film that depends on an audience's immediate recognition of the psychoanalytic clichés Adorno critiques so unsparingly—has there ever been a more memorable cinematic representation of a "mother fixation"?—it is also a film that ends with a demolition of those clichés, particularly in its conclusion, where the pseudo-explanatory natterings of the psychiatrist are contrasted with the uncanny internal voice of "Mrs. Bates" speaking from within her son Norman, clearly defining the utter inadequacy of the language of psychoanalytic explication, in contrast to the forceful irrationality of the discourse of madness itself.

It is in *Vertigo*, however, that Hitchcock gives his most thorough and subversive account of psychiatry, psychoanalysis, and their role in establishing and maintaining a therapeutic culture. In a sense, *Vertigo* may be seen as a disenchanted version of *Spellbound*—a story in which only the criminality of analytic insights are portrayed; but I want to suggest here that *Vertigo* might be seen as a meditation on the cultural consequences of the act *Spellbound* performs, the assimilation of the doctrines of psychoanalysis into American mass culture and popular consciousness. In *Vertigo*, as in *Spellbound*, solving a crime and curing a neurosis are plotted against each other, but here Hitchcock suggests the affinity between the two the better to split them asunder, to suggest that while a mystery-story may be given a solution, "psychic conflicts" may not be so simply resolved. In contrast, they are shown to be fundamentally mysterious, unresolvable, incomprehensible: in a word, vertiginous. More important, Hitchcock is here interested in delineating the implications of this vertiginousness in their full social range and cultural specificity. Throughout the film, Hitchcock seeks to depict a culture in which the doctrines of psychoanalysis stand at the problematic center of a wide range of institutions and practices—in which, in fact, the therapeutic agenda has been elevated into nothing less than an ethos, a reflexive, and hence all-powerful, means of explicating the mysteries of the psyche and the uncertainties of the world. Thus, for example, when Gavin Elster, the film's suave villain, asks the film's protagonist, Scottie (James Stewart), how he would respond to Elster's proposition that his wife was possessed by a figure from "out of the past," Scottie's response is as immediate as it is telling: "Well, I'd say take her to the nearest psychiatrist, or psychologist, or neurologist, or psychoan— . . . or maybe just the plain family doctor. I'd have him look at you, too." Scottie's immediate response to the mysterious, the bizarre, the uncanny, in other words, is not merely to reject it, or even to say "you're crazy," but to advise Elster to get some therapy, and the sooner the better. It is not the least of the film's many ironies that it is Scottie, not Elster, who is driven to a psychiatrist's care, and by Elster's cunning use of Scottie's own psychic infirmities against him; it is doubly ironic that when Scottie is treated for his insanity, the outcome is nothing short of disastrous.

Indeed, throughout the film, we witness through Scottie's own experience the full range of analytic discourses and therapeutic institutions Scottie alludes to here; and we learn repeatedly the inefficacy of both a thoroughly popularized psychoanalytic discourse and official mechanisms of cure informed by them. In the first full scene of the film, for example, Scottie is racked with guilt feelings by a fellow officer's death, arguably caused by Scottie's newly discovered vertigo. When his motherly friend Midge (Barbara Bel Geddes) tells him not to feel responsible, she explicitly invokes therapeutic authority to buttress her arguments: "The doctors explained it to you. It wasn't your fault," she tells him, later adding that she has consulted her own doctor, whose advice she paraphrases as follows: "You've got it [vertigo] and there's no losing it. . . . Only another emotional shock will do it [cure the vertigo] and probably won't." "The hard-headed Scot," as he is called later by the harder-headed (and harder-hearted) Gavin Elster, refuses to believe Midge; "I won't crack up," he tells her, but then he proceeds to do just that. Setting himself a course of self-cure by physical therapy—ascending a kitchen chair and looking "up and down, up and down"—he fails his own test miserably, swooning into Midge's maternal arms the moment he rises too high and glances down, into the street below.

This opening scene establishes the patterns that the rest of the movie will play out: A hero on the verge—and soon to be over the edge—of insanity calls into motion various therapeutic mechanisms that attempt to name his guilt and then cure him of his neuroses, to assure him that he should not feel guilty for his own failures and to provide him a mechanism for curing their symptomatic manifestation. But these mechanisms quickly fail, leaving him more perilously positioned than he was before he had invoked them. Early in the film, we suspect that the problem may result from Scottie and Midge's lack of psychological sophistication—from their naive attempts to understand and cure Scottie's disturbed psyche by diagnostic proxy or by that fashionable tendency of the 1940s psychoanalytic boom, self-therapy. But later we learn that the psychiatric establishment fares little better. About midway through the film, thinking that his vertigo has prevented him from rescuing "Madeleine"—the woman he falsely believes to be Elster's wife—from spirit-induced suicide, Scottie goes completely insane, lapsing into a state of trancelike catatonia. The ever helpful Midge arrives at the hospital where he is institutionalized carrying a Mozart record, which, she tells Scottie, is what "the lady in musical therapy" has prescribed to aid Scottie's recovery—"the broom that sweeps the cobwebs clean." The turn to music therapy is doomed from the start. In the film's first scene, Scottie makes a point of his disinclination for classical music by asking Midge to turn off a tape of J. C. Bach playing in her apartment. At the time, he seems to be trying to divert attention from a particularly vexing moment in their conversation, but later on in the film, that moment works with telling economy to adumbrate the failure of the kind of therapy Midge attempts to assist—and hence that of all the therapies the film represents. For if even the notion of music therapy (which did indeed enjoy a brief vogue in the 1950s, largely as a means of calming unruly patients in mental institutions) is presented by Midge as being slightly comical—"They have music for dipsomaniacs, music for melancholiacs, music for hypochondriacs. I wonder what would happen if someone got their files mixed up"—Scottie's failure to respond to either Midge or Mozart forces us to recognize that the problems here extend beyond music therapy itself to any system of thought that thinks it can cure the mysteries of mental life by neatly categorizing them and then proposing the appropriate therapeutic intervention and cure. In direct contravention of *Spellbound*, in other words, *Vertigo* proposes that mental "illness" is fundamentally disjunct from physical illness; neither diagnosis nor cure is rapid, certain, or even—it increasingly seems—possible.

This suggestion becomes clearer in the film's next scene, in which Midge consults the psychiatrist in charge of Scottie's case. For no less ridiculous than the discourse of music therapy is the discourse of this bespectacled doctor, who solemnly asserts that Scottie is "suffering from acute melancholia, together with a guilt complex," then translates into layman's terms: "He blames himself for what happened to the woman." Here, as in Midge's parody of music therapy, the discourse of psychoanalysis is fully transformed into a banal nonlanguage, one that promises extensive explanatory power but instead devolves into misleading mumbo-jumbo. Indeed, more problematically, the doctor's jargon blinds him to what the film insists are the realities of the case, as we learn when Midge offers her own diagnosis: "I can give you one thing—he was in love with that woman. And he still is." The nameless psychiatrist can respond to Midge's diagnosis only by suggesting the inadequacy of his own: "Well, that does complicate things." And he can only suggest the inadequacy of his own care by answering Midge's question "How long is it going to take to pull him out of this?" with a statement that begins with pseudo-scientific precision and ends with a carefully hedged confession of his own irrelevance: "Well, it's hard to say. At least six months, perhaps a year. It really could depend on him." Midge's final comment in the scene—and, for that matter, in the film, from which, like the fool in *Lear*, she disappears halfway—summarizes the utter irrelevance of the formal, official, in-

Analysis—interminable

stitutionalized mechanisms of therapy and of cure: "And you know something, doctor, I don't think Mozart is going to help at all." Neither, we infer, is poor Scottie's psychiatrist. Our last view of Midge stresses the power madness exerts over Scottie for the rest of the film. We see Midge walking away from the psychiatrist's office sadly, melancholically, and in solitude down a once busy corridor with a large window at its end; the shot is held until she reaches its end, then fades to blackness. The corridor not only represents the solitude of Scottie's consciousness—for Scottie, there is no light at the end of the tunnel; it also reproduces a darkened, dimmed version of the scene of "Madeleine"'s dream (about which I will say more later); moreover, the shot, like "Madeleine"'s dream, reproduces on a horizontal axis the image of Scottie's vertigo. Midge, the shot suggests to us, is fully swallowed up by Scottie's madness and obsession—as are the normative principles of sanity she represents.

But if official means of analytic inquiry into the mysteries of Scottie's psyche fail in this film, others, by now fully canonized by the conventions of the Hollywood cinema, fare little better. I am referring here to the powerful homology the movie establishes, and plays off, between detective work and psychoanalytic cure. That homology we have seen instituted so powerfully by *Spellbound* is not only a sign of both the depths to which therapeutic culture has penetrated the conventions of mass culture; it is, more powerfully, a sign of Hitchcock's interest in altering those conventions so as to interrogate the therapeutic ethos itself. For in this film, it is precisely through the connection between his vocation as a detective and his attempts at cure that Scottie is first driven mad, then cured of his madness, then driven insane one last, irrevocable time.

The culturally resonant, and Hollywood-ratified, homology between detective work and psychoanalysis extends into virtually every aspect of Scottie's experience in the film—with ironical, and ultimately tragic, results. It is first established early on in the film, before Scottie's obsession with Carlotta/Madeleine/Judy takes him over completely. In his scene with the therapeutically inclined Midge—just before she informs him that she has spoken with her own doctor about his "case"—Hitchcock poses Scottie in an analytic attitude; he frames Scottie leaning back on a leather couch, interrogating Midge, like any stereotypical shrink, about her sex life. "How's your love life, Midge?" he asks; and, after a brief attempt to change the subject, she responds to the analytic cue with an appropriately therapeutic response. "Normal," she responds with some discomfort before turning back to her work—a look she well should display, since Midge was not only Scottie's college sweetheart but is still obviously, transparently in love with him. (The discomfort is emphasized later in the scene, when, in responding to a particularly pointed question from Scottie, Midge's apparent equanimity is shattered and she looks up from her desk; her uneasiness is further emphasized by an extreme close-up of her face from a slightly superior angle, subjecting her to the relentless interrogation not only of Scottie but also of Hitchcock's camera itself.) And Scottie continues the session with the standard question of 1950s analysis: "And when are you going to get married?"—a question that, ironically, then produces the counter-transferential remembrance that Scottie himself was Midge's intended. And indeed, we recognize at this moment that the entire scene is ironically reflexive. Just as Hitchcock's camera places Scottie in the position of the analysand, not the analyst—on the couch, not behind it—so the questions he asks Midge apply most powerfully to himself, not to her. If there is any character in the film whose "normality" is in question, it is Scottie, not Midge, and if there is any character to whom applies the hidden agenda behind the question "When are you going to get married?"—i.e., "What are your true sexual inclinations?"—it is the paralyzed, fixated, and obsessively scopophilic Scottie himself.

This scene produces a paradigm that Scottie will follow out for the rest of the film. Scottie attempts simultaneously to discover the truth about and so to cure others—employing means that freely mix the methodology of the psychoanalyst and the detective in the manner so influentially instantiated by *Spellbound*—but ends up only hiding the truth from, and failing to cure, himself. Such a pattern, for example, structures the bizarre and ultimately tragic love affair between Scottie and that figure he knows as "Madeleine." In a remarkable series of scenes, "Madeleine" gradually reveals to Scottie the details of a dream intended to lure him to the site where he is to witness what he is to believe is "Madeleine's" suicide. As does Peterson's with Ballantine, Scottie's infatuation with "Madeleine" merges with, is expressed by, his fascination with reading, understanding, interpreting her dream—in short, with playing amateur analyst. In doing so, he acts out of the belief we have seen in *Spellbound* and in post-*Spellbound* Hollywood psychoanalysis films: that in discovering the actual scenes or events the dream work veils and represents, "Madeleine" will be cured of her mental distress, purged of her psychic traumas—in this case, her suicidal impulses. He will show her that she is not, as she tells Scottie, going "mad, mad, mad," by reading through the veil of her dream, as Dr. Peterson did, to the real places and events they represent. "If I can just find a key," Scottie exclaims with equal degrees of optimism and desperation, "something to explain it." What he doesn't realize, however, is that the dream that so fascinates him isn't really Madeleine's, and that instead of leading to psychic release, bringing that dream into the light of day will lead to the very madness and death the dream represents. The dream, that is to say, is on a superficial level really Gavin Elster's, who, we are to believe, has concocted it in order to lead Scottie to the bell tower where the body of his wife—the real Madeleine—will be substituted for that of Judy and thrown to the ground. But more important, and more ironically, the dream is most profoundly Scottie's own. The topography of the dream, a long corridor leading to an open grave into which "Madeleine" fears she will plunge, tropes the topography of Scottie's fixation as well—rotating the nightmarish vision of Scottie's vertigo by 90 degrees, the dream transforms a vertical vortex into a horizontal one; and the fear it represents—the lure of death, the call of the tomb—is a representation of the fear of his own annihilation that stands at the center of his own vertigo. And, indeed, after "Madeleine's" "death," the dream does indeed quite literally become Scottie's; it passes directly into his own oneiric life and is represented at the climax of a remarkable dream sequence (and one, it should be added, that is far superior to the Dali-designed extravaganza in *Spellbound*), in which Scottie sees his body tumbling into Carlotta Valdez's tomb, his disembodied head screaming with horror in the midst of the darkness, then a shadowy body—possibly the policeman's, probably his own—hurtling from the bell tower. At this moment, we recognize that, far from being her own or Elster's product, "Madeleine"'s dream was always already part of Scottie's internal life; indeed, we realize that it is precisely through her unfolding of Scottie's own unconscious fixations to him that "Madeleine" has fascinated and entrapped him. And it is this fact that most effectively dismantles the *Spellbound* paradigm of analysis and cure. Scottie thinks that he is drawn— transferentially, erotically, like Ingrid Bergman—into the analysis and cure of another; in reality, he is sucked counter-transferentially, if equally erotically, into the mysterious abyss that is himself.

The imperative of solving the mystery that is Madeleine passes, during the second half of the movie, into Scottie's fetishistic fixation with re-creating Judy in Madeleine's image, the psychic ramifications of which and their implications for theorizing the nature and ramifications of Hitchcock's cinema itself have been so extensively treated as to demand no further comment from me. What I would like to focus on here, however, are the ramifications of Scottie's attempts to cure himself—a cure that, again in the best Hollywood tradition, seems to conflate the "solving" of a crime and the "resolving" of a mental conflict. In many ways, Scottie's final effort at self-cure, auto-therapy (a "wild psychoanalysis" indeed), although obviously closest in spirit to the detective's solution of a crime, is represented by Hitchcock as a demented, parodic version of an analytic "breakthrough." He takes Judy, whom he now recognizes to have impersonated "Madeleine," back to the bell tower, the site of his earlier trauma in order to reveal the truth about the past and so release him from his obsessions. And again his efforts are depicted by the film as therapeutic in nature—at once the climax of his efforts to "cure" himself and the repetition of his efforts to cure the fictitious Madeleine. For the point of bringing Judy back to the bell tower is not only to return to the "scene of the crime"—the explanation Scottie gives Judy; it is to re-create the language, the gestures, even the physical actions of "Madeleine"'s "suicide," so as—or so he says—to be "free" of his extreme, by now psychopathic "guilt complex," just as he had hoped to free "Madeleine" of her own fixations by bringing her face to face with the "real" site her dreams have represented. "There's one final thing I have to do—and then I'll be free of the past. . . . I have to go back into the past one more time, just once more, and when it's done, we'll be free," he tells Judy, echoing exactly the words he spoke to "Madeleine" as he urged her to repeat her dream to him. And as he half-leads, half-drags Judy/Madeleine back up the bell tower, Judy reveals to him—or, rather, he reveals to himself, with her increasingly desperate responses serving as confirmation—that he was indeed not responsible for Madeleine's death, that he was the victim of a monstrous plot. And as in *Spellbound*, where Dr. Peterson brings her patient to the site of his trauma in order to bring to life his repressed memories, the effects of this maneuver seem to be cathartic, curative. In good Freudian fashion, repetition is replaced by recollection, and recollection is followed by working-through: When Scottie successfully retells the narrative of his gulling, his neurotic symptom, his vertigo, disappears, signifying not only his successful resolution of his guilt complex over the death of "Madeleine" but also the original guilt occasioned by the death of the policeman. Scottie has, like all good Hollywood shrink/detectives, solved the crime and cured the patient by discovering the true facts of the case, facts that had been veiled by the mysterious mechanisms of mental dysfunction.

But as every viewer of *Vertigo* knows, the film refuses to end on this affirmative note. After the story has fully emerged—and as Scottie and Judy passionately embrace—a mysterious figure appears and Judy flings herself off the tower, just as "Madeleine" had appeared to do and as the policeman had actually done. And Scottie is plunged back into the madness he has seemed, finally to escape; he stands on the edge of the tower, like a stickless scarecrow, his body slumped and his arms akimbo, perhaps to follow Judy and hurtle himself off the side of the tower, or perhaps—at best—to fall into the abyss of madness itself. And at this moment, for the first and fullest time in his cinematic career, Hitchcock fully severs the narrative and ideological strands that he had seemed to be working to tie together—and that had been tied firmly together in the Hollywood film from the time of *Spellbound* on: Scottie has indeed solved the crime, but he has done the very opposite of curing himself, and psychoanalysis and crime detection turn out to be very much at odds with one another. Indeed, far from returning to the past in order to free himself from it—the psychoanalytic imperative he had cited as the ground of his detective work at the end of the film—Scottie has re-created a traumatic event in order to cause it to repeat itself, and to repeat itself with the ironic difference that the very crime he had falsely felt guilty for he is now truly guilty of. "One doesn't often get a second chance," he tells Judy as he drags her up the tower. "You're my second chance, Judy, you're my second chance," he maniacally chants as he pulls her up the last, steepest steps of the tower. Both the words he speaks and his repetition of them enforce on a verbal level the ironic lesson of the film's narrative: The compulsion to repeat and its companion, the death drive, rule Scottie even as—especially when—he seeks to explicate and defuse the power of the past. Seeking to break his own fixation by identifying Judy's guilt and eliciting her confession, Scottie unwittingly causes her death and, in so doing, brings about the very action he had sought to explain, expatiate, and annul.

And it is at this moment that the full dimensions of Hitchcock's critique of therapeutic culture become clear—and clearly paradoxical. To deal with the second issue first: We recognize at its conclusion that for all its rather mordant and indeed contemptuous treatment of psychoanalytic discourse and the therapeutic institutions informed by them, Hitchcock's film is not incompatible with high Freudianism—far from it. If Hitchcock critiques the tame Freudianism of the American psychological establishment or the even more thoroughly domesticated pop-Freudianism of the Hollywood film, he does not do so by turning away from Freud entirely—by turning, for example, to the Gothic madness-as-spiritual-possession paradigms that predate pop-Freudianism and have, in recent years, supplemented it; indeed, this paradigm is explicitly rejected in *Vertigo* by its representation of Gavin Elster's malevolent scripting of the Carlotta Valdez scenario. (Elster seems to have seen Hitchcock's *Rebecca* one too many times.) Rather, Hitchcock's cinema stages an extraordinarily complex return to Freud, or, more specifically, to the aspects of Freud that were studiously ignored in both the official and the mass-cultural American transformations of psychoanalytic theory. For when Hitchcock turns to critique the popular American mania for psychoanalysis, he articulates the lessons we may also find in the weird, the uncanny, the late Freud: the Freud of the metapsychological and culturally despairing writings like *Civilization and Its Discontents*, *Beyond the Pleasure Principle*, and *Analysis Terminable and Interminable*. The analogy between the two is as precise as it is unexpected: Hitchcock, like this Freud, sees the compulsion to repeat as being so powerful as to be irresistible, infecting even, and indeed quite precisely, the efforts to escape it; the death drive as so potent as to be irreversible, drawing not only Scottie but also Judy (who has a chance to leave town when Scottie discovers her identity but chooses not to) into the beckoning abyss of the grave; and the possibilities that, through therapy, the mastery of the rational ego can be asserted over these dark necessities as a particularly pernicious snare, defeated by the intransigencies of the death drive and the inevitabilities of the compulsion to repeat.

And, most importantly like this Freud: In doing so, Hitchcock seeks to position himself as a pessimistic critic of modern culture—and specifically modern American culture, American culture understood as the locus of a debased modernity itself. Ironically enough, given Freud's gloomy meditations on the American propensity for transforming what he increasingly saw as his grim tragic lessons in necessity into pragmatic insipidities, it is the cultural dominance of Freudian thought in postwar American culture that provides him with a particularly effective avenue for this mode of critique. The American "triumph of the therapeutic" affords Hitchcock a means of showing that what were culturally defined as the very means of psychic liberation were in fact only the most cunning of ruses by which those irrationalities could exert their power. In *Spellbound*, Hitchcock—and the American popular culture to which he spoke so powerfully—held out the possibility that psychoanalysis when broadly accepted and thoroughly understood could provide a solution to all problems, personal and social; that "psychic conflicts" were easily resolved and cure was as simple as the solving of a Hollywood mystery. In *Vertigo*, Hitchcock critiques—a better word might be demolishes—this very notion; he suggests that while psychoanalysis may have moved from a cultural mystery to a cultural commonplace, its insights institutionalized within structures like the psychiatric profession and American mass culture, its promises, or, rather, the promises of its American spokesmen and salesmen, could never be realized. Indeed, the very hope for cure, the very expectation that "guilt" can be internalized as a "complex" and then resolved by the unveiling of a repressed childhood trauma, is demonstrated by Hitchcock to be the very means by which Scottie is entrapped and Judy destroyed—the very means, that is to say, by which human beings are condemned to the criminality and madness they have turned to therapeutic institutions in order to escape.

And here the analogy to Adorno with which I began returns in an even more forceful manner, for like Adorno's, Hitchcock's cultural critique is based on what Adorno calls "the abyss of the self"—the adherence to a vertiginous model of selfhood that stresses the power of unconscious desires, wishes, and impulses and the impossibility of ever achieving any but the most perilous and transitory escapes from their demands and imperatives. And since not only Adorno but generations of Freudian fundamentalists who have followed him have been frequently criticized for the limitations of this model of selfhood—largely, indeed, for the ahistoricism of this model, its assumption that the Freudian model is valid for all psyches and genders, rather than a culturally specific hermeneutic that emerges from and is valid only in terms of a given historical moment—it is only fair to conclude by assessing Hitchcock in the same terms. To a certain extent, this critique is valuable and important; it reminds us that however differently *Spellbound* and *Vertigo* may approach the issue of cure, they are united in their appreciation of the unconscious's uncanny power. Neither the therapeutic complacency of *Spellbound* nor the therapeutic agitation of *Vertigo* can question the essential grounds on which the "triumph of the therapeutic" is wrought—the primacy of a historically unchanging, indeed a historically transcendent, unconscious. Indeed, in this sense, *Vertigo's* therapeutic pessimism only confirms the essential claims it seems to question; the *triumph* of the therapeutic may be called into question, but the essential conceptual structure that underlies its social hegemony—the "terror before the abyss of the self" that Adorno describes and *Vertigo* literalizes—is not.

But this critique, while important to bear in mind, is also limited: In the name of historical specificity, it bulldozes into oblivion the historicity of the gesture it claims to question. To understand both *Spellbound* and *Vertigo* as historically specific acts is to inquire not only about the historical blinders of *Vertigo* but also its powers of historical insight. Swimming against the mainstream, Hitchcock crafts a critique of American therapeutic culture as startling and passionate as those that were to follow his in the 1960s and early 1970s. And it might also be said that even in the 1990s—with psychobabble books proliferating on the best-seller lists, credentialed analysts dispensing advice on Top 40 radio, and a TV sex-talk show hosted by a therapist with an accent even more outrageous than Ingrid Bergman's—Hitchcock's understanding and critique of the interpenetration of the therapeutic ethos and the institutions of the culture industry has lost neither its relevance nor its cogency.

Notes

1. See Rieff, *The Triumph of the Therapeutic* (New York: Harper and Row, 1966), and the final chapter, "The Rise of Psychological Man," in *Freud: The Mind of a Moralist* (New

York: Viking, 1959). The sociological critique Rieff offers here has been historicized by T. J. Jackson Lears, who traces the rise of a therapeutic ethos to transformations in late-nineteenth-century religious doctrine in *No Place of Grace: Antimodernism and the Transformation of American Culture* (New York: Pantheon, 1981) and describes its intersection with the advertising revolution of the 1920s in "From Salvation to Self-Realization: Advertising and the Therapeutic Roots of the Consumer Culture, 1880–1930," in *The Culture of Consumption: Critical Essays in American History, 1880–1980*, ed. Richard Fox and T. J. Jackson Lears (New York: Pantheon, 1983). And it also informs the jeremiads of Christopher Lasch; see especially *The Culture of Narcissism: American Life In An Age of Diminished Expectations* (New York: Norton, 1978).

2. See Nathan Hale, *Freud and the Americans: The Beginnings of Psychoanalysis in the United States, 1876–1917* (New York: Pantheon, 1971), and *The Rise and Crisis of Psychoanalysis in the United States: Freud and the Americans, 1917–1985* (New York: Oxford University Press, 1995). Also useful is Irving Schneider, "Images of the Mind: Psychiatry in the Commercial Film," *American Journal of Psychiatry* 134 (1977): 613–19; I was directed to this article by Leslie Fishbein's programmatic but intelligent essay "*The Snake Pit*: The Sexist Nature of Sanity," in *Hollywood as Historian: American Film in Cultural Context*, ed. Peter Rollins (Lexington: University Press of Kentucky, 1983), 134–58.

3. Francis Still Wickware, "Psychoanalysis," *Life*, February 3, 1947. This feature article—one of many to be found in middlebrow journals during these years—is accompanied by the following telling headline: "Through books and movies, millions are discovering that they have 'unconscious minds' where strange impulses lurk. Getting rid of 'repressions' may take years, cost thousands."

4. See Peter Biskind, *Seeing Is Believing: How Hollywood Taught Us to Stop Worrying and Love the Fifties* (New York: Pantheon, 1983), 23–34.

5. Both the point and the quotation may be found in Lawrence Leff, *Hitchcock and Selznick* (New York: Weidenfeld and Nicholson, 1987), 234.

6. Krin and Glen Gabbard, *Psychiatry and the Cinema* (Chicago: University of Chicago Press, 1987).

7. Mary Ann Doane, *The Desire to Desire: The Woman's Film of the Forties* (Bloomington: Indiana University Press, 1987), 47. This is perhaps the place to comment briefly on this essay's attitude toward the project Doane so eloquently represents—a psychoanalytically inflected feminist film criticism that juxtaposes the discursive enterprise of Freud and Lacan against those of film to interrogate the representation of sexual difference and the construction of the male and female spectator by the narrative devices and cinematic apparatus of film. While acknowledging my debt to this tradition, I have tried to stay outside its coordinates, for I wish to interrogate the psychoanalytic project from an angle that would encompass the historical process of the institutionalization of psychoanalysis in American culture at large; and from this angle, the canonization of psychoanalysis as a—as the—privileged methodology of feminist academic film criticism in the late 1970s and early 1980s is undoubtedly a part (best understood, perhaps, as analogous to the cult of analysis among American intellectuals in the 1920s and 1930s). For a fine reading of the concerns of this essay from within the linguistic and analytical coordinates of psychoanalytically inflected feminist film criticism, see Thyrza Goodeve, "Desiring Narrative/Curing Vertigo," *Praxis* 1 (Spring/Summer 1987): 78–98.

8. Leff, *Hitchcock and Selznick*, 115.

9. Howard Faulkner and Virginia Pruitt, eds., *The Selected Correspondence of Karl A. Menninger, 1919–1945* (New Haven: Yale University Press, 1988), 402–3. Subsequent citations to the correspondence between Selznick, Menninger, Mankiewicz, Romm, and Bartemeier will refer to this edition.

10. For more details on the indefatigable (and quite commonsensical) Romm, as well as her complicated relation with the Selznicks/Mayers, see Steven Farber and Marc Green, *Hollywood on the Couch* (New York: W. Morrow, 1993), esp. pp. 37–55, and David Thomson, *Showman: The Life of David O. Selznick* (New York: Knopf, 1992), esp. pp. 423–29.

11. The film's attitude toward what *Life* magazine referred to as "the mystery of transference" deserves more comment than I can give it here. The film establishes a link between transference, counter-transference, and erotic love and suggests what later Hitchcock films make explicit—that such a transferential love is accompanied by strong impulses toward erotic domination and even violence. But it is crucial here that the analyst be female and the analysand male; violence and the will to dominate can be neutralized, read as signs of a negative transference only—as when Ingrid Bergman tells Gregory Peck, after he expresses irritation at her probings of his unconscious mind, "Darling, you'll be angrier at me yet."

12. I am arguing somewhat against the grain here, since Hitchcock himself is on record as seeing the psychoanalytic elements of the film as its least successful dimension—as not even a successful "MacGuffin." To a certain extent, one cannot argue with him, or with critics like Thomas Hyde, who argues that the "psychoanalytic practice [in the film] is a vehicle for making an artistic statement; it is both MacGuffin and metaphor" ("The Moral Universe of Hitchcock's *Spellbound*," in *A Hitchcock Reader*, ed Marshall Deutelbaum and Leland Poague [Ames: Iowa State University Press, 1966], 154). But what I find most compelling about the film is not so much the success or failure of the film's use of psychoanalysis but the consequences of that adaptation within both the Hollywood cinema and American culture.

5

Hitchcock's Washington
Spectatorship, Ideology, and the "Homosexual Menace" in Strangers on a Train

Robert J. Corber

> A curious freemasonry exists among underground workers and sympathizers [of the Communist party]. They can identify each other (and be identified by their enemies) on casual meeting by the use of certain phrases, the names of certain friends, by certain enthusiasms and certain silences. It is reminiscent of nothing so much as the famous scene in Proust where the Baron de Charlus and the tailor Jupien suddenly recognize their common corruption.
>
> —Arthur Schlesinger Jr., *The Vital Center* (1949)

Set in Washington, D.C., Alfred Hitchcock's *Strangers on a Train* (1951) abounds with images of the federal government. In shot after shot, the dome of the Capitol building appears in the background brilliantly lit up, and the Jefferson Memorial provides the setting for a suspenseful encounter between the all-American hero, Guy Haines (Farley Granger), and the murderous villain, Bruno Anthony (Robert Walker). The function of these monumental backdrops is not readily apparent. Although national monuments often figure prominently in Hitchcock's films, they usually have an obvious connection to the plot. In the climactic scene of *North by Northwest* (1959), for example, the American agent Eve Kandall (Eva Marie Saint) dangles perilously from Mount Rushmore. Her suspension from the monument translates into visual terms the cold-war conflict at the heart of the film: Mount Rushmore stands for the democratic principles at stake in the recovery of the microfilm stolen by the Communist spies. But the images of the federal government in *Strangers on a Train* bear no obvious relation to the plot. There are no Communist spies conspiring to overthrow the American government, only a psychopathic killer who tries to blackmail a champion tennis player into committing murder. Why, then, does the film abound with images that constantly remind the spectator that the film is set in the nation's capital?

In a cursory but suggestive reading of *Strangers on a Train*, Alain Marty provides a possible explanation for the film's constant reminders of its own setting. Although Marty does not specifically discuss the film's recurrent use of national monuments or the significance of its setting in the nation's capital, he links the film to the anti-Communist hysteria unleashed by the McCarthy hearings. He suggests that the film registers "the more or less unconscious preoccupations of public opinion in the 1950s."[1] Stressing the subject's often unconscious engagement with the discursive practices that structure its relation to the world, he argues persuasively that the film encodes Hitchcock's own paranoia about Communist infiltration of the American government. But despite Marty's attempt to historicize the film by locating it in the cold-war politics of the 1950s, he never specifically engages the film's topographical referent, its setting. The film emerges from his reading as a kind of mythical allegory. He argues that the film tries to show that "American society must be purged from top (Bruno) to bottom (Miriam) whatever the social cost" (124). Even the all-American Guy Haines must prove himself before he can assume his rightful place in the ruling class, for he undergoes a series of tests, "like a medieval knight" (121). Marty's reading, in other words, inadvertently reproduces the reductive categories of cold-war political discourse. It represents the cold war as a struggle between good and evil, heroes and villains.

Despite its hasty retreat to political allegory, however, Marty's Althusserian reading of *Strangers on a Train* represents a welcome departure from the rigid psychoanalytic approach to classical Hollywood cinema that has dominated Hitchcock criticism. This approach tends to ignore the historical specificity of male subjectivity, its construction in relation to historically specific institutions, discourses, and practices. Raymond Bellour, for example, in a series of textual analyses deeply indebted to Lacanian theories of the cinematic apparatus, has argued somewhat abstractly that Hitchcock's Oedipalized narratives constantly restage the subject's entry into the Symbolic order.[2] He claims that because Hitchcock's films are constructed along an Oedipal trajectory, they insert the male spectator into a fixed, stable subject position. The hero's sadistic pleasure in the woman's fragmented body supposedly guarantees the coherence and totality of his own, thereby allowing him to return her look without fear of castration. Bellour also argues that these films restage the mirror phase as defined by Lacanian psychoanalysis. Because the spectator misrecognizes the hero's bodily coherence as his own, he eludes the threat of castration signified by the image of the woman on the screen.

Feminist film critics have been quick to point out the limitations of this narrow approach to Hitchcock's films. They have shown that Bellour's use of psychoanalysis elides the differences between male and female subjectivity.[3] For if, as Bellour claims, voyeurism and fetishism are the dominant codes of Hitchcock's films, then the only position of subjectivity they make available to the female spectator is a masochistic one. While some feminist film critics accept the argument that spectatorial pleasure is, in Mary Ann Doane's words, "indissociable from pain," others argue that the female spectator's subjective engagement with the filmic text is more complicated.[4] Teresa de Lauretis, for example, claims that the female spectator identifies with the active and desiring male subject as well as with the passive and fetishized object of his gaze.[5] Tania Modleski also emphasizes the female spectator's shifting identifications. She suggests that Hitchcock's films narrativize the female as well as the male Oedipal trajectory, thereby allowing for the limited expression of a specifically female desire.[6]

Feminist film critics, then, have not so much rejected the model of filmic pleasure proposed by Lacanian theories of the cinematic apparatus as they have expanded it to include the production of an active and desiring female subject. For although they conceive of the process of identification as a sexually differentiated one, they follow Bellour's example in proposing a monolithic view of male subjectivity. They assume that the male spectator is not only heterosexual but unequivocally so, and they limit the possibility of occupying multiple identificatory positions to the female spectator.[7] Consequently, they tend to see the male spectator's insertion into a fixed, stable heterosexual subject position as inevitable. But in stressing the fixity of the male spectator's identification with the hero, they overlook the polymorphous sexualities circulating through the filmic text. As I will show, an alternative reading of psychoanalytic theory suggests that we should regard the male spectator's identification with the hero of the classical text as fluid and unstable. Moreover, their application of psychoanalysis to Hitchcock's Oedipalized narratives seems circular. For Hitchcock's films have an ideological investment in ratifying a psychoanalytic understanding of male subjectivity. One of the ways in which Hitchcock's films try to contain the play of sexualities circulating through the cinematic apparatus is by narrativizing the male Oedipal trajectory. In identifying with the hero, the male spectator becomes complicit with the production of his own Oedipalized subjectivity. Obviously, Hitchcock's films must engage the male spectator libidinally if they are to ensure his submission to their discursive structure.[8] The male spectator must first desire his own Oedipalization before he will consent to it. Yet by relying on the process of identification as their primary mode of address, Hitchcock's films threaten to disrupt their own ideological project.

Imported from psychoanalytic discourse, the concept of identification has remained largely unexamined in Lacanian film theory. Although psychoanalytically oriented film theorists emphasize the importance of identification in the construction of the male heterosexual subject, they ignore the concrete historical forces that condition it, and they oversimplify the role Freud assigned to it in the male Oedipal trajectory. Freud conceived of identification as a defense against the boy's homosexual object cathexis with the father. In *The Ego and the Id*, he defines identification as a melancholic structure that compensates the boy for his loss of the father as an object choice. Freud argues that the boy frequently adopts a "feminine attitude" toward the father during the pre-Oedipal phase and fantasizes about taking the place of the mother. But in order for him to resolve the Oedipus complex, he must renounce these fantasies. Unless he represses his attachment to the father and fixes his affections on the mother, he will retain the polymorphous sexuality of the pre-Oedipal phase. He reconciles himself to this loss by incorporating the father into his ego, which reinforces his primary identification with the father. Freud explains that in assuming the features of the lost object, the ego "is forcing itself, so to speak, upon the id as a love-object and is trying to make good the id's loss by saying: 'Look, you can love me too I am so like the object.' "9

Insofar as this psychoanalytic model of identification clarifies the primary mode of address of classical Hollywood cinema and its codes, it suggests that rather than inserting the male spectator into a fixed, stable heterosexual subject position, Hitchcock's films return him to the polymorphous sexuality of the pre-Oedipal phase. For according to Freudian theory, the male spectator's identification with the hero of the classical text involves the repression of a potentially destabilizing homosexual object cathexis: He unconsciously desires the hero of the classical text, or else he would not identify with him. Identification acts as a defense against a homosexual object cathexis. The culturally sanctioned prohibition of homosexuality requires the male spectator to abandon his object relation to the hero. To compensate for this loss, he incorporates the hero into his ego: He does not desire the hero; he *is* the hero. But this does not mean that he wholly relinquishes his homosexual object choice. Rather, it continues to exist in his unconscious, where it becomes a potential obstacle to the formation of a fixed heterosexual identity. The melancholic structure of identification guarantees the preservation of the object relation to the hero in the unconscious. Thus, in addressing the male spectator as a subject, cinematic discourse establishes a homosexual object relation between him and the hero that it must then repress. As the primary mode of address of classical Hollywood cinema, identification restages the male spectator's feminine attitude toward the father in the pre-Oedipal phase, thereby encouraging the formation of a polymorphous, rather than a fixed, heterosexual identity. Obviously, Hitchcock's films must limit the effects of this aspect of identification if they are to insert the male spectator into an Oedipalized subject position.

To show how Hitchcock's films contain the potentially disruptive effects of their own mode of address, I will follow Alain Marty's lead and situate *Strangers on a Train* in relation to cold-war politics. But whereas Marty links *Strangers on a Train* to the anti-Communist crusade, I will focus on the cold-war construction of "the homosexual" as a national-security risk. This shift in focus has several advantages. First, it furthers recent attempts to historicize the spectatorial subject. I will show that the spectator's subjective engagement with Hitchcock's film was determined by a multiplicity of discursive practices, political as well as medical, that defined homosexuality as pathological. Second, emphasizing the homophobic politics of the postwar period will clarify the paranoia about male heterosexuality encoded in the film. At the same time that it tries to insert the male spectator into an Oedipalized subject position, *Strangers on a Train* represents the achievement of a fixed heterosexual identity as virtually impossible. I will argue that this paranoia is directly related to cold-war fears that homosexuals were indistinguishable from heterosexuals and had infiltrated all levels of American society. Finally, locating the film in its cold-war context will shed more light on the heterosexual panic of the period. In particular, it will clarify the significance of the juridical construction of "the homosexual" as a security risk. Because this construction involved the appropriation of a medical model of same-sex eroticism, it resulted in a virtually unprecedented alliance between juridical and medical discourses. To counteract the pioneering attempts of gay men and women to define themselves as an oppressed minority with their own history and culture, the government appealed to medical evidence supposedly demonstrating that homosexuals and lesbians had no outward characteristics or physical traits that distinguished them from heterosexuals, but because this evidence acknowledged the resistance of sexuality to containment through representation, it called into question the fixity of male and female heterosexual identities. Thus, I will use *Strangers on a Train* to examine the relation between the politics of spectatorship and the crisis over national security. I want to show that in the cold-war era the construction of male and female subjectivity was conditioned by the identification of homosexuality and lesbianism as threats to the nation's security.

The Kinsey Reports and the Homosexualization of the American Male

On February 28, 1950, John Peurifoy, a State Department official, made a revelation that would not only intensify allegations that the employment practices of the Truman administration recklessly endangered national security but also precipitate a juridical crisis that threatened to undermine the government's power to regulate same-sex practices.[10] Under sharp questioning by the Senate Appropriations Committee, Peurifoy disclosed that the State Department had recently dismissed several employees on charges of homosexuality. Republican leaders, already engaged in a campaign to discredit the Truman administration over its national security policies, seized the opportunity to embarrass the president further. Exploiting Peurifoy's disclosure, they accused the president of tolerating homosexual employees in the federal government. Senator Joseph McCarthy charged that the State Department had reinstated a known homosexual despite the growing crisis over national security. Suddenly, homosexuals were said to pose as great a threat to the government as members of the Communist Party. When the chief officer of the District of Columbia vice squad testified before a Senate committee that thousands of "sexual deviates" were employed by the federal government and had been arrested for cruising in the city's parks, Senator Kenneth Wherry, the Republican floor leader, demanded a full-scale Senate investigation. How could thousands of "sexual deviates" with police records be employed by the government without the government knowing it?

It would be difficult to exaggerate the significance of the ensuing investigation undertaken by the Senate Appropriations Committee into same-sex behavior. To begin with, the discovery that there were "deviates" who could "pass" as heterosexuals, thereby escaping detection, led to a redefinition of homosexual and lesbian identities. The report issued by the Senate Appropriations Committee disputed the popular stereotypes of the effeminate homosexual and the masculine lesbian. Many of the legal and medical "experts" who testified before the committee claimed that there were "no outward characteristics or physical traits" that positively identified gay men and women.[11] Thus, effeminate men or masculine women were not necessarily homosexual or lesbian: "The fact is that many male homosexuals are very masculine in their physical appearance and general demeanor, and many female homosexuals have every appearance of femininity in their outward behavior" (2–3). This testimony encouraged the medicalization of the juridical discourse on sex. For if the government could not identify homosexual and lesbian employees, how could it regulate their behavior? Moreover, even if it could identify them, how could it legally expel them when, except for their sexual orientation, they appeared "normal"? To support its claims that lesbians and gay men did indeed constitute a security risk, the committee appealed to a medical model of same-sex eroticism. It tried to show that homosexuals and lesbians were by definition emotionally unstable and should therefore "be considered as proper cases for medical and psychiatric treatment" (3). This meant that even those gay men and women who seemed "normal" should be expelled from the government. They were as emotionally unstable as more stereotypical homosexuals and lesbians and were therefore just as vulnerable to the "blandishments of the foreign espionage agent" (5). If the government could not expel "passing" lesbians and gay men on the basis of their behavior, it could do so on the basis of their psychological profile. Indeed, their very "normalcy" was a sign that they were disturbed.

How do we account for the emergence of gays and lesbians as security risks? Historians of American sexuality generally agree that Alfred Kinsey's reports on male and female sexuality, published in 1948 and 1953, respectively, forced Americans to reexamine the established norms of male and female sexual behavior.[12] Widely discussed in the news media, Kinsey's reports contained startling findings that seemed to confirm psychoanalytic theories that stressed the instability of sexual identities. The incidence of same-sex behavior among the men and women interviewed for the reports was unexpectedly high. Among the men, for example, 50 percent admitted to being aroused by members of their own sex, 37 percent reported having had at least one postadolescent homosexual experience leading to orgasm, and 4 percent claimed to be exclusively homosexual. Perhaps the most startling of Kinsey's findings was that "persons with homosexual histories are to be found in every age group, in every social level, in every conceivable occupation, in cities and on farms, and in the most remote areas of the country," a finding that added new meaning to the patriotic phrase "from sea to shining sea."[13] The high incidence of homosexuality led Kinsey to conclude that homosexual behavior was an "inherent physiological capacity" (659–60) that could not be suppressed and should therefore be tolerated.

Historians of American sexuality may be right in claiming that the Kinsey reports eventually undermined the restrictive norms of male and female behavior in postwar America, thereby making possible the sexual liberation movements of the 1960s, but their most immediate impact was to exacerbate the emergent heterosexual panic. Kinsey's findings that the sexual identities of most Americans varied during their lifetimes only reinforced fears that homosexuals and lesbians had infiltrated the government and threatened to subvert it from within. For if Kinsey was correct, if homosexuality and lesbianism did indeed constitute an "inherent physiological capacity" that could not be contained, then gay men and women would have little difficulty converting straight employees to their "perverted" practices. The knowledge that many "normal" men and women had once been so converted, even if they were not now engaging in same-sex practices, made this vulnerablity to sexual conversion seem even more acute. The report of the Senate Appropriations Committee claimed that "one homosexual can pollute a Government office" (20). The continued employment of lesbians and gay men, in other words, threatened to result in a homosexualization of American society. The report cited legal and medical evidence supposedly showing that homosexuals and lesbians "will frequently attempt to entice normal individuals to engage in perverted practices. This is particularly true in the case of young and impressionable people who might come under the influence of a pervert" (4).

Kinsey's reports, then, inadvertently contributed to the growing juridical crisis over the politics of sexual practice. Confronted by the evidence of widespread homosexual and lesbian activity among "average" American men and women, the government appealed to the psychiatric discourse on same-sex eroticism, lest Kinsey's findings encourage greater tolerance of homosexuals and lesbians. The Senate Appropriations Committee was especially determined to counteract the evidence suggesting that there was little to distinguish gay men and women from straights except for their sexual orientation. It accepted the finding that homosexuals could be masculine, but it continued to treat homosexuality as a form of gender inversion. The masculine homosexual emerged as particularly threatening. Dividing the male homosexual population according to the binarisms that governed the production of gender, it claimed that the active gay man "exhibits no traces of femininity in his speech and or mannerisms which would disclose his homosexuality. This active type is almost exclusively attracted to the passive type of homosexual or to young men or boys who are not necessarily homosexual but who are effeminate in general appearance or behavior" (3). Thus, the committee continued to rely on homophobic stereotypes to categorize homosexual behavior. The effeminate gay man, whose behavior corresponded to those stereotypes, was supposedly more "normal" than the masculine gay man. The masculine gay man, on the other hand, could avoid detection. Because he was active rather than passive, his masculinity conflicted with his sexual orientation. In this way, the committee tried indirectly to recuperate Kinsey's findings for the continued medicalization of same-sex eroticism. It positioned lesbians and gay men who did not correspond to the stereotypes as even more threatening than those who did.

This is not to suggest that Kinsey's findings were solely responsible for the postwar crisis over the government employment of an indeterminate group of gay men and women who could pass. The emergence of politicized gay and lesbian communities in large urban areas also contributed to the construction of "the homosexual" and "the lesbian" as security risks. For it was in the postwar period that middle-class gay and lesbian professionals in cities such as Los Angeles and New York first began to define themselves as members of an oppressed minority. Rejecting the medicalization of same-sex behavior, these gay and lesbian professionals pioneered a minoritarian, or subcultural, model of same-sex eroticism. For them, gay men and women were not "sick" but different. They had a history and a culture that extended beyond the bars and bathhouses that had traditionally provided urban gay men and women with a sense of collective identity. This history and culture encompassed all aspects of their lives, including their careers. The pseudonymous Donald Webster Corey, for example, in *The Homosexual in America* (1951), argued that homosexuals and lesbians shared more than a common sexual identity. They were members of an oppressed minority whose rights had been systematically violated by the American government: "Our minority status is similar, in a variety of respects, to that of national, religious and other ethnic groups; in the denial of civil liberties; in the legal, extra-legal and quasi-legal discrimination; in the assignment of an inferior social position; in the exclusion from the mainstream of life and culture."[14]

The Mattachine Society, the first homosexual and lesbian rights group founded in the postwar period, similarly emphasized the common history of oppression uniting gay men and women. As former members of the Communist Party, the founders of the society—Henry Hay, Bob Hull, and Chuck Rowland—were committed to theorizing homosexual and lesbian oppression from a Marxist perspective. They felt that gay men and women who passed as middle-class heterosexual professionals were victims of false consciousness and did not realize that they were oppressed, despite their wealth and privilege. When the society began to recruit members in 1950, it established consciousness-raising groups that encouraged the participants to see themselves as members of an oppressed minority regardless of their status as professionals. Not surprisingly, Hay, Hull, and Rowland encountered significant opposition to their essentialist claims about distinct lesbian and gay identities. Even those members who were sympathetic to their claims hesitated to embrace their position. They worried that the attempt to define a distinct gay and lesbian culture would only isolate them further from mainstream American life. But the majority of newly recruited members simply rejected the idea that they were fundamentally different from heterosexuals. Although they agreed that they had certain interests in common with other homosexuals and lesbians, they insisted that the only thing that distinguished them from heterosexual professionals was their sexual orientation. After a protracted struggle with Hay, Hull, and Rowland, these members assumed leadership of the society and stated categorically that "the sex variant is no different from anyone else except in the object of his [sic] sexual expression."[15]

Historians of the homophile movement usually explain this struggle over how to define lesbianism and homosexuality within the Mattachine Society in terms of a "retreat to respectability."[16] For these historians, the members of the Mattachine Society who rejected the founders' minoritarian claims wanted to be accepted into, rather than excluded from, mainstream American society; thus, they were unwilling to challenge existing social structures. Yet this explanation oversimplifies the resistance encountered by the founders. For the divisions within the society suggest that lesbian and gay professionals occupied a multiplicity of competing subject positions. The lawyers, doctors, and other professionals recruited by Hay, Hull, and Rowland resisted the argument that they were essentially different from heterosexuals with similar backgrounds because that argument failed to describe their own lived experience. Unless their behavior corresponded to the stereotype of the "fairy" or the "dyke," they could pass in straight America. Consequently, they did not experience the disjunction between their personal and professional lives as a contradiction. Thus, to claim that the rejection of a minoritarian model of same-sex eroticism in the 1950s constituted a form of false consciousness and/or denial is to minimize the extent to which the relation between gay men and women and their sexuality was overdetermined. The members who eventually gained control of the Mattachine Society had no interest in radically challenging existing social structures, because those structures allowed them to practice their sexuality without seriously endangering their professional status.

The emergence of a minoritarian model of same-sex eroticism also left its mark on the report of the Senate Appropriations Committee. By invoking psychiatric categories, the committee tried to indirectly contain the attempts of middle-class gay men and women to define themselves as members of an oppressed minority. It insisted that homosexuality and lesbianism constituted aberrant psychological conditions. Because they suffered from an arrested sexual development, homosexuals and lesbians could supposedly be cured of their "perverted" practices. Citing medical evidence, the committee claimed that homosexuals and lesbians could be cured "if they [had] a genuine desire to be cured" (3). The committee defined gay men and women, in other words, as "sick" or recalcitrant heterosexuals who refused to grow up. Such a definition indirectly countered the argument that lesbians and gay men were systematically oppressed by society. If lesbians and gay men felt alienated from mainstream America, that was because they were maladjusted; their problems were personal rather than political and were best remedied in a doctor's office. Thus, the homophile movement's minoritarian claims emerged as another indication of just how "abnormal" gays and lesbians were. The medical model defined homosexuality and lesbianism as developmental disorders rather than as categories of identity similar to other categories of identity such as race, gender, and nationality.

In the postwar period, then, homosexuality and lesbianism became sites of extended ideological struggle among competing political interests. On the one hand, juridical discourse appropriated the medical model of same-sex eroticism to justify the government expulsion of lesbians and gay men; on the other hand, middle-class lesbians and gay men began to contest the pathologizing of same-sex practices and to define themselves as an oppressed minority. The problem with the first of these constructions was that it appropriated rather than disputed Kinsey's findings. To justify its claims that even gay men and women who appeared "normal" constituted a security risk, it invoked medical findings that all human sexuality was fluid and polymorphous. For this reason, it left heterosexuals in a vulnerable and embattled position. In assuming that many heterosexuals might succumb to the "blandishments" of gay men and women, it encouraged heterosexual panic. The problem with the second of these constructions was that it assumed that it had a potential constituency in all lesbians and gay men. It failed to consider the overdetermination of gay and lesbian identities and simply took for granted that there was an automatic connection between an individual's sexuality and her/his politics. Many of the members recruited by the Mattachine Society proved just as susceptible to anti-Communist propaganda as more mainstream Americans and had no desire to theorize their own oppression from a

Marxist perspective that seemed at odds with the nation's security interests. Rather than making a connection between the anti-Communism and homophobia sweeping the nation, these members threw their support behind the government's campaign to rid American society of Communist influence. They proposed requiring loyalty oaths and establishing a committee to investigate members suspected of Communist sympathies. These members saw themselves primarily as vulnerable middle-class professionals whose entitlement was threated by the growing influence of the Communist Party. Their identities as members of an oppressed minority were secondary to their identities as patriotic Americans.

A question remains, however: Why would the government appeal to scientific findings that encouraged heterosexual panic? What did it gain by acknowledging the resistance of sexuality to containment through representation? The codification of lesbian and gay identities according to a medical model of same-sex eroticism might, after all, have reassured heterosexuals of the fundamental differences between them and passing lesbians and gay men. Such a model conceived of all gay men and women as sick, whether they appeared "normal" or not. But the government invoked scientific findings that posited the instability of all sexual identities, gay or straight. It wanted to justify the expulsion of gays and lesbians by claiming that they might pervert straight employees if they remained in the government. Thus, at the same time that the government claimed that gays and lesbians were fundamentally different from heterosexuals, it also argued that heterosexuals were vulnerable to sexual conversion. Yet it was precisely for this reason that the alliance between medical and juridical discourses provided a particularly effective mechanism of social control. For it allowed the government to do more than regulate the behavior of an indeterminate group of gays and lesbians. Historians generally agree that the postwar years were a period of almost unprecedented social and sexual upheaval. Returning soldiers often had difficulty readjusting to civilian life, and many women resented the pressure to return to the domestic sphere.[17] Moreover, many homosexuals and lesbians came out for the first time during the war and, upon returning home, settled in urban centers where they participated in the gay and lesbian subcultures.[18] The construction of gays and lesbians as security risks helped to contain these dramatic shifts in attitudes and behaviors. It not only politicized the sexual practices of an indeterminate group of gay men and women by linking them to the crisis over national security but also coerced heterosexuals into policing their own behavior. Suddenly, there was a connection between an individual's politics and her/his sexual identity. Membership in the Communist Party and other left-wing political organizations indicated that the individual was not only unpatriotric but potentially perverted as well. Thus, if an individual's sexual orientation could no longer be determined by her/his lack of conformity to the norms of male and female behavior, it could be by her/his politics.

Hitchcock and the Heterosexualization of Spectatorship

Hitchcock's *Strangers on a Train* participated in these attempts to contain the political and sexual upheavals of the postwar period through the deployment of homophobia. Based loosely on a Patricia Highsmith novel of the same name, it identified individual conformity to the political and sexual norms sanctioned by the national security state as an act of supreme patriotism. In Highsmith's blatantly homophobic novel, a fledgling architect, Guy Haines, befriends Charles Bruno, a spoiled mama's boy from Long Island, on a train while traveling from New York to Texas. Over drinks in the dining car, Guy tells Bruno that he is returning home to Texas to divorce his wife, Miriam, who is pregnant with another man's baby. When he expresses his fear that Miriam might refuse to grant him a divorce, thereby jeopardizing his first architectural commission, Bruno proposes exchanging murders. Bruno will murder Miriam, if Guy will murder Bruno's father. Throughout the scenes on the train, Guy becomes increasingly uncomfortable with Bruno's flirtatious behavior. When Bruno suggests that they spend a couple of days together in Santa Fe, Guy snaps: "Pick up somebody else."[19] It is not until Bruno makes his murderous proposal, however, that Guy becomes truly alarmed by his familiarity. When he leaves Bruno's compartment, he regrets that he has left behind his volume of Plato, Highsmith's not-so-subtle clue that Guy is latently homosexual: "He didn't like the idea of its spending the night in Bruno's room, or of Bruno's touching it and opening it" (32). Guy rejects Bruno's proposal unequivocally, but Bruno ignores his protestations and kills Miriam when he discovers that she has indeed refused to give Guy a divorce. He then blackmails Guy into killing his father by threatening to implicate him in Miriam's murder.

Although Hitchcock's film retains the basic outline of Highsmith's novel, it makes several important changes. Rather than a fledgling architect, its Guy Haines is a champion tennis player who intends to enter politics after his final match at Forest Hills. His girlfriend, Ann (Ruth Roman), is not a wealthy socialite but the daughter of a powerful senator, and he resists Bruno's attempts to blackmail him into carrying out his part of their "bargain." But the film's most significant change is in translating the action from New York and Connecticut to Washington, D.C. The film's setting in the nation's capital casts the homosexual subplot in a wholly new light. The encounter between the strangers on the train has a political resonance lacking in the novel, for it narrativizes the "homosexual menace" as defined by contemporary juridical discourse.[20] To begin with, it translates into visual terms the juridical crisis precipitated by the discovery that gays and lesbians could look and behave like heterosexuals. Hitchcock's Guy Haines certainly does not look homosexual. In his dark wool tweeds and V-neck sweater, he appears too clean-cut and all-American to threaten national security. Yet it is he who initiates the meeting with Bruno: He accidentally kicks Bruno while crossing his legs. Moreover, Hitchcock's scenarization of the encounter on the train immediately identifies Guy as a potential security risk. Bruno recognizes Guy because he has seen his picture in the society pages of the newspaper. (Bruno apparently does not read the sport pages, which is probably intended as another indication that he is homosexual). It is common knowledge that Guy wants to divorce Miriam (Laura Elliot) and marry Ann in order to further his political ambitions. Thus, the meeting between him and Bruno exposes him to the threat of blackmail.

Cold-war political discourse made Hitchcock's attempts to represent Guy and Bruno as homosexuals extremely problematic. As I have already noted, the report issued by the Senate Appropriations Committee claimed that lesbians and gay men could avoid detection by passing. But if lesbians and gay men could pass, how could they be distinguished from heterosexuals at the level of cinematic representation? One of the ways Hitchcock tries to resolve this dilemma is by adhering to the stereotype of the effeminate homosexual. His representation of Bruno seems to insist that there *are* outward characteristics and physical traits that positively identify gay men. The famous opening shots in which the camera tracks Guy's and Bruno's feet as they rush from opposite sides of Union Station imme- diately identify Bruno as outside mainstream American society. In marked con- strast to Guy, who wears dark wool trousers and wing-tipped shoes, Bruno wears striped trousers and pair of saddle shoes. Bruno's unsolicited confessions to Guy on the train further mark him as homosexual. He is overly dependent on his mother. He explains to Guy that his monogrammed tie clip is a gift from his mother. A later shot shot of him lounging in a silk robe in the richly appointed living room of his father's estate while his mother manicures his nails only rein- forces the impression that he is a mama's boy who is insufficiently masculine.

But the growing crisis over the government employment of passing gays and lesbians problematized Hitchcock's use of the traditional signifiers of homosexu- ality in classical Hollywood film. As we saw above, effeminate behavior did not necessarily indicate that a man was homosexual. Thus, Hitchcock tries to secure his representation of Bruno as "the homosexual" of cold-war political discourse by invoking the medical model of homosexuality. Insofar as it stresses Bruno's emo- tional dependence on his mother (Marion Lorne), the film encourages a psycho- analytic interpretation of his behavior. Bruno appears to suffer from an unresolved Oedipus complex. His fantasies of replacing the father threaten to become reality. Moreover, the film implies that his mother is responsible for his arrested sexual development, which is recontained by his final "arrest" by the police at the end of the film. She encourages his dependence on her by constantly mediating be- tween him and his disapproving father. The shot of her manicuring his nails is especially incriminating. She meticulously prepares his hands for strangling Miriam.[21]

Hitchcock's film, then, invokes the homophobic categories of cold-war po- litical discourse to secure its representation of Bruno as the emotionally unstable homosexual who threatens national security. Bruno first tries to pervert Guy and then to implicate him in Miriam's murder when he refuses to abide by the terms of their "agreement" on the train. Hitchcock condenses this scenarization of the homosexual menace into one of the film's most powerful images. At one point in the film, the camera tracks Guy as he walks toward the Jefferson Memorial with a police detective. When Guy suddenly turns his head and looks outside the frame, the camera follows the direction of his gaze and pans the Jefferson Memorial. The composition of this shot immediately focuses our eye on Bruno. Unlike the other figures in the shot, he stands near the center of the frame, motionless and looking straight into the camera. He has apparently been following Guy and now watches him from the steps of the memorial. Although Bruno is dwarfed by the memorial's massive columns and seemingly endless rows of steps, the stark contrast between his dark silhouette and the gleaming white marble makes the government appear vulnerable and unprotected. Bruno emerges as a blight on the government. His menacing presence on the steps of the memorial amounts to blackmail. It reminds Guy, the would-be senator, that he cannot expose Bruno as Miriam's murderer without incriminating himself. This scene is especially powerful because it is shot from Guy's point of view. The spectator shares Guy's shock of recognition when Guy realizes that Bruno is watching him. The dizzying movement of the camera as it pans the memorial (repeated when Guy's taxi pulls away from the steps) only reinforces this shock: The spectator's look is momentarily dislocated. In this way, the film positions the spectator as "the heterosexual" of contemporary juridical discourse who is threatened by the homosexual menace. Like Guy, the spectator is susceptible to blackmail because of the instability (literalized by the camera's movement) of her/his sexual identity.

But Hitchcock's representation of the homosexual menace is more complicated than this analysis implies. According to the Senate Appropriations Committee, it is the homosexual or lesbian employee who is susceptible to blackmail, not the "normal" individual whom he or she perverts. In the film, however, it is Guy, not Bruno, who emerges as the potential security risk; he is the one compromised by the encounter on the train. In this respect, the film complicates the homophobic categories of cold-war political discourse. Whereas the Senate Appropriations Committee tried to show that homosexuals and lesbians frequently seduced their impressionable young coworkers, Hitchcock's film makes little distinction between Guy and Bruno. To be sure, Guy would never murder Miriam himself, but he clearly desires her death and allows Bruno to "seduce" him. For example, after learning that Miriam has decided not to give him a divorce, he calls Ann from the train station and tells her that he "could strangle her [Miriam's] little neck." A train hurtles by as he says the words, recalling Bruno's murderous proposal.

He also seems to indicate his consent to the terms of Bruno's proposal when he accidentally leaves his lighter in Bruno's compartment. Marked "A to G," the lighter is the film's substitute for the volume of Plato in Highsmith's novel and functions as a signifier of the instability of Guy's sexual identity. Originally a token of Ann's love for him, it now becomes a token of his love for Bruno. In the context of the encounter on the train, the A on the lighter is ambiguous. It stands not only for Ann but also for Bruno (whose last name in the film is Anthony). Thus the markings can be interpreted to mean that Guy would consider Miriam's murder a token of Bruno's love for him ("Anthony to Guy"). Miriam's death, after all, would enable Guy to marry Ann and achieve his political ambitions. This is certainly how Bruno interprets the markings on the lighter. After Guy leaves his compartment, Bruno examines the lighter before pocketing it and says, "Crisscross." Bruno's comment could of course merely refer to the crossed tennis rackets engraved on the lighter, but "crisscross" is also the term he uses to describe the exchange of murders. Bruno, then, has some justification for believing that Guy has agreed to the terms of his proposal. Yet Guy leaves the lighter in Bruno's compartment not so much to indicate his consent to the exchange of the murders as to redefine their relationship. As I have already suggested, the A is ambiguous. It stands for Ann as well as for Bruno, which makes it possible to interpret the markings on the lighter in a different way. Guy would accept Miriam's murder as a token of Bruno's love for him because it would normativize their relationship by triangulating it through Ann.[22] By eliminating the obstacles to Guy and Ann's marriage, Bruno would in a sense be giving Ann to Guy ("A to G") as well as making her into a guy. Reduced to an object of exchange between the two men, Ann would become a substitute for Bruno. Guy uses the lighter, in other words, to redefine the terms of the exchange. He and Bruno will exchange Ann rather than the murders.

In this respect, the film goes even further than the national security state in attempting to police male same-sex behavior. The Senate Appropriations Committee distinguished sharply between "latent" and "overt" homosexuals. It limited its investigation to overt homosexuals, or homosexuals who openly engaged in same-sex practices, and ignored those who "knowingly or unknowingly have tendencies or inclinations toward homosexuality and other types of sex perversion, but who, by the exercise of self-restraint or for other reasons, do not indulge in overt acts of perversion" (2). It refused, in other words, to pathologize traditionally accepted forms of male homoeroticism such as those in which two men mediated their desire for each other through the exchange of a woman. By contrast, Hitchcock's film insists that homosexuality is homosexuality, whether it involves the exchange of a woman or not. Guy remains outside the law, despite his attempts to normativize his relationship with Bruno. In shot after shot, Guy's actions mimic Bruno's, thereby reducing him to Bruno's double. The crosscuts that link the two men in the film repeat formally the crisscross that links them in the plot. A shot of Bruno looking at his watch crosscuts to one of Guy looking at his. In the scene in which Bruno informs Guy that he has strangled Miriam, the composition of the shots visually expresses Guy's complicity with the murder. The camera shows him and Bruno standing next to each other behind the bars of a wrought-iron gate that casts its shadows across their bodies. Close-ups of his face as he listens in horror to Bruno's description of Miriam's death alternate with close-ups of Bruno talking excitedly. The shot/reverse shot structure of this sequence makes Guy and Bruno seem virtually interchangeable: Guy too belongs behind bars. Guy's doubling of Bruno culminates in the scenes of Guy's final tennis match at Forest Hills. Shots of Bruno frantically searching for Guy's lighter, which he has accidentally dropped down a sewer, are crosscut with shots of Guy desperately trying to beat his opponent. In these scenes, Guy seems to have become Bruno. He is active rather than passive. His determination to win the match surprises the tennis announcer: Guy usually plays with a "watch-and-wait" strategy, but his desire to win has made him uncharacteristically "grim and determined."

In representing Guy as Bruno's double, Hitchcock encourages the spectator to interpret his behavior psychoanalytically. Guy's doubling of Bruno recalls the mirror stage as defined by Lacanian psychoanalysis. According to Lacan, during the mirror stage, the subject exchanges a fragmented bodily image for a coherent, unified one when it recognizes its own image in a mirror or in another body (usually the mother's). This exteriorization of the subject, its projection outward,

Guy and Bruno: virtually interchangeable

enables the subject to conceive of the body as finite rather than as continuous with the mother, thereby establishing a boundary between inside and outside: The subject becomes an object that can be incorporated and mimicked. Thus, Guy's doubling of Bruno is one of the preconditions of his entry into the Symbolic order. In mimicking Bruno's actions, Guy achieves a unified and coherent identity. Guy must first project himself outward before he can master his transgressive desires. Recognizing himself in Bruno enables Guy to displace those desires onto him. He does not desire Miriam's death—Bruno does; he does not desire Bruno—Bruno desires him. Moreover, Guy's mimicking of Bruno shows that he has relinquished the polymorphous sexuality of the pre-Oedipal phase. Guy's doubling of Bruno conforms to the Freudian model of identification described above. It indicates that he no longer desires Bruno but identifies with him. The culturally sanctioned prohibition of homosexuality forces Guy to renounce Bruno as an object choice, and he compensates for his loss by incorporating Bruno into his ego. He no longer adopts a "feminine attitude" toward Bruno but is determined to beat his opponent in the tennis match so that he can prevent Bruno from planting the lighter at the scene of the murder.

The film, then, follows the example of contemporary juridical discourse in privileging a psychoanalytic understanding of male subjectivity. It tries to show that in order for the male subject to achieve a fixed heterosexual identity, he must successfully negotiate the Oedipus complex. For if Guy must pass through the mirror stage before he can enter the Symbolic order, so too must he elide the threat of castration signified by Miriam and her transgressive sexuality. Mary Ann Doane has shown that glasses worn by women in classical Hollywood film indicate an active looking "or even simply the fact of seeing as opposed to being seen."[23] Doane stresses the epistemological rather than the sexual implications of such looking, but her analysis still seems applicable to Miriam, whose glasses signify plenitude rather than lack. Miriam represents the sexually "deviant" woman demonized by cold-war political discourse because she refuses to restrict her sexuality to the privatized space of the nuclear family. The subject of her own desire, she circulates freely among men. She returns the male gaze rather than submitting to it passively and refuses to function as an object of Guy's desire and his alone. The scenes in which Bruno follows her at the amusement park are constructed in such a way as to excuse her murder. Because they are shot almost wholly from Bruno's point of view, the spectator identifies with Bruno, who seems both attracted to and repelled by her. Although she has come to the park with two other men, she seems to want Bruno to pick her up. She constantly looks to see if he is still following her. When she buys an ice cream cone, she turns toward him and licks it suggestively, staring straight into the camera. In other words, she is "asking for it." Because her sexuality is castrating, she deserves to die. We are meant to accept her death as a precondition for Guy's entry into full masculinity as signified in the Symbolic order. Significantly, when Bruno tells Guy that he strangled Miriam, he gives his glasses to him as though they are a kind of trophy or prize; in so doing, he returns her look to him. Her cracked glasses are the mark of her castration and thus guarantee Guy's totality and coherence. He can now return her look without fear of castration.

This does not mean that Guy achieves a fixed, stable heterosexual identity. In narrativizing the postwar crisis over the politics of sexual practice, Hitchcock follows the example of contemporary juridical discourse by representing all sexuality as polymorphous. Despite Guy's determination to prevent Bruno from planting the incriminating lighter at the murder scene, he continues to adopt a "feminine attitude" toward him. He never makes a choice between Ann or Bruno; rather, the choice is made for him. He continues to mimic Bruno even in the final shots. He pursues Bruno through the amusement park just as Bruno once pursued Miriam. Bruno also seems to control the action in these shots. He nearly overwhelms Guy during their struggle on the merry-go-round, and Guy retrieves the lighter only when the merry-go-round crushes Bruno to death.[24] Thus, Bruno's death functions as a kind of deus-ex-machina conclusion to Guy's Oedipal journey. Bruno is a powerful figure who constantly threatens to seize control of the narrative. He is more charismatic than the all-American Guy, and his potentially destabilizing presence can be contained only by his violent expulsion from the diegesis, just as the potentially destabilizing presence of homosexuals and lesbians could be contained only by their violent expulsion from the government. Rather than Guy resolving his Oedipus complex, it is resolved for him. This becomes apparent in the final shot, where we see Guy and Ann sitting on a train. Guy's Oedipal journey seems to have come to an end, for he appears to have entered the Symbolic order. Ann is sitting in the place where Bruno sat when he proposed exchanging murders with Guy, and thus she seems to have replaced him as an object of Guy's desire. Yet when a priest leans over to ask Guy if he is Guy Haines the champion tennis player, Guy, about to reply yes, has second thoughts and quickly changes places. In concluding the film in this way, Hitchcock stresses the tenuousness of Guy's Oedipal resolution. Although Guy's Oedipal journey seems to have come to an end, he remains susceptible to, if not allured by, the "homosexual menace." He cannot trust even a representative of the very institution that sanctions monogamous heterosexuality.

In this way, the film ratifies the report issued by the Senate Appropriations Committee. It shows that heterosexuals are indeed susceptible to sexual conversion. But whereas the report argued that the expulsion of lesbians and gay men from the government would counteract the "homosexual menace," the film questions whether the threatened homosexualization of American society can be prevented. Guy's relationship with Bruno is normativized only when Bruno is crushed to death by the merry-go-round.[25] The crisis over the government employment of gays and lesbians appears to justify extreme measures. Miriam's murder and Bruno's death are both necessary to prevent Guy's homosexualization. In what is perhaps the film's most famous shot, we see Miriam's murder reflected in her own glasses, which have fallen to the ground. Here the camera reappropriates Miriam's look. The act of seeing belongs to the camera, not to her. As a woman she is meant to be seen rather than to see. But with this shot the film also implicates itself in the production of a female subject who is desired rather than desiring. In reappropriating Miriam's look, the film endorses her castration (and by implication the castration of all women who dare to resist confinement to the domestic sphere). As I have already noted, the film seems to suggest that the stability of American society depends on the female subject's restricting her sexuality to the privatized space of the nuclear family. The desiring female subject signifies plenitude rather than lack, thereby threatening the male subject with castration: She refuses to function as an accessory to his Oedipal trajectory. In other words, Hitchcock attributes the homosexual menace not so much to the gay men and women who avoided detection as to those heterosexual women who positioned themselves as subjects of desire. Miriam's unwillingness to occupy a passive position in relation to desire forces Guy to consent to Bruno's murderous proposal. Guy's inability to contain Miriam's desire within the domestic sphere signifies his castration. Thus, if the female subject persists in occupying an active position in relation to desire, she must be forcibly subjected to the binary logic of male heterosexual desire.

That the film does indeed attribute the crisis over national security to those heterosexual women who resisted returning to the domestic sphere is nowhere more apparent than in its representation of Ann's sister, Barbara (Patricia Hitchcock). Barbara bears a close physical resemblance to Miriam, which Bruno notices when he first meets her at one of Guy's tennis matches. Barbara's glasses remind him of Miriam, and he is momentarily transported to the murder scene. The camera cuts from a shot of Bruno looking at Barbara to a shot of her returning his gaze. A shot of the lighter then appears, superimposed over Barbara's image. But Barbara's resemblance to Miriam is more than physical, for, like Miriam, she positions herself as a desiring subject. Although she is not even remotely promiscuous, she occupies an active position in relation to desire, constantly flirting with the detective assigned to shadow Guy. Thus, she threatens to end up like Miriam (a woman she describes as a "tramp," implying that she deserved to die) and must be forcibly subjected to the binary structure of postwar gender relations. The similarities between her and Miriam become obvious even to her in the scene in which Bruno nearly strangles Mrs. Cunningham to death at Senator Morton's party. When Bruno realizes that Barbara is watching him, he becomes delirious and begins to strangle Mrs. Cunningham in earnest; Barbara's presence reminds him of the murder, and he imagines that he is strangling Miriam. Barbara feels as though Bruno were strangling her and becomes terrified. When Ann asks her what happened, she stammers, "His hands were on her neck, but he was strangling me. . . . Ann, he was strangling me!" Thus, Barbara interprets Bruno's nearly fatal stran-

gling of Mrs. Cunningham as a warning. In positioning herself as a desiring subject, Barbara, like Miriam, is "asking for it."

Ultimately, then, *Strangers on a Train* suggests that the solution to the crisis
over national security lay not so much in the government expulsion of lesbians
and gay men as in a stricter regulation of female sexuality. Hitchcock tries to
show that it was not the gay men and women employed by the government who
threatened national security, but heterosexual women who did not want to return
to the domestic sphere. I argued above that the shot of Miriam's murder in her
glasses seems to acknowledge the film's complicity with the production of a female
subject who is desired rather than desiring. In reappropriating Miriam's look (and,
by extension, the look of the female spectator), the film returns the scopophilic
pleasures of the cinematic apparatus to the male heterosexual spectator. Now I
would like to argue that this moment of self-reflexivity calls attention to the
operations whereby the film tries to insert the spectator into a fixed, stable subject
position. The spectator does not see Miriam's murder directly. Her glasses act as
a mirror in which her castration (and, by extension, the castration of the female
spectator) becomes visible. In this respect, the shot acknowledges the film's complicity with the specular logic of the mirror stage as defined by Lacanian psychoanalysis. The film structures the spectator's gaze according to a specific mode of
apprehension. In subjecting the spectator to this mode of apprehension, it restages
her/his entry into the Symbolic order. It provides the spectator with the categories
of seeing through which s/he becomes visible not only to her/himself but to other
spectators as well. In this way, the film ensures that the spectator will be satisfied
that s/he has been adequately reflected on the screen. The spectator's engagement
with the film virtually guarantees the production of Oedipalized male and female
subjects less vulnerable to the "homosexual menace." Because of the film's narra-
tivization of the crisis over national security, the spectator submits to the specular
logic of its mode of address and recognizes her/himself reflected on the screen.
Like the characters with whom s/he identifies, the spectator is susceptible to the
homosexual menace and therefore willingly acquiesces to her/his heterosexualization, which becomes the ultimate patriotic act.

But this moment of self-reflexivity also indicates a crisis in the film's own
system of representation. The film must call attention to its own operations, lest
the spectator not realize that s/he is meant to see her/himself reflected in the
characters on the screen. Moreover, the film must supplement its own operations
by invoking other discursive practices. To guarantee the spectator's heterosexualization, it enlists the homophobic categories of cold-war political discourse. But
why would the film distrust the logic of its own specular regime? Apparently, the
proliferation of competing constructions of same-sex eroticism threatened to disrupt the discursive structure of classical Hollywood cinema. As we saw above, the
process of identification involves the repression of a potentially destabilizing homosexual object cathexis between spectator and hero. The male spectator must

first desire the hero before he can identify with him. The widespread paranoia about male heterosexual identities in cold-war America rendered this aspect of identification extremely problematic. By encouraging the male spectator to iden- tify with the hero, the film threatened to reinforce his sexual instability.[26] At- tempts to redefine gay men and women as members of an oppressed minority only added to this crisis in cinematic representation. Constructed across a mul- tiplicity of competing discourses, the spectator might reject the subject position made available to her/him by the film. Thus, by invoking the juridical construction of "the homosexual," the film tried to contain the spectator's political and sexual indeterminacy. It appropriated the nationalistic discourses that constructed the cold-war subject in order to promote the spectator's heterosexualization. Even gay men and women committed to delegitimating the medicalization of same-sex erot- icism had difficulty resisting appeals to their patriotism.

Notes

1. Alain Marty, "L'inconnu du Nord-Express et le Maccarthisme," Son et Image 2 (1980): 117 (my translation). All further references will be cited in the text.

2. For Bellour's analysis of North by Northwest, see "Le blocage symbolique," Communi- cations 23 (1975): 235–50. For his analysis of Marnie, see "Hitchcock, the Enunciator," Camera Obscura 2 (1977): 66–87. For his analysis of Psycho, see "Psychosis, Neurosis, Perversion," Camera Obscura 3–4 (1979): 66–103.

3. For feminist critiques of Bellour, see Jacqueline Rose, "Paranoia and the Film Sys- tem," in Feminism and Film Theory, ed. Constance Penley (New York: Routledge, 1988), 57– 68, and Susan Lurie, "The Construction of the Castrated Woman in Psychoanalysis and Cinema," Discourse 4 (1981–82): 52–74. See also Janet Bergstrom, "Enunciation and Sexual Difference," in Penley, Feminism and Film Theory, 159–88.

4. Mary Ann Doane, The Desire to Desire: The Woman's Film of the 1940s (Bloomington: Indiana University Press, 1987), 16. See also Laura Mulvey, "Visual Pleasure and Narrative Cinema," in Penley, Feminism and Film Theory, 57–68, and her "Afterthoughts on 'Visual Pleasure and Narrative Cinema' Inspired by Duel in the Sun" in ibid., 69–79.

5. Teresa de Lauretis, Alice Doesn't: Feminism, Semiotics, Cinema (Bloomington: Indiana University Press, 1984), 103–57.

6. Tania Modleski, The Women Who Knew Too Much: Hitchcock and Feminist Theory (New York: Methuen, 1988), 1–15.

7. There are some exceptions. For theories of male spectatorship that stress male masochism, see D. N. Rodowick, "The Difficulty of Difference," Wide Angle 5 (1982): 4– 15, and Janet Bergstrom, "Sexuality at a Loss: The Films of F. W. Murnau," Poetics Today 6 (1985): 185–203. See also Gaylyn Studlar, In the Realm of Pleasure (Urbana: University of Illinois Press, 1988), and Kaja Silverman, "Masochism and Male Subjectivity," Camera Ob- scura 17 (1988): 31–66. For a forceful feminist critique of these theories, see Modleski, The Women Who Knew Too Much, 9–13. The problem with these theories, including Modleski's critique of them, is that they restrict the male spectator's bisexuality to his masochistic attachment to the mother during the pre-Oedipal phase, and they ignore his pre-Oedipal

attachment to the father, with its fantasies of replacing the mother. As a result, they repress the homoerotics of spectatorial pleasure. As I will show, an alternative reading of psychoanalytic theory suggests that the male spectator's identification with the hero involves the repression of a homosexual object cathexis that recalls his pre-Oedipal attachment to the father.

8. Insofar as the filmic text engages the male spectator libidinally, it can be said to function as a machinery for ideological investment that makes the spectator's insertion into the sex-gender system not only desirable but pleasurable. For a discussion of this aspect of textual practice in general, see Fredric Jameson, *The Political Unconscious: Narrative as a Socially Symbolic Act* (Ithaca: Cornell University Press, 1981), 17–102. For a discussion of it as it relates specifically to classical Hollywood cinema, see Kaja Silverman, *Male Subjectivity at the Margins* (New York: Routledge, 1992), 52–121.

9. Sigmund Freud, *The Ego and the Id*, trans. Joan Riviere (New York: Norton, 1960), 20.

10. For more detailed chronologies of these events, see John D'Emilio, *Sexual Politics, Sexual Communities: The Making of a Homosexual Minority in the United States, 1940–1970* (Chicago: University of Chicago Press, 1983), 40–53; John D'Emilio and Estelle Freedman, *Intimate Matters: A History of Sexuality in America* (New York: Harper, 1988), 288–95; and Allan Bérubé, *Coming Out under Fire: The History of Gay Men and Women in World War Two* (New York: Free Press, 1990), 255–70.

11. *The Employment of Homosexuals and Other Sex Perverts in Government* (Washington: Government Printing Office, 1950), 2. Hereafter all Senate Appropriations Committee citations refer to this edition.

12. See D'Emilio and Freedman, *Intimate Matters*, 275–300.

13. Alfred Kinsey et al., *Sexual Behavior in the Human Male* (Philadelphia: Saunders, 1948), 627. Hereafter all Kinsey citations refer to this edition.

14. Quoted in D'Emilio, *Sexual Politics, Sexual Communities*, 33.

15. Quoted in ibid., 81.

16. See ibid., 75–91. See also Toby Marotta, *The Politics of Homosexuality: How Lesbians and Gay Men Have Made Themselves a Political and Social Force in Modern America* (Boston: Houghton Mifflin, 1981), 1–68.

17. For a discussion of the impact of this social and sexual upheaval on cinematic representation, see Silverman, *Male Subjectivity at the Margins*, 52–121, and Dana Polan, *Power and Paranoia: History, Narrative, and the American Cinema, 1940–50* (New York: Columbia University Press, 1986), 251–308.

18. See D'Emilio, *Sexual Politics, Sexual Communities*, 9–53, and Bérubé, *Coming Out under Fire*, 175–201.

19. Patricia Highsmith, *Strangers on a Train* (London: Penguin, 1988), 27. Hereafter all Highsmith citations refer to this edition.

20. Although critics of *Strangers on a Train* have neglected its relation to the "homosexual menace," they have long noted its homosexual subplot. See in particular Vito Russo, *The Celluloid Closet: Homosexuality in the Movies*, rev. ed. (New York: Harper, 1987), 94–95, 99. Russo cites evidence that Robert Walker deliberately played Bruno Anthony as a homosexual. See also Donald Spoto, *The Art of Alfred Hitchcock* (New York: Doubleday, 1979), 209–17, and Marty, "L'inconnu du Nord-Express," 120.

21. Insofar as Bruno's relationship with his mother constitutes a form of "momism," Hitchcock's film indicates another possible dimension to the representations of momism in cold-war movies discussed by Michael Rogin in *Ronald Reagan, The Movie: And Other Episodes of Political Demonology* (Berkeley and Los Angeles: University of California Press, 1987), 236–71. The demonization of the mother in cold-war movies may also encode anxieties over the homosexual menace.

22. For a discussion of the triangulation of male desire that sees it as normative, see Rene Girard, *Deceit, Desire, and the Novel: Self and Other in Literary Structure*, trans. Yvonee Freccero (Baltimore: Johns Hopkins University Press, 1965). For an important feminist revision and application of Girard's mimetic theory of desire, see Eve Kosofsky Sedgwick, *Between Men: English Literature and Male Homosocial Desire* (New York: Columbia University Press, 1985), 21–27. See also Toril Moi, "The Missing Mother: The Oedipal Rivalries of Rene Girard," *Diacritics* 12 (1982): 21–32.

23. Mary Ann Doane, "Film and Masquerade—Theorizing the Female Spectator," *Screen* 23 (1982): 72–87.

24. When I presented an earlier version of this chapter at Dartmouth College, a member of the audience informed me that the term "merry-go-round" was used in the 1950s to refer to the gay male subculture. If this is so, then the merry-go-round in the final scene provides another indication that Bruno is meant to represent "the homosexual" of postwar juridical discourse.

25. In this respect, Bruno is merely one of a long line of psychopathic gay men and women who die violently in Hollywood films. For a "necrology" of gay and lesbian characters who meet violent deaths in Hollywood films, see Russo, *The Celluloid Closet*, 347–49. Russo compares the psychopathic gay and lesbian killers who populated postwar Hollywood films to the stereotypical black characters played by Butterfly McQueen, Hattie McDaniel, and Stepin Fetchit in the 1930s and 1940s. But clearly more is involved here than the perpetuation of homophobic stereotypes. Films such as *Strangers on a Train* in which the gay or lesbian killer is more charismatic than the heroes and heroines are perhaps best understood as heterosexual paranoid fantasies about the instability of the sex-gender system.

26. Contributing to this potentially destabilizing aspect of identification was the disparity between Robert Walker's and Farley Granger's screen images. Granger was perhaps best known for his role in an earlier Hitchcock production, *Rope* (1948), in which he played David Kentley, Shaw Brandon's homosexual lover, and it seems likely that contemporary spectators would have seen a parallel between his role as Kentley and his role as Guy. Moreover, he seemed passive and ineffectual compared to the more charismatic Walker, whose performance won praise from critics. Hitchcock was apparently concerned about this. In his interview with François Truffaut, he commented: "I must say that I . . . wasn't too pleased with Farley Granger; he's a good actor, but I would have liked to see William Holden in the part because he's stronger. In this kind of story the stronger the hero, the more effective the situation" (François Truffaut, *Hitchcock: The Definitive Study of Alfred Hitchcock by François Truffaut*, rev. ed. [New York: Simon, 1983], 199).

6

Rear-View Mirror
Hitchcock, Poe, and the Flaneur in America

Dana Brand

As many of the essays in this volume make clear, the films of Alfred Hitchcock's American period are shaped by his direct and imaginative experience of America and his interest in American films. While little can be known with certainty about Hitchcock's familiarity with American literature, one thing that is known is that Hitchcock acknowledged a significant imaginative debt to an American writer, Edgar Allan Poe. In a 1961 essay entitled "Why I Am Afraid of the Dark," Hitchcock described how he discovered the works of Poe at the age of sixteen, after reading an account of Poe's life. "Very likely," Hitchcock wrote,

> it's because I was so taken with the Poe stories that I later made suspense films. I don't want to seem immodest, but I can't help comparing what I've tried to put in my films with what Edgar Allan Poe put in his novels (sic): a completely unbelievable story told to the readers with such a spellbinding logic that you get the impression that the same thing could happen to you tomorrow. . . . I believe Poe has a special place in the world of literature. He's at the same time certainly a romantic and a herald of modern literature.[1]

As a herald of modern literature, Poe's influence on him was, Hitchcock wrote, indirect as well as direct. Poe, Hitchcock suggests, was responsible for Baudelaire, whom Hitchcock calls, in this essay, "the French Edgar Allan Poe."[2] Surrealism, a major influence on Hitchcock, was also, in Hitchcock's words, "born from the work of Poe as much as Lautreamont."[3]

Some of Hitchcock's best work in America is clearly influenced by Poe. The first two episodes directed by Hitchcock for his television series were relatively straightforward modern adaptations of Poe's stories "The Premature Burial" and

"William Wilson." *Strangers on a Train*, as Spoto has suggested, owes much to "William Wilson,"[4] and it seems to me that the plot and atmosphere of *Vertigo* owe a great deal to Poe's story "Ligeia." Like *Vertigo*, "Ligeia" is set in a world of towers, mists, and high rooms suffused with strange light. Anticipating *Vertigo*, it deals with the obsessive effort of its narrator to reincarnate his magnificent, mysterious first wife into the body of his unloved and more prosaic second wife. In the final sentences of the story, the apparent and unexplainable success of the narrator's effort is represented by his "observation" that the corpse of his second wife has returned to life, with the distinctive hair color of the first wife. Even in films that do not owe as clear a debt to Poe as these, one is frequently reminded, throughout Hitchcock's films, of situations and images familiar from Poe's work (e.g., suggestions of "The Tell-Tale Heart" in *Rope*, "The Raven" in *Psycho*, etc.).

In this essay, I will explore an aspect of Hitchcock's interaction with Poe. I will argue that the setting, images, and preoccupations of *Rear Window* echo those of Poe's stories "The Man of the Crowd" and "The Murders in the Rue Morgue." Like these Poe stories, *Rear Window* is concerned with the dynamics of a kind of urban spectatorship that was a prominent feature of the fiction and periodical essays of Poe's time. By considering Hitchcock's film in relation to these Poe stories and the urban cultural context in which they were produced, I hope to offer a new perspective on *Rear Window*, a perspective that may help to identify the place of the film within the culture of modern cities and within Hitchcock's own implicit analysis of American civilization.

Like *Rear Window*, "The Man of the Crowd" opens with the introduction of a convalescent who, bored with his enforced inactivity, entertains himself by observing the people he sees outside his window. Poe's narrator sits in the bay window of a London coffee shop, and as the story opens, he seems entirely confident of his ability to read the crowd that passes, to determine the character and profession of individuals by recognizing certain unvarying and unmistakable signs. At times, it even seems to him as if he can "read the history of long years in a single glance."[5] His extraordinary assertion of power, his distance, and his casual composure would have been very familiar to readers of English, French, and American periodicals in the first half of the nineteenth century.[6] In France, writers who adopted this persona were known as flaneurs. As the French word implies, such writers conventionally presented themselves as idlers who, while strolling or observing a crowd from a panoramic vantage, offered an image of the crowd as a friendly, predictable, and easily legible text. Celebrating randomness, while creating the impression of order, the fluid yet composed consciousness of the flaneur was identified by Charles Baudelaire, in his essay "The Painter of Modern Life," as the ideal consciousness of modernity. It was this form of consciousness, Baudelaire argued, that was most suited to the observation and representation of the spectacle of nineteenth-century commercial and metropolitan life.

The figure of the flaneur is most familiar to contemporary cultural critics from Walter Benjamin's writings about Baudelaire.[7] Benjamin's treatment of the flaneur focuses on the social and political meanings of the flaneur's reassuring image of urban life. As Benjamin writes, the flaneurs offered a form of literature that achieved the same effects as a panorama or diorama.[8] Enjoying their greatest degree of popularity at the same time as panoramas and dioramas, the flaneur's urban scenes offered, like these other forms of representation, a view of urban life as a harmonious collection of rational and predictable processes that could be understood and encompassed at a glance. Sharing the flaneur's perspective, bourgeois readers could enjoy a sense of the urban crowd, Benjamin suggests, as a collection of unthreatening, "harmless oddballs"[9] whom one could regard with a kind of paternalistic affection. The flaneur, in other words, would seem to say, as L.B. Jeffries says to Stella when she reproaches him for his invisible surveillance of his neighbors: "It was only a little bit of innocent fun. I love my neighbors like a father."

In the way that he feels and the way that he acts, L. B. Jeffries is a traditional flaneur. Like the narrator of Poe's "The Man of the Crowd," Jeffries has no difficulty reading his neighbors at a single glance. Sharing his perspective, we immediately seem to understand the situations of Miss Lonelyhearts, Miss Torso, the newlyweds, and so on, just as Poe's narrator claims to be able to divide the crowd into professional and moral types on the basis of easily recognizable signs. In addition to being transparent, the city of L. B. Jeffries has the dioramic regularity typical of the literature of the flaneur. In the opening sections of *Rear Window*, Hitchcock achieved, more than in any of his other films, an ideal of a dioramic film that he once described to François Truffaut: "I'd like to do twenty-four hours in the life of a city," he said, "and I can see the whole picture from beginning to end. It's full of incidents, full of backgrounds, a complete cyclic movement. It starts out at five A.M., at daybreak." Hitchcock goes on to describe how he'd show the cyclical process of the day: "the way fresh food is turned to waste. . . . You could take it through the whole city, look at everything, film everything, and show all of that."[10] When we see, in the opening frames of *Rear Window*, the cat, the milkman, the alarms going off one by one, the uncovering of the birdcage, Miss Torso doing her morning exercises, we see a process that we imagine is the same every single morning. We feel we have a handle on such a world, a world that, like the London of Dickens's "The Streets-Morning,"[11] goes through the same emotions every day. We are, as with any flaneur's sketch, reassured. And Hitchcock reinforces our sense of clockwork regularity by offering shots of measuring devices, clocks, watches, thermometers. Things are so predictable in the early portions of the film that everything we see appears to be a visual elaboration of the reading we have just made of the measuring device. This is 9 A.M. This is midnight. This is a 92-degree day. This is an 80-degree evening. The particular importance of these measuring devices is suggested by Hitchcock's appearance in the film as someone winding the song-writer's clock.

The dioramic qualities of Jeffries's courtyard place it within the tradition of the flaneur. It is also, however, part of another pattern present throughout the film. The clockwork courtyard may also be connected, in Hitchcock's conception, with other American systems of regularization. The film contains several references to the stock market. Lisa asks Jeff to guess how much her dress cost. Ignoring the personal meaning of the fact that she's worn such an expensive dress for him, Jeff tries to arrive at an actual figure, figuring in the airplane flight, import duties, hidden taxes, and profit markup. When she tells him that the dress is a steal at $1,100, he says it ought to be listed on the stock exchange. This exchange immediately follows Stella's account of how she predicted the stock market crash by observing how often the president of General Motors went to the bathroom in the course of a day. This peculiar prominence of the stock market in the opening scenes of the film, accompanied as it is by all of the imagery of quantification, suggests that in constructing his portrait of America, Hitchcock was influenced not only by Poe but by a conception of America he may have encountered in Baudelaire's writings on Poe.

As Hitchcock's previously quoted comments about Poe make clear, he had, in 1961, something more like a French than, at that time, an American understanding of Poe's importance. Hitchcock even claims to have read Baudelaire's translations of Poe into French. If he had read Baudelaire's prefaces to these translations, and in fact, if he had read, as he says, any account of Poe's life around 1915, when virtually all available accounts of Poe's life were influenced by Baudelaire's interpretation of it, he would have been familiar with a model for understanding Poe as a critic of American culture that might have some relevance for understanding Hitchcock as a critic of American culture. Poe was an implicit critic of American culture, according to Baudelaire, because in so many of his stories he unravels specious systems for understanding reality. American culture, according to Baudelaire, was a network of such systems. It was, according to Baudelaire, "a vast cage, a great counting-house,"[12] whose relentlessly calculating and naive reduction were in large part responsible for Poe's self-destruction.[13]

In the opening scenes of Rear Window, everything in this little corner of American certainly seems to be measurable, quantifiable, and predictable. Like Poe, Hitchcock was fascinated by systematic efforts to impose regularity upon the irregular. Again, like Poe, he devoted much of his artistic energy to exploring the tendency of such systems to collapse. As Poe does in "The Man of the Crowd," Hitchcock in Rear Window undermines the flaneur's confident, paternalistic sense of power over his field of vision. In doing so, he offers, like Poe, a complex analysis of some of the inadequacies of this form of urban spectatorship. At the same time, he offers a corresponding analysis of some of the inadequacies of the naive and narcissistic systems with which Americans, and particularly American men, try to establish control over reality.

Easily legible and behaving like a diorama, the courtyard of *Rear Window* not only exemplifies the process of reduction typical of the flaneur and the diorama. It also exemplifies the typologizing and reductive devices of an American ordering system that owes something to these nineteenth-century forms. The cinema, and particularly the American cinema, has always and inevitably made use of the same typologizing devices as the flaneur and the dioramas. Film is the legitimate successor to these earlier forms of image culture, and as twentieth-century viewers, we accept the absurd transparency and regularity of this courtyard not because we are familiar with the conventions of the flaneur but because we have seen so many Hollywood movies. We are always aware that what we see on the screen is not Greenwich Village but a highly artificial Hollywood set of a courtyard in Greenwich Village. Jeffries's world is a colorful and cleaned-up bohemia, half of whose inhabitants are artists and half of whose inhabitants are the sort of ordinary people that artists need to have around to watch. In the manner of the typological urban pastorals of the 1930s and 1940s, everyone really can be summed up in a sentence or so. In any case, this is just half of *Rear Window*'s New York. The other half is the world of Lisa Fremont, which is also familiar from Hollywood films. This is the glamorous Hollywood image of New York as the capital of fashion, of dinners at Twenty One, of dresses that cost over a thousand dollars. And surely we can accept the premise that one of our New York types, the glamorously adventurous bohemian, has fallen in love with another, the beautiful fashion model. There is a nostalgia built into the texture of this world that is as potent as the rural nostalgia of *The Trouble with Harry*. And like that rural idyll, and like all of the specious systems in Poe's stories, it is set up to be undermined.

In "The Man of the Crowd," the flaneur narrator becomes bored with the regularity and predictability of the diorama to which he has reduced the urban crowd. To relieve his boredom, he imagines that there is something extraordinarily anomalous about one of the passing faces, that of an old man. He quickly, and with no evidence whatsoever, convinces himself that the old man is guilty of some terrible crime. Though he is recovering from a serious illness, he leaves the coffeehouse to pursue the old man, to see if he can discover his secret. The narrator's effort becomes compulsive, and he follows the old man through cold and rainy streets for two days, at the end of which he has still seen nothing to vindicate his assumption that a crime has been committed. Finally, the narrator abandons his quest, declaring simply and unconvincingly that the old man is the type and genius of deep crime. Though the narrator finds nothing to convict the old man of a crime, his pursuit does enable the reader to observe that the narrator has in fact found in the old man a mirror of his own obsessive activity. The old man is unable to be alone. Terrified of boredom, he is compulsively curious. He

The narrative elements of Rear Window: *the flaneur, the female, the diorama*

seeks oblivion in the perpetual rush of urban stimuli. He interacts with nothing, but he must fill his consciousness with every scrap of movement, light, and color he can find. In this way, he provides an image of the impersonal, compulsively curious spectatorship of the flaneur narrator, an image of the process taken one step further, to the point where nothing but the detachment and curiosity remain, to the point where the intellectual control has been lost.[14]

By finding a repressed image of himself in the old man, the narrator of "The Man of the Crowd" is doing something that Baudelaire recognized as part of the essence of the flaneur's sketch. In the poem "Crowds" in *Paris Spleen*, Baudelaire describes how a crowd offers a spectator the opportunity to "relish a debauch of vitality at the expense of the human species." The creative mind in the crowd "enjoys the incomparable privilege of being able to be himself or someone else, as he chooses. Like those wandering souls who go looking for a body, he enters as he likes into each man's personality" and so enjoys the "singular intoxication" of "universal communion."[15] For the spectator, as Baudelaire writes in "The Painter of Modern Life," the crowd is a "vast mirror," [16] a projection of one's own life upon the faces of others. The truthfulness of the projection is irrelevant, as Baudelaire asserts in a *Paris Spleen* poem entitled "Windows." After making up a story of an old woman he observes from his rear window, Baudelaire's flaneur anticipates a reader's objection: "Perhaps you will say 'Are you sure that your story is the real one?' But what does it matter what reality is outside myself, so long as it has helped me to live, to feel that I am, and what I am?"[17]

In "The Man of the Crowd," the flaneur's tendency to turn a face in a crowd into a mirror acquires a much more sinister meaning than it traditionally has. The flaneur in this story cannot recognize what he himself is doing, but he feels that what he sees in his mirror is some sort of crime. His process of self-projection is unselfconscious. All the narrator knows is that a "criminal" mystery suddenly appears in the middle of his pleasantly predictable city, causing him to lose the satisfied yet slightly bored composure he had been enjoying. As the narrator obsessively pursues the old man through the streets of London, Poe is able to offer an analysis of the narrator's complacency, suggesting that the crowd is not in fact legible and the narrator's spectatorship is not in fact innocent. The dynamic of *Rear Window* is strikingly similar to this.

Like the narrator of "The Man of the Crowd," L. B. Jeffries becomes bored with the transparency and accessibility of his text, and he imagines the sudden appearance of an anomaly. Like the narrator of "The Man of the Crowd," his spectatorship changes from amused and diffident regard to an obsessive desire to solve a mystery. Like Poe's narrator, he decides, without any evidence, that someone is guilty of a serious crime. I state the issue in this way because I think that the film makes perfectly clear to us, through Doyle's interrogation, that Jeffries is simply having a stationary imaginative adventure, on the order of what the speaker of the *Paris Spleen* poem enjoys as he watches the old woman from his window.[18] Although our identification with Jeffries's point of view obscures the fact, no one can see what Jeffries has seen and reasonably conclude that Lars Thorwald has murdered his wife.

Having reached an unfounded conclusion, and waiting for its confirmation, Jeffries, like the narrator of "The Man of the Crowd," wishes to change from a flaneur into a detective. His motivations are no different from the motivations of Auguste Dupin, Poe's detective. Dupin solve mysteries for the same reason that the flaneur looks into faces: to satisfy a morally detached curiosity. As Dupin says of the murders in the Rue Morgue: "As for these murders, let us enter into some examinations for ourselves, before we make up an opinion respecting them. An inquiry will afford us some amusement."[19] What distinguishes the detective from the flaneur is that he seems to undertake a more challenging task. Unlike the flaneur, he acknowledges the mystery and the destabilizing or threatening character of what he originally confronts. Often, in the genre of the detective story, the mystery to be solved is, like the mystery of "The Man of the Crowd," an emblem of something that the detective cannot see within him or herself. *Rear Window* has the same projective structure as "The Murders in the Rue Morgue." Just as Auguste Dupin constructs, as Hitchcock would say, a "completely unbelievable" explanation of a crime that mirrors, in certain ways, his own "crime" and situation,[20] what L. B. Jeffries sees across the courtyard is a reflection of the emotional sterility and figurative violence of his spectatorial narcissism.

Thorwald, Jeffries imagines, has murdered his wife and cut her into pieces. Jeffries is doing everything he can to avoid having a wife, and in several of his activities, as well as throughout the film in general, there are numerous references to the literal and figurative dismemberment of women, as there are throughout "The Murders in the Rue Morgue." The central event generating " "The Murders in the Rue Morgue" is the brutal murder and dismemberment of two women, one of whom has been thrown out of the window of her apartment into an interior courtyard, where her head falls off. Jeffries regularly observes three women across the courtyard. He calls one of these Miss Torso and another Miss Lonelyhearts, and the third is literally cut into pieces. When Lisa asks Stella if she ever takes off her wedding ring, Stella replies that the only way the ring would ever be separated from her is if someone were to cut her finger off. Of course, the burial of Mrs. Thorwald's head in the garden is entirely gratuitous and really very unconvincing in terms of anything we can see about Thorwald's motivation. Why would he bother to bury it? Why would he expose himself to the possibility that the dog might discover it? There are no convincing answers to these questions. But we don't ask them as we're watching the film. As we wonder, however, what piece of Mrs. Thorwald is buried in the garden, we remain aware of this fundamental paradigm of dismemberment.

Jeffries's spectatorship, like that of the flaneur, is a form of dismemberment. He sees little pieces of people's lives and imagines that these pieces are the whole. This process is characteristic of his profession, which tries to pass off striking images of something at a particular dramatic moment as a representation of the totality of what is being photographed. It is clear, from early on in the film, that Jeffries is only concerned with the pieces into which he can fragment the world. The figuratively violent character of his photography is suggested, I think, by the obscure prominence, in many of the shots of the apartment, of a framed negative of a photograph of a woman's head, much like the one Thorwald has in the hatbox, which, as the opening narrative shot instructs us, is a photograph Jeffries took for the front cover of *Life* magazine. This negative, in which, of course, the woman appears ghostlike, corpselike, is visible during much of the scene in which Lisa originally presents herself, and in which we see how indifferent Jeff is to her. She stands in front of it, and beside the magazine, when she introduces herself as Lisa Carol Fremont, and this may remind us of the astonishing shot in which she first appears, in which she smoothly approaches the awakening Jeffries, like a woman's head on the cover of the magazine. Lisa's white filmy shawl is placed in front of the negative, as we see when she picks it up to wrap herself in it, preparing to take her disappointed departure. Later, Lisa places her open overnight case, containing her filmy nightgown, directly in front of the negative. In this gesture, it is as if Lisa becomes the negative, a white, filmy, shrouded image, part of Jeffries's collection of images, but definitely, and if he has his way, permanently on the other side of the camera lens.

Not having any success as an image, in spite of all of her efforts to make herself into a well-lit visual spectacle, Lisa finally figures out that the only way to win the love of a male spectatorial narcissist is to get on his side of his various phallic lenses. Although Lisa originally puts up perfectly reasonable resistance to the Thorwald theory, she pretends to be converted to it after seeing Thorwald securing a large chest with rope. This bit of "proof," which is even less convincing than those she has just rejected, becomes her pretext for saying to Jeffries: "Tell me everything you've seen and what you think it means." From this point on, she is joined to Jeffries by her commitment to his theory. She proudly and, I think, ironically announces to Doyle, "We think Thorwald is guilty," and using her "feminine intuition," she begins, within the parameters of Jeffries's theory, to invent evidence as creative and unconvincing as his own. (There are, after all, all sorts of reasons why a woman might take off her wedding ring.) Becoming part of Jeff's creative activity, Lisa becomes a party to the act of dismemberment. The nature and degree of her involvement is suggested by the fact that she offers to go out and dig where the little dog had been digging, in the expectation that she will in fact encounter the dismembered remains of Mrs. Thorwald. Her offer to do this, her insistence that she "always wanted to meet Mrs. Thorwald," is of course absurd for such a fastidious woman, but it shows how comfortable she has become with Jeffries's act of dismemberment. From here, it's just a small step to actually climbing the fire escape into Thorwald's apartment, in the nylons and heels and high-fashion dress Jeff had scorned, in order to demonstrate that her otherness and her femaleness do not in fact prevent her from becoming the physical extension of Jeff's imaginative desire. When this union is complete, Jeff finally shows some response to her. His creative act has brought them together, but only by making her a part of him.

To suggest the sterility of Jeff's creative accomplishment, Hitchcock inserts, into the background of the film, two alternate images of creative representation. There is, first of all, the songwriter who works throughout the film to perfect the song that will save Miss Lonelyhearts and enable her to meet the songwriter. Then, there is the only female creator of images in the film, the sculptress, who is shown at one point working, beneath Miss Torso's apartment, immediately to the left of Miss Lonelyheart's apartment, on a sculpture of a female torso with a large hole where the heart should be. When someone stops and asks the name of the sculpture, she says that it's called *Hunger*. This hunger can certainly be associated with the hunger felt by Lisa and by her two reflections across the courtyard, Miss Torso and Miss Lonelyhearts.

These two alternate possibilities, of representation for the sake of expression and representation for the purpose of bringing people together, are off to the side, present but not prominent in this film. At the center of our attention has been a creation that has come into being for its own sake, something born of a desire to play, something interesting and compelling, and very much a part of a venerable tradition of urban spectatorship in the Western world over the past three centuries. At the same time, however, Hitchcock's American flaneur exemplifies the callous, lonely, and figuratively violent narcissism that Hitchcock, in so many of his films of the 1950s, from *Strangers on a Train* to *Vertigo*, found at the core of the idealized personality of the American male. This is a narcissism born of both an obsessive desire for mastery and an obsessive fear of stasis, and it is found, Hitchcock suggests, in all quintessentially American environments and in all quintessentially American venues for adventure.

Hitchcock, of course, wipes away the implications of what he's created by actually producing a corpse at the end of this film. Hitchcock had to end the film in this way, of course. If Lars Thorwald had not killed his wife, the characters with which we have been sympathizing would indeed be "ghouls," as Lisa Fremont suggests at one point. The bizarrely inappropriate ending returns the courtyard to the dynamic order it had at the beginning, and it reinforces this order by resolving everyone's love problems in what appears to be a satisfactory comedic way. This apparent surrender to the conventions of Hollywood film would seem at first to suggest the power and the inescapability of the reductive systems that enclose American life and art. But Hitchcock, like Poe, always finds a way of suggesting the speciousness of apparent order. He comments on the character of his ending by showing, in the final scene, some painters "whitewashing" the walls of Thorwald's apartment. And Lisa, in spite of her new attire and reading matter, has hardly been turned into Jeff's reflection, as she affirms when she reaches for her copy of *Harper's Bazaar*. The world, in the end, cannot be made into a mirror, by a flaneur or any other kind of male narcissist. It is unknowable, intractable, and irregular. Any apparent reduction of it to a clockwork mechanism is as artificial as the extraordinary and self-consciously artificial set upon which *Rear Window* is filmed.

Notes

1. Cited in Donald Spoto, *The Art of Alfred Hitchcock: Fifty Years of His Motion Pictures* (Garden City, N.Y.: Doubleday & Company, 1979), 39.

2. Ibid., 40.

3. Ibid.

4. Ibid., 329.

5. Edgar Allan Poe, *Collected Works of Edgar Allan Poe*, ed. Thomas Ollive Mabbot (Cambridge: Harvard University Press, 1978), 2: 511.

6. From the writings of Baudelaire, Benjamin, and others, the flaneur has been understood for some time as an important part of the literary culture of early- to mid-nineteenth-century Paris. In the first four chapters of my book *The Spectator and the City in*

Nineteenth-Century American Literature (New York: Cambridge University Press, 1991), I discuss the evolution of the flaneur in the English-speaking world, demonstrating that by the time Poe was writing, the flaneur was as important and influential in the culture of Great Britain and the United States as he was in France.

7. Benjamin first discussed the flaneur in an essay entitled "The *Flaneur*," which was originally intended to be the second of three essays in a work entitled "The Paris of the Second Empire in Baudelaire," which was itself intended to be the second of three parts of a work on Charles Baudelaire that Benjamin decided, in the late 1930s, to produce from the materials he had collected for his projected "Paris Arcades" project. This work was to have offered an image of the culture of commodity capitalism by exploring the connections between such cultural products as the flaneur, the arcades, the panoramas, dioramas, world expositions, etc. In response to Adorno's critique of his essay, Benjamin wrote "Some Motifs of Baudelaire" to replace "The *Flaneur*" as the second essay of "The Paris of the Second Empire in Baudelaire." Both of these essays have been published in Benjamin's *Charles Baudelaire; Lyric Poet in the Era of High Capitalism*, trans. Harry Zohn (London: New Left Books, 1973).

8. Though panoramas and dioramas came in a variety of forms, most panoramas were 360-degree cylindrical paintings, and most dioramas were series of interacting flat painted surfaces that were movable and that would reveal different features depending upon changes in lighting. Both were extremely popular in the early nineteenth century, and both were used most frequently to provide schematic reductive representations of urban environments or exceptionally dense nonurban environments (like battlefields). For the fullest account of their development and vogue, see Richard D. Altick, *The Shows of London* (Cambridge: Harvard University Press, 1978). For a discussion of their relationship to the flaneur, see Brand, *Spectator*, 7–8, 51–55, and 74–75.

9. Benjamin. *Charles Baudelaire*, 39.

10. François Truffaut, *Hitchcock*, with the collaboration of Helen G. Scott (New York: Simon and Schuster, 1966), 241.

11. This essay, in Dickens's *Sketches by Boz*, is one of the best examples of the genre of the flaneur's sketch in English. It describes, in panoramic fashion, all that might be seen on a typical morning in London.

12. Charles Baudelaire, *Baudelaire on Poe*, trans. and ed. Lois and Fancis E. Hyslop Jr. (State College, Pa.: Bald Eagle Press, 1952), 39.

13. In ibid., see "Edgar Allan Poe: His Life and Works (1852)," 38–40; "Edgar Allan Poe: His Life and Works (1856)," 92–94; and "New Notes on Edgar Poe," 129–32.

14. For a fuller discussion of this process, see Brand, *Spectator*, 79–90.

15. Charles Baudelaire, *Paris Spleen*, trans. Louise Varese (New York: New Directions, 1970), 20.

16. Baudelaire, *Baudelaire on Poe*, 9.

17. Baudelaire, *Paris Spleen*, 77.

18. Hitchcock's own sense that Jeffries's activity is simply a fantasy motivated by boredom and curiosity rather than a serious effort to bring a criminal to justice is indicated by the following exchange from the interviews that he gave to François Truffaut: "(Truffaut): At the end of *Rear Window*, when the killer comes into Stewart's room, he says to him 'What do you want of me?' and Stewart doesn't answer because, in fact his actions are

unjustified; they're motivated by sheer curiosity. (Hitchcock): That's right, and he deserves what's happening to him" (Truffaut, *Hitchcock*, 162).

19. Poe, *Collected Works*, 2: 546. As a professional photographer, Jeffries seems to be motivated by the same morally distanced, adventurous curiosity as Dupin. He is extremely disappointed that his injury will prevent him from recording images of Kashmir going up in smoke.

20. The fact that Dupin is mirrored in the mystery he solves has often been noted in the criticism of this story. See, for example, Richard Wilbur, "The Poe Mystery Case," in *Responses: Prose Pieces, 1953–1976* (New York: Harcourt, Brace, and Jovanovich, 1976).

7

Hitchcock and American Character
The Comedy of Self-Construction in
North by Northwest

Richard H. Millington

At least since Tocqueville, the nature and condition of the "American character" has been an irresistible subject to analysts, both imported and domestic, of American culture. Hitchcock's strongest American films can best be seen as an extraordinary contribution—arguably, the richest twentieth-century contribution—to this enterprise. Indeed, the issues defined in *Democracy in America*—the relation between the configuration of a culture and the inner life of its inhabitants; the possibilities for freedom a community makes possible; the ways in which, despite the manifest protection of political freedoms, authority is exercised and inhibition generated—seem also to quicken Hitchcock's richest American movies, which attempt to arrive at an account of the distinctive condition of American middle-class culture by examining the forms of emotion and behavior that give shape to character. Movies like *Shadow of a Doubt, Notorious, Rear Window, The Wrong Man, Vertigo*, and *Psycho* explore the varieties of middle-class entrapment, following their troubled protagonists as they negotiate a terrain configured by the interlinked authority structures—psychic, familial, social, sexual—that endanger pleasure and freedom. In this essay I will look at a work that provides a comic counterweight to this tragic or admonitory strain within Hitchcock's films, that sets out to rescue its American characters from their capacity for self-entrapment and from the culture that so successfully invites them to it. *North by Northwest*, in dialogue, we might say, with the films that precede and follow it, proposes a strategy for recovering imaginative agency, for reclaiming the pleasures of being a subject.[1]

North by Northwest emerges from the most influential criticism as an allegory of maturation. For Robin Wood, for Stanley Cavell, for Lesley Brill, the film is a work of considerable moral beauty. Cary Grant's Roger Thornhill and Eva Marie Saint's Eve Kendall move, through the instructive trials the plot supplies, from inner emptiness to a fully achieved selfhood expressed by their joint recovery of freedom of action and the capacity to love. Raymond Bellour's prestigious reading of the film brilliantly recounts the same psychological trajectory but robs it, quite delightfully, of its aura of achievement: Thornhill's career within the film replays, as it must, the Oedipal scenario that instructs the desirous male, under threat of castration, to accede to the paternal "law" that at once produces the orthodox couple and sponsors conventional Hollywood narrative.[2] I have in mind a different way of understanding the deepest interests of Hitchcock's narrative. While *North by Northwest* is undoubtedly a movie about the construction of character, Hitchcock—his exile's eye alert to the way selfhood expresses cultural location—conceives and presents that process as inseparable from the places in which it occurs. The film is, I will be arguing, not only a psychological allegory of maturity but a historical or "anthropological" allegory of the relation between character and culture; its central subject is not selfhood but ideology, and its relation to that ideology is not symptomatic but analytic.[3]

"I don't like the way Teddy Roosevelt is looking at me"

The movie that would become *North by Northwest* began as a set of ideas for scenes in places that seem definitively American: a chase across the face of Mount Rushmore, a car coming off the assembly line in Detroit with a corpse inside. The plot elements were added as ingenuity allowed, and Ernest Lehman began his sustained work on the script with visits to the final locations.[4] Literally, in the genesis of the screen play, story was driven by place. I want to argue that this is also true more deeply and interestingly: that the concept of an American "place" or "space"—America conceived as a particular ideological location or configuration, and exercising a shaping power on what happens within it—drives the action and generates the meanings of the film.

The film's famous opening sequence is designed to construct an equation between the organization of space and the conditions of identity in the modern American city. The flat green screen of the titles gives way to a grid, which in turn emerges as the vertiginous, reflecting face of a New York skyscraper. Next, a series of urban vignettes interprets city life as a set of struggles to occupy a place—a cab, an elevator, the stairs to the subway. The sequence ends with this film's heuristic cameo: a shot of Hitchcock excluded by the shutting doors of a bus. The juxtaposition of the grid and these struggles for position suggests that the conditions of life the sequence evokes have reduced identity to the occupation of a niche within the maze. Cary Grant's Roger Thornhill is presented as at once a master and symptom of this cultural situation. Adept at skillful positioning, he steals a cab for his tired secretary and shuffles the cards of his social and libidinal itinerary; yet, in the inner life, as in Gertrude Stein's Oakland, there is no there there—or, to borrow a figure from the movie, in Thornhill as in Kaplan's hotel room, there's no one home. The mistake in identification that launches the plot neatly illustrates this relation between place and identity: When Thornhill stands up to send a telegram as the bellboy pages a George Kaplan, Kaplan he becomes. Lest we miss this logic, both "Thornhill" and "Townsend," the two most prominent names in the early going, might signify either places or people; this ambiguity is emphasized by the shot of the "Townsend" sign that locates us at the mansion, which reads as the name of the place but turns out to name its owner—whose name and place, of course, have been taken by someone else.

The link between the organization of space and the conditions of identity established in the opening sequence sets in motion the film's sustained effort to render a cultural situation visually and spatially, to establish the emblematic landscape that will guide us through the film's allegory of the condition of American middle-class culture. In addition to the image of the grid, the film's spatial vocabulary contains another crucial element: While the woman or man on the street struggles for position, and while Thornhill undergoes his lesson in the vicissitudes of American identity, someone is looking on from above. A position exists outside the grid, in possession of the downward view of the skyscraper that opens the film. This position of surveillance is repeatedly made visible in the form of, or as a reference to, a shot from a high angle. We encounter these shots at the Townsend mansion, when Vandamm offers Thornhill the "opportunity of surviving the evening"; at the UN, in the spectacular shot that nearly loses the speck that is Thornhill in the architectural geometry; during the meeting of Intelligence bureaucrats that consigns Thornhill to oblivion ("Good-bye Mr. Thornhill, wherever you are"); and at Vandamm's house in Rapid City, when it underscores the plan to drop Eve Kendall from the airplane. The position from which such shots can be made is occupied by the plane that attacks Thornhill at the crossroads and by the presidential faces on Mt. Rushmore. In each case, the possession of the high angle is linked to the exercise of power: to the machinations of Vandamm; to the more insidious, because ostensibly benevolent and rational, power of the Professor; to the abstracted form of cultural authority of which Mt. Rushmore is the monumental fetish. Indeed, the film's refusal to distinguish between these various versions of power suggests that this position of "altitude" represents, most significantly, the nature of authority in modern democratic culture—powerfully immanent but always elusive, never fully located in any of its avatars but always, as it were, "in the air." No wonder Thornhill remarks, late in the film, "I don't like the way Teddy Roosevelt is looking at me."[5]

As the film unfolds, Hitchcock comes to use particular places almost as quotations, which, taken together, establish the "direction" and meaning of the film's journeying. For the testing of Roger Thornhill's character unfolds as a series of

ordeals in places that trace out the mythological history of American individualism. The crossroads among the cornfields at "Prairie Stop" thus locates Thornhill's
story in terrain that is less Oedipal than "national," evoking the storylines com-
posing the narrative of essential Americanness: the move west, the reclamation of
the frontier by laconic pioneer farmers, the notion that the Middle West—here
stripped down to iconic simplicity—is the realest America there is. The north-
westerly trajectory of his subsequent journey moves Thornhill still deeper into
the terrain of American mythology as he heads for Rapid City and Mt. Rushmore's
stupefying monument to the national character. When located within the landscape I have been describing, the itinerary that the critical tradition has interpreted—whether approvingly or cynically—in terms of personal growth or maturation emerges as a simultaneous, ironic meditation on the condition of the
American character.

"A bedroom on the Twentieth Century"

When Thornhill asks the ticket agent at Grand Central Station for "a
bedroom on the Twentieth Century," Lehman's phrase—like the settings I have
been discussing—reaches beyond the literal toward a kind of representativeness,
suggesting a link between the bedroom of private experence and the overarching
condition of middle-class life in America. The script, like the film's visual order,
is rich in such invitations to cultural interpretation, as in the emphasis on theat-
ricality in Vandamm's interview with Thornhill, which links identity with the
playing of assigned roles, or in the tendency of the characters to make remarks
that reach out of the diegetic frame ("Train's a little unsteady." "Who isn't?"). It
is this relation between the "personal" stories of love and maturation and the film's
sustained evocation of the ideological context in which they unfold—a relation
only passingly explored by previous readings of the film—that I will now explore.
Once we become alert to the ideological interests of *North by Northwest*, the
characters played by Cary Grant and Eva Marie Saint emerge as interestingly
overdetermined; they represent not only particular psychological "types" or issues
but the present condition of American culture, and the meanings of their trials
are simultaneously private and social. Let us begin by attending to what might
be called the cultural "provenance" of Cary Grant's Roger Thornhill. As we have
already begun to see—and as the psychological interpretations have of course
observed—Thornhill represents the attenuation of identity that is endemic to the
world of *North by Northwest*; his difficulty in proving that he is who he claims to
be reminds us of the "given-ness" and insubstantiality of identity, and Thornhill's
"personalized" matchbook—R-O-T, two initials with a zero in the middle—is
offered as the emblem of this condition. But the film presents Thornhill's identity
problem not simply as a given, nor as the product of the "immaturity" hinted at

in his relation to "mother," but as distinctly the effect and expression of a particular set of cultural circumstances. Two of the most emphasized components of the character of Roger Thornhill—and they are interesting precisely through their interconnection—are his work identity as an advertising man and the history of his relationships to women. As an advertising man, a creator of demand—a role the film is pointedly and recurrently interested in—Thornhill is perhaps the quintessential cultural worker in the consumption-driven economy that comes to characterize the America of the postwar years; this is, of course, the same "psychological" economy of which Hollywood is one of the capitals. What links advertising and women, both within Thornhill's psyche and in the culture at large, are a story about love and a particular way of imagining the body. For all his manifest sophistication, Thornhill is curiously receptive to advertising's constitutive promise that selfhood can be refashioned—made more desirable—by insubstantial means, like buying a car; feeling "heavyish," he has his secretary leave a note on his desk instructing him to "think thin." Correspondingly, and as in advertising, women seem to exist in his mind as a set of fetishized and interchangeable "pieces"—hence the note that directs a box of candy to his current love interest: "For your sweet tooth and all your other sweet parts." For the twice-married Thornhill, love, like identity itself, has been subject to attenuation. And, as an advertising man, he has been a purveyor of this reduction, editing love down to a commodified seduction scenario, endlessly replayable with conveniently interchangeable parts—customarily blondes at this moment in cultural history. As we will see, he will experience, in the plot's unfolding, an uncomfortable connection between his work life and his private history.[6]

We seem to know less about the character of Eve Kendall, but I think her representativeness might be said in part to inhere in that very emptiness or elusiveness, for it is the part of women in Thornhill's world to "float," to be defined by the roles assigned them in the scenarios of male desire, scenarios that themselves supply advertising's most cherished plots. Thus, both the Professor and Vandamm, in their interchangeable plots, use her (in a way reminiscent of Ingrid Bergman's role in *Notorious*) as an erotic commodity, to be exchanged between men in an effort to produce "information," the supreme—and supremely empty—commodity in this world's evacuated moral and political economy. As she comes into focus as a person rather than a predetermined role or function, Eve Kendall emerges as a compendium of the contradictory views of women at this particular moment in American history. Thus, Eve explains herself in terms of what might be called a history of disappointed domesticity; she has been propelled into her current role by the emptying out, by "men who don't believe in marriage," of a once authentic female identity. But her association with consumption and commodification seems to notate the way domesticity is shifting from a form of female moral authority to a role as the supervisor of the family's consumption, and that titillation—playing the dual roles of consumer and desired object—is one of the new duties of the angel of the house. It is symptomatic of these confusions that what Eve is offered as a moralized career—"the first time anyone had asked me to do something worthwhile"—is a role as a "tramp." However one unravels this knot of cultural associations, it is clear that her ostensibly private history, like Thornhill's, dovetails significantly with shifting identities in American consumer culture. Yet if, by virtue of the role she plays, we know less about Eve than about Thornhill, she might be said to know more about herself; unlike Thornhill, who remains for a long time oblivious to the attenuated condition of his character, Eve, as a conscious player of roles, must suffer—and this is lucidly played by Eva Marie Saint—the double consciousness that attends her conversion into a commodity.[7]

Both Grant's corporation man and Saint's commodified woman, then, are carefully located at a particular moment in the history of American culture and come to represent the contemporary condition of middle-class identity. The film's pointed location of these characters within a distinctive historical context, moreover, suggests that they are who they are not because of an accident of personal circumstance or the unchangeable dictates of psychic need but because of the condition of the culture they inhabit and, symptomlike, represent. The action that brings them together is similarly representative, reaching beyond the romantic thriller's customary symbiosis of love and suspense plots to interrogate the narratives that shape our cultural situation. We are alerted to this larger range of reference by means of a tactic we might call "cultural quotation," the deployment of scenes or images—Mt. Rushmore is the most obvious example—that evoke specific cultural contexts that, in turn, need to become part of our interpretation of the film's range of meanings.[8] Here I wish to examine the way Hitchcock plays and plays off the narrative of seduction, so central to both advertising and the movies, in two scenes on the Twentieth Century Limited—the conversation on the dining car and the bedroom scene that delivers its consummation.

The dinner scene, with its own musical theme and its discrete, familiar narrative, has the feel of a set piece or interlude within the unfolding of the suspense plot. What I want to argue for, though, is its quality of "quotedness"; in effect, it is a commercial interruption. What we are witnessing, in the innuendo-laden conversation that gradually confirms for Thornhill his own irresistibility, is the full unfolding of the masterplot of the television commercial, the production of that moment in which one's extraordinary desirability, enhanced or produced by whatever product one has applied or ingested, is, at last, acknowledged. The unfolding seduction scenario is not only uncannily familiar to anyone who has watched television or thumbed through magazines—and here we might remind ourselves of Hitchcock's habit of commenting on advertising in the lead-ins to his TV show—but is written, played, and shot so as to emphasize its derivation. As the scene unfolds, the predictable innuendos develop a "scripted" quality, which the actors acknowledge: "You know what I mean?" "Let me think. . . . I know exactly what you mean." (This "quoted" or scripted quality is further emphasized by the last exchange in the dialogue, when Grant mistakenly interprets Kendall's advice not to order dessert—motivated by the approach of the state police—as a predictable part of the script of sexual urgency: "I get the message.") Thornhill's delight at being in the middle of a story he must have sold many times is tempered by a certain incredulity about how smoothly it's going—the point, it seems to me, of the double, triple, and quadruple takes Grant so exquisitely performs. Thornhill, on his way to being seduced to death, is getting the ad man's comeuppance.

The climax of this scene is still more insistently allusive—or derivative. When Thornhill lights Eve's cigarette, in confirmation of the lovemaking to come, he evokes not only the television commercial but the lyricism of smoking in the high romantic vocabulary of the movies—think of Paul Heinreid and the double light-up of *Now Voyager*. When Eve responds by taking his hand and, with Hermann's music pumping away in the background, blows out the match, she, in turn, summons up what one would have to call the screen's rich tradition—the whistling scene in *To Have and Have Not* comes to mind—of metaphorical blow jobs (a move that seems to shock even Thornhill, presumably accustomed to the limits of writing for TV). Even Hitchcock's camera seems to be quoting here; the camera begins to treat Eve in a new way, pulling slightly back from the close-ups and two-shots, which have been rendering Eve as a player in the scene, equal in command to Grant, to a familiar, voyeuristic distance—the customary position of the spectator within advertising—in order to render her as the portrait of available longing characteristic of that idiom's presentation of women.[9] The tactic of "cultural quotation" I have been illustrating here thus brings to our awareness the set of conditions and influences—most notably a commodified sexuality, and the commercial media that provide its sustaining narratives—that are helping to create the behavior we witness, the kinds of characters Grant and Saint have come to inhabit, and the narratives they find themselves operating within.

The dinner scene, then, locates us at a familiar stop not simply on love's cinematic itinerary but within the larger trajectory of American cultural history. And when we actually arrive in the Twentieth Century's mobile bedroom, this insistent strain of cultural reference, linking advertising and a fragmentary view of the female body, at once culminates and explodes. Thus, the early moments of Thornhill and Kendall's kiss consist of her tribute to his prowess as an ad man, while he sustains the tedious, fetishistic patter of 1950s eroticism: "I'm a big girl." "Yes, and in all the right places." "You have taste in clothes, taste in women." "Yes. I like your flavor." Yet in the middle of this all-too-familiar bedroom scene, something surprising begins to happen. As the kiss builds momentum, the visual idiom changes emphatically. The camera violates the flattering conventions of presenting stars at romance—the tactics of camera angle, lighting, and focus that invite voyeuristic identification or yearning—in order to render the physical ex-

Cultural quotation: the masterplot of the television commercial

perience of bodies moving in a small place. There are too many elbows and hands, and the actors seem to crowd the camera, which keeps maneuvering to keep them in sight while getting out of their way; the shots are often quite unflattering, lampooning Grant's customary physical grace and making Saint look rather mouthy and ordinary. I am suggesting that, like Hitchcock's rendering of the kiss itself, Thornhill and Kendall break out of their established "idiom," that from the extraordinary, awkward physicality of the embrace emerges a countercurrent to the emptiness of the encounter. These two simulacra, this is to say, suddenly discover themselves as bodies, and out of this moment of incarnation—or, more precisely, out of the gap between their constraining language and their uncontained, unframeable physicality—emerges the possibility of a form of character not fully driven or determined by the collection of ideological narratives in which they have been embedded. It is as though, under the cultural conditions Hitchcock has been evoking, identity can only be rescued or recovered by pressing it back to its origins in bodily weight or volume, and the subsequent reconstruction of American character the film describes takes the form of a series of physical trials that will test and confirm upon the body the characters' achievement of a more authentic selfhood. The two lovers break out of their idiom verbally as well when they discuss their impending lovemaking as a form of murder ("Are you going to murder me?" "Shall I?" "Please do")—a highly figurative and surprising exchange that momentarily explodes the prefabricated frame by hinting at the destabilizing experience of an unpredictable desire.

The love story of *North by Northwest,* I am arguing, is simultaneously personal and cultural—not, as Bellour claims, because the movie, like the culture whose agent it is, must inevitably ride the rails of the stereotyped narrative of desire's disciplining, but because the film understands love as, simultaneously, our most determined and most authentic experience, in which we are most permeable to ideological narratives and surprised into the possession of something that might disrupt or counter them. Hitchcock, this is to say, is using the culturally shaped yearning that makes us want the success of the romance between Thornhill and Kendall—our generic desire and our desire for genre—to invite us both to notice the narratives that condition that yearning and to glimpse the possibility of their disruption. The exhilarating actions taken by the characters, especially by Thornhill, to rescue and reclaim the possibility discovered in that awkward embrace comprise Hitchcock's answer to the question of whether—and how—American character might be rescued from the constraints the film so richly describes.

Bodies, Effigies, Monuments

It has been my claim that the "personal" or "psychological" story of *North by Northwest* unfolds within and finds its meaning in relation to an orbit of cultural reference; together these interlocking allegories—one about the development of Thornhill and Kendall as characters, the other about the shaping of identity within American middle-class culture—compose a diagnosis of the condition of American character and a meditation on how this condition might be cured. The story told by the romantic thriller—of the escape from the villain and the emergence of love—becomes simultaneously a story about the possibility of agency, about the conditions that make meaningful action possible within a culture configured in the way the movie has been showing us. Building on the moment of incarnation we have been examining, Hitchcock casts this diagnostic and curative narrative, on both the personal and the cultural level, as a story about the body: its current and customary condition, its possible reclamation, its achievement of a renewed capacity for motion.

Once Roger Thornhill has resumed possession of his body during the embrace on the Twentieth Century Limited, he begins to function as the hero of a modernized quest romance. The plot calls forth from him a series of exemplary trials that chart his achievement of a newly substantial character by testing his possession of his body and, simultaneously, his capacity to sustain love. The first stop on Grant's itinerary of incarnation is, of course, the prairie crossroads where he is attacked by the crop duster. The location invites us to see this moment as, in both psychological and cultural terms, a return to the beginning: The stripped-down, evacuated landscape suggests the arid terrain of Thornhill's interior, and, as I have already suggested, it evokes one of the foundation-scenes of the my-thology of American self-making. The treatment of this attack emphasizes, along with Thornhill's shift from being acted upon to taking action, his possession of a body. To have a body, in this first instance, is to be a target. Grant's evasion of the plane's attack is played so as to emphasize his newly acquired substantiality: the weight of his body as it crashes to the ground; its momentum as (in a mem-orable image), with his face in the dirt, Grant's airborne legs sustain the trajectory of his dive; its capacity for motion (and the limits of that capacity) as he races the plane to the road; its susceptibility to dirt and friction. With his "incarnation," Thornhill has discovered that he, in the most visceral way, has something to protect; when the crop duster materializes out of the ideological sky, "thinking thin" will no longer do the trick.

The auction scene—about which there will be more to say later—completes the film's diagnosis of what ails Roger Thornhill. This sequence begins with a lingering close-up of Vandamm's hand, in proclamation of his proprietorship, ca-ressing Eve Kendall's neck. The intensity of Thornhill's horror and rage, this subjective shot suggests, is generated less by a generic romantic betrayal than by the violation of his incipient experience of incarnation. What he sees—and the surround of the auction, with its buying and selling of beautiful objects, makes this perception inescapable—is that Eve is not an embodied person but an object of exchange, an effigy. (The dialogue, too, emphasizes the prominence of com-modification in Thornhill's feelings of betrayal: "I bet you paid plenty for this little piece of sculpture. . . . She's worth every dollar of it. . . . She puts her heart into her work . . . her whole body.") The experience that had seemed to bring him to himself was itself already emptied out; in a modernization of the ancient sin of demonality, he has made love to a commodity. In this fashion he receives the final, illuminating blow in the punishment of a marketeer; expert at the cre-ation of commodities out of bodies, he suffers the full meaning of that process.

Still, like the bedroom scene, this moment of bleak diagnosis begins to unfold the possibility of a cure, which continues to be figured in terms of "embodiedness." Just as the thrust and torsion of Thornhill's evasions in the cornfield signify the beginnings of substantial character, so his rage against Kendall, his need to hurt her—and her answering, imprudent inability *not* to retaliate—testify (against the force of the auction) to a coming into possession of an "unplotted" identity, a form of selfhood discovered to be there precisely through its ability to be hurt.[10] The importance of this moment is confirmed when Thornhill and Kendall allude to it in the forest scene, late in the film. Their avowal of love, in a beautifully written exchange, takes the form of a recital of the pain they have caused one another: "I did treat you miserably." "Ah yes. I hated you for it." "Well, I used some pretty harsh words. I'm sorry." "They hurt deeply."

In psychological terms, then, this is Hitchcock's diagnosis of the condition of his two main characters: Roger Thornhill and Eve Kendall suffer from a kind of weightlessness, their emotional lives reduced to their passive playing out of the attenuated scenarios of desire their culture seems to sponsor, their moral lives recruited to a kind of gender-defined careerism that substitutes its own internal momentum for any lucid or identifiable value. The only way to counter this attenuation of identity is through a turn toward the body, an emblematic repossession of the physical self, as though a reclaimed identity might be founded on the body's intractable physical mass and rebuilt from the ground up. While I have already argued for the representativeness of their condition—and while the dinner scene, with its evocation of the commercial, suggests a cultural etiology for personal behavior—the story of what happens to these individual bodies is enfolded within a still fuller argument about the relation between character and culture—an argument that takes the form of an investigation into the kinds of bodies American culture characteristically manufactures.

This account of the condition of the body cultural begins with the design of the credit sequence. As befits the logic of ideological analysis, which will see behavior as overdetermined, the images occupy the same space as, and unfold simultaneously with, the psychological and cultural allegories we have been following. The spectacular moment when the green screen emerges as the reflecting surface of a New York office building not only establishes the "grid" as the essential form of modern American life; it simultaneously reminds us of one of film's essential powers, the capacity to create on a flat screen the illusion of three-dimensionality, an imaginary bodily volume. This reminder that an actual flatness underlies the world of depths and volumes that invites the complex acts of identification that movies call forth introduces us to the possibility that another form of psychological volume or presence—identity, character—may be similarly illusory. And in the film proper this opening hint of the manufacture of identity—by inflation, as it were—takes the form of a recurrent attention to the size, content, and condition of bodies—and to representations of the body—that we encounter on the screen.[11]

The trajectory of images I have in mind stretches from this opening innuendo to the massive presidential faces that supply the terrain for the plot's climactic struggles; let me recount its crucial moments. Taken together, these images constitute what might be called a discourse of the effigy in *North by Northwest*. These moments draw some of their meaning from the ideological organization of space within the film. The position of "height" associated with cultural authority carries with it an attendant feeling of scope or size that is finally figured forth in the images of Mt. Rushmore; the inflated selfhood notated by images of the effigy is connected, then, to the nature of authority within the world the film implies. While I have already discussed the bedroom scene as an ideological drama, the moment of incarnation or embodiment I have analyzed carries with it the suggestion that both Thornhill and Kendall—their inner lives thinned out by their roles as "agents" of the cultural narratives they represent—have been (and might well remain) effigies, hollowed-out simulacra that only seem three-dimensional. Both Grant and Saint, it seems to me, play their earlier scenes together so as to suggest not fully present or consistent characters, but double beings who consist of an effigy inhabited by a miniature consciousness flickeringly aware of its own inauthenticity—an implication achieved, in both performances, by eye move-ments that hint at a fugitive awareness or sadness, independent of their role-playing, looking out, like a tiny watcher at a window, of the inflated bodies they inhabit.[12]

It is this implication of a gap in "size" between the body that inhabits its customary ideological position and the miniature consciousness that might con-stitute a distinctive individual identity that leads to and makes sense out of the scene of Thornhill shaving with Kendall's tiny razor—the next "stop" in the film's metaphorical exploration of the condition of American selfhood. Like the film's other vignettes of ideological commentary, this moment is carefully composed but marginal to the advancement of the plot. The sequence builds to a shot of Grant deploying the tiny razor upon his suddenly massive face; the stroke leaves in its wake a tiny Chaplinesque mustache, and, when Thornhill, shocked or struck by the effect, displays the razor to the equally surprised man at the next sink, this moment is identified as an emblem, a moment of recognition we need to see and think about. In part, this shot emphasizes the mismatch between the relative "sizes" of the projected and interior selves I have just referred to; it reminds us that Thornhill is still an effigy of himself. But it also reaches ahead to the faces on Mt. Rushmore, implying that Thornhill's visage would fit among them, that his inflated condition is somehow linked or analogous to theirs.[13] In the context of Thornhill's retracing of the westerly itinerary of heroic American individualism, the implication that these outsized tributes to the national spirit are similarly inflated suggests a mismatch, analogous to the gap within Thornhill's character, between the mythology of a robust and untrammeled American individualism and the actual conditions of identity—so richly specified by the film—endemic to American life.

Just as the shaving scene wittily implies that Thornhill and Rushmore's pres-idential effigies are brothers under the skin, so the auction links Eve Kendall—marked as Vandamm's possession in the shot I have already discussed—with the statuette Vandamm purchases at the auction. The implication of this miniaturi-zation is similar, it seems to me, to Thornhill's inflation: If identity consists of an emptiness contained within a bodily shell, the "volume" of its bodily container may fluctuate wildly without increasing or decreasing the amount of character enclosed. If we look forward, though, to the shot late in the film in which the statuette breaks open to reveal several strips of film inside, the figurine might be said to represent not only the commodification of the body but the role of various ideological narratives—TV commercials, movies—in manufacturing the condition of effigy-ness the film is exploring.[14] Taken together, the analogies established, by means of this simulacral imagery, between the private predicament of Kendall and Thornhill and the general condition of what might be called the "body cultural" suggest that their individual condition of attenuation is also national, that American culture has become a machine that produces effigies—the grotesque national product, as it were. This sequence of images, along with the other tactics of ideological allusion I have been noting, sustains a reference to the cultural that invites us, as we compose our understanding of the cause and meaning of the story we witness, to move beyond the narrowly psychologizing, individualistic explanations so characteristic of middle-class culture (by and large the perspective the critical tradition offers us) toward an awareness of the presence and power of the ideologically inflected narratives we live within. And it is precisely this kind of conceptual move—outside the frame—that Thornhill and Kendall will make as they struggle to evade the authorities that so hotly pursue them.

Slanting the Truth

Tell all the Truth but tell it slant—
Success in Circuit lies

Emily Dickinson, poem 1129

The film's compelling diagnosis of the mutual evacuation of American middle-class character and culture inevitably poses the question of cure: How might these "agents" of the cultural system recover an agency they can call their own? Hitchcock brings *North by Northwest* to a close not by proposing a solution but by evoking and exemplifying a stance toward experience—expressed by Roger Thornhill's actions and implied by his own stylistic tactics—that, in reference to the film's cultural geometry and in homage to Dickinson's poem, I will call "slanting."

As Thornhill conducts his mock pilgrimage toward Mt. Rushmore, he takes possession, in ironic counterpoint to the monument's mythic inflation, of a newly defined capacity for action, implying, as he does so, the possibility of a differently configured American character. Thornhill's new maneuverability is expressed in part as a capacity for improvisation. Purged, we might say, of his past as an adman, Thornhill stops protesting that he is not George Kaplan and begins to "play off" that role; with increasing force and skill, he composes his own strategies and sets an independent agenda—a tendency that culminates in his determination to thwart the Professor's plot as well as Vandamm's. Part of Thornhill's rescue of Eve, of course, consists of a performance—his staging of Kaplan's apparent death. While it may seem odd to link a newly discovered talent for role-playing with the solidifying of one's character, Hitchcock's implicit argument seems to run this way: Improvisation is a form of acting that, by its very nature, at once confers an awareness of the act of performance and implies the existence of a base of selfhood to improvise from. Thornhill's trouble—indeed, the film implies that it is the trouble with middle-class America—has been his unreflective assumption of a role—and an attendant set of emotions—that has been given by ideology, a situation that his interchangeability with Kaplan forces him to acknowledge. Being "mistaken" for Kaplan confers the admonitory self-loss, and eventually the self-consciousness, that seems to be, for Hitchcock, the beginning of autonomy.[15] While this move toward action undoubtedly represents Thornhill's "growth" as a character, it is important to see that this growth takes the form of an enhanced capacity for self-conscious performance rather than a simple return to an original or essential selfhood.

Two other features of Thornhill's maneuvers contribute, like the emphasis on improvisation, to giving his actions an instructive or allegorical force. The first is the emphasis on bodily pain. I have already argued that the attack of the crop duster is shot so as to emphasize the wear and tear exacted upon Thornhill's body, and in subsequent scenes, Thornhill sustains an impressive amount of damage: the bruise suffered when he falls while faking his death (commented upon in the conversation on emotional wounding that takes place in the forest); the punch delivered by the ham-handed ranger; the hand bleeding from his scramble up the rocky foundation of Vandamm's house; Leonard's attempt to crush his fingers as he and Eve hang suspended from the monument. Given the diagnosis of attenuated identity the film has established, Thornhill's capacity to absorb punishment is a sign of good health. This emphasis on the actuality of Thornhill's body testifies to his successful escape from the culture of the effigy the film has been diagnosing. The once inflated Thornhillian edifice has been cut down to size, its capacity to bleed proclaiming a new match between inner and outer selves. But Hitchcock's very insistence on the bodily here—inherently paradoxical in the medium of film—reminds us of the difficulty of his achievement; intriguingly, the success of the rescue is endangered when Thornhill's image, reflected in the screen of the living-room TV—an emblem of the hollowed-out selfhood Thornhill is escaping—is glimpsed by Vandamm's housekeeper-henchwoman.[16]

As significant as Thornhill's shift from passivity to action, from effigy to body, is the distinctive form that his action takes. Beginning with his maneuvers in the cornfield, Thornhill's actions begin to assume, in keeping with the movie's title, a diagonal or "slanting" trajectory, cutting across the ideological "grid" Hitchcock establishes early in the film (and reestablishes in the shot of the cornfield/crossroads). As he discovers his character—his body and his capacity for action—he stops struggling to obtain or regain his compartment in the grid and begins to conceive a path of his own. This "slanting" motion thus draws on the cultural geometry established at the start of the film and culminates in Thornhill's climb

Thornhill: sustaining an impressive amount of bodily damage

up the vectorlike buttresses and vertiginous stone walls—which refer us to the face of the skyscraper in the opening sequence—of Vandamm's house. These images of diagonal counter-movement complete, in visual terms, the ideological allegory that Hitchcock sets in motion at the beginning of the film, suggesting that Thornhill has begun to move against the ideological grain and evoking, emblematically, the possibility of a freer relation to the invisible structures that give shape to middle-class life.

The fullest demonstration of the kind of "slanting" relation to cultural authority Hitchcock has in mind is provided in the auction scene. Here Thornhill, combining his newly discovered talent for improvisation and the astute use of his body, saves himself by disrupting the auction and causing his own arrest. Implicit in the ingenuity and wit of Thornhill's performance—throwing himself, as a human monkey wrench, into the works—is the kind of analytic relation to experience the film is recommending to its viewers, for Thornhill's trashing of the auction depends on his understanding of the structure of rules that operates in the "institution" of the auction and his consequent ability to "play off" those rules for his own ends.

Thornhill's achievement of a newly critical awareness of his cultural situation is confirmed when he switches from thwarting Vandamm's plan to subverting the Professor's. In the now familiar position of having been lied to by his government, Thornhill abandons his role as the Professor's proxy and, in constructing his own plot to rescue Eve, becomes his own agent. The insight implied by Thornhill's subversive behavior—that, seen from an independent point of view, Vandamm and the Professor are interchangeable—has some interesting political resonances. For one thing, it identifies the Professor—and the kind of "faceless," egoless, "expert" form of governmental authority he represents—as yet another effigy, his aura of self-submerging seriousness and quasi-academic expertise concealing a relation to Eve as exploitative as Vandamm's. Moreover, Thornhill's rejoinder to the Professor's justification of his lie on the grounds of "national security"—"Maybe it's time you started losing a few cold wars"—challenges the tendency to value abstractions, like "information," over persons that is the hallmark of twentieth-century political authority—something that Hitchcock also questions in *Notorious*. The skepticism about the "national interest" suggested by Thornhill's behavior is reinforced when Thornhill refers to the microfilm-filled statuette as "the pumpkin," an allusion, of course, to Whittaker Chambers's testimony in the Alger Hiss case and, through that, to McCarthyism's empty but viciously potent paranoia—the MacGuffin with teeth—about "internal security." There is, finally, a kind of relation between these explicitly political moments in the film and the analysis of the endangerment of identity that is its more central subject; in each case, the person has been lost or subordinated to a process of inflation or abstraction; the character of politics and the politics of character are similarly in need of rehabilitation.

The maneuvers Thornhill teaches himself, then, not only describe a tactics of self-recovery but define a stance toward the experience of living within American culture, a strategy for the reclamation of "American character." The capacity for analysis that Thornhill achieves and enacts, his ability to see the covert shapes and structures that ideology gives to experience, is precisely what his situation demands—and insofar as his situation represents our own, it is the ability that we, too, must discover if we are to recover our own American characters from the condition the film makes manifest. The action that confers and confirms character in *North by Northwest*, then, is imagined as a kind of purposeful obliquity, a tactic of "cutting across" the ideological grid—of saying "in your face," as it were, to Teddy Roosevelt.[17]

It is not necessary, it seems to me, to exaggerate the "subversiveness" of *North by Northwest* to admire—or learn from—its examination of American character. For if the film is lucidly about American middle-class culture, it is also of it, believing, as far as one can tell, in the curative power of love and the transformative power of an enhanced self-awareness. But if the exhilarating possibilities of a freed-up consciousness are celebrated through Grant/Thornhill's performance, the film also contains—in what might be called its stance toward itself—an acknowledgment of the complexity of its enterprise, an understanding of the relation between popular art and ideology arguably more capacious than that customarily provided by film studies.[18] We have been following a string of allusions that bring the terms of Hitchcock's art into pointed relation to the themes of the narrative: the production of volume out of flatness; the creation of characters or "identities"; the meaning of framing and being "framed"; the relation between acting and "acting"; the construction of plots of seduction.[19] Taken together, these allusions to the work of filmmaking do more than testify to Hitchcock's possession of a degree of self-consciousness worthy of an "artist." Rather, in the sustained awareness they invite of this movie's own participation in the image culture it is diagnosing, these allusions compose a complex acknowledgment of an inevitable—but not an inevitably entrapped or empty—"insidedness": Like the selves we inhabit, the film is always inside the culture it might nevertheless describe and disrupt. The joke that ends the movie provides, in effect, a valedictory illustration of this paradoxical stance. As Leonard Leff's account of the filming of *North by Northwest* reveals, Hitchcock was plagued during the last days of shooting by warnings from the Production Code Administration, forwarded by anxious studio executives, against including any signs of impending sexual activity in the closing scene; they insisted, for instance, that the lovers be dressed in daytime apparel. Hitchcock's recourse to metaphor, which of course conjures up a more distinct and vivid image of the sexual act than Grant and Saint in pajamas, manages to defeat and lampoon the censors while ostensibly cooperating with them.[20] That is to say, the film enacts its own sustained illustration of the lucid self-awareness it is recommending to us. In *North by Northwest*, Hitchcock invents—and exemplifies—an American character "at large" and in motion, relational rather than static, called into being by the performances it improvises—love, perhaps, the chief among them—in its sustained awareness of the shaping power of the ideological narratives among which we must maneuver.

Notes

1. As Rupert Wilkinson demonstrates, a renewed preoccupation with American character emerges among intellectuals, both "public" and academic, in the 1950s. Books like David Riesman's *The Lonely Crowd* (1950), William Whyte's *The Organization Man* (1956), and Vance Packard's *The Hidden Persuaders* (1957), along with essays by David Potter, Seymour Martin Lipset, and George Pierson—typically emphasizing the endangered or emptied-out quality of modern American selfhood—provide what might be called the intellectual context for Hitchcock's movie. See Rupert Wilkinson, *The Pursuit of American Character* (New York: Harper and Row, 1988), chap. 2.

2. Robin Wood, *Hitchcock's Films Revisited* (New York: Columbia University Press, 1989), 131–41; Stanley Cavell, "*North by Northwest*," in *A Hitchcock Reader*, ed. Marshall Deutelbaum and Leland Poague (Ames: Iowa State University Press, 1986); Lesley Brill,

The Hitchcock Romance: Love and Irony in Hitchcock's Films (Princeton: Princeton University Press, 1988), chap. 1; Raymond Bellour, "Le blocage symbolique," *Communications* 23 (1975): 235–350. The film, of course, figures in other notable arguments: William Rothman and Marian Keane see the film as Hitchcock's meditation on his career, and on the conditions and responsibilities of film authorship; George M. Wilson, setting aside the maturity theme, interprets it as a philosophical investigation, via Thornhill's predicament, of a particular modern "epistemic situation," the "devious conflations of appearance with reality," which makes the problem of reading the film generatively resemble the problem of reading reality. See Rothman, "*North by Northwest*: Hitchcock's Monument to the Hitchcock Film," *NDQ* 51 (1983): 11–23; Keane, "The Designs of Authorship: An Essay on *North by Northwest*," *Wide Angle* 4 (1980): 44–52; Wilson, *Narration in Light* (Baltimore: Johns Hopkins University Press, 1986), chap. 4. Anyone working on the film will be grateful for James Naremore's excellent critical "edition" of the film in the Rutgers Films in Print series: *North by Northwest* (New Brunswick, N.J.: Rutgers University Press, 1993).

3. Both Bellour and Cavell make passing reference to the "American-ness" of the narrative, but in each case questions of ideology are distinctly secondary to the issue of psychological development (Bellour, "Le blocage symbolique," 262; Cavell, "North by Northwest," 263.) Two significant exceptions to the critical indifference to the film's portrayal of American culture are recent essays by Slavoj Žižek and Fredric Jameson. Žižek places the film, cryptically but intriguingly, in the "sociological" framework of Hitchcock's examination of "the three successive forms of the libidinal structure of the subject exhibited in capitalist society during the past century," in this case "pathological narcissism" (Žižek, "The Hitchcockian Blot" [1991], reprinted in Naremore, *North by Northwest*, 225–27). Jameson analyzes the way ideology is rendered by what he calls the "spatial system" of the film, especially its treatment of the culturally central but deceptive opposition between public and private. Jameson's very abstract analysis defies brief summary, but, unlike me, he is distinctly uninterested in the "banal" question of the thematic meaning of the movie's spaces or in the possibility that Hitchcock may have meant to say something in particular about American culture through his representation of its characteristic places. Jameson, "Spatial Systems in *North by Northwest*," in *Everything You Always Wanted to Know about Lacan (But Were Afraid to Ask Hitchcock)*, ed. Slavoj Žižek (London: Verso, 1992), 47–72. For a fuller criticism of Jameson's attitude toward Hitchcock, see Tania Modleski, *The Women Who Knew Too Much: Hitchcock and Feminist Theory* (New York: Routledge, 1989), 119–20. Perhaps this is the place to register a midwesterner's protest against geographical chauvinism: Jameson thinks that Mt. Rushmore is located in Cedar Rapids, Iowa, while Keane places the film's closing scene in Grand Rapids, Michigan.

4. See John Brady, "An Interview with Ernest Lehman," reprinted in Naremore, *North by Northwest*, 186–88.

5. One might think here of Tocqueville's account of the "tyranny of the majority," of Foucault's emphasis on the historical shift from punishment to surveillance, and of Richard Sennett's analysis of the elusiveness of present-day forms of power in *Authority* (New York: Vintage, 1981), esp. chap. 5. My interpretation of this motif might be compared to that of Keane, who sees these shots as an indication of Hitchcock's authorial presence, registering his opposition to the Professor and Vandamm (46); to that of Bellour, who argues that in their suggestion of a fall from a precipice, they evoke the threat of death and

castration (250); to that of Jameson, who analyzes them as signals regarding the nature of the film's "spatial system" (59–61). Hitchcock continues to send such postcards from the ideological throughout the film. Consider, for instance, the ballet of twirling redcaps that accompanies Thornhill's escape from the police at the Chicago railroad station—another notation of the endemic confusion of position, in this case established by the work uniform of the porters, and identity in the film's world.

6. William Rothman remarks that "in the new America of *North by Northwest*, advertising is everywhere. America has become a place, the film continually reminds us, where human beings and works of art alike are reduced to objects bought and sold" ("*North by Northwest*," 12). Hitchcock briefly considered recasting the opening of the film to emphasize even more strongly Thornhill's connection to advertising, proposing to begin the movie by showing Thornhill at work in his office, with the opening titles appearing on the layout cards he's examining. See Leonard J. Leff, "Hitchcock at Metro," in Deutelbaum and Poague, *A Hitchcock Reader*, 55. In 1957, Vance Packard published *The Hidden Persuaders*, a runaway best-seller that warned of the threat to individuality, democracy, and traditional American self-reliance posed by the psychological manipulations of advertisers deeply versed in the "science" of "motivational research." For the argument and impact of Packard's book, see Daniel Horowitz, *Vance Packard and American Social Criticism* (Chapel Hill: University of North Carolina Press, 1994), 104–9.

7. For a richly observed analysis of Hitchcock's presentation of Eve Kendall, see Rothman, "*North by Northwest*," 15–22. For an account of the vicissitudes of middle-class women's roles in twentieth-century America, see Elaine Tyler May, *Homeward Bound: American Families in the cold war Era* (New York: Basic Books, 1988).

8. This is a widely used, insufficiently noticed element of Hitchcock's film composition. Think, for example, of the meaning carried by domestic furnishings in *Shadow of a Doubt*, or by the interior and roadside settings of the early scenes of *Psycho*.

9. The classic analysis of this aspect of advertising is provided in John Berger, *Ways of Seeing* (London: British Broadcasting Corporation and Penguin Books, 1972), chaps. 3 and 7.

10. George M. Wilson observes that at this moment Eve's feelings for Thornhill "rend the role she plays for Vandamm" (*Narration in Light*, 76).

11. Marian Keane argues that the credit sequence alerts us to film's capacity to conjure depth out of flatness ("Designs of Authorship," 49).

12. William Rothman provides, on behalf of a different argument about its force, a fine description of the implication of "double-consciousness" achieved by Hitchcock's camera and Saint's performance ("*North by Northwest*," 18–19).

13. Stanley Cavell ingeniously discusses the link between Grant's face and the monument as part of his analysis of the film's self-consciousness about the conditions of film acting. See "*North by Northwest*," 256. As one might expect, this scene, in Raymond Bellour's view, crystallizes the threat of castration that's been implicit all along. See "Le blocage symbolique," 252–53.

14. See George M. Wilson's interpretation of this emblem—"Films are the stuff that reality is made of"—in *Narration in Light*, 81.

15. The concept of an improvisatory identity I am describing here is more fully worked out in *The Trouble with Harry* (1955), in which a set of characters evade the inhibitory

authority represented by Harry's corpse (an avatar of the super-ego, now happily killed off) by at once playing and subverting the various character "types" that they have assumed but that fail, nevertheless, fully to contain them or to predict their actions. It is intriguing that in making this film Hitchcock transplants a British novel to another definitively American locale—the New England village, the starting point for the myth of American individualism that he interrogates in North by Northwest.

16. If we follow Wood, Rothman, and others in thinking about the history of particular actors within Hitchcock's movies, we might invoke Grant's portrayal of Dev Devlin in Notorious as an earlier instance of this metaphor of embodiedness. Grant gives Devlin's twin entrapments—in his role as a government agent, and in a brittle and self-poisoning masculinity—distinctive bodily form, it seems to me, by expressing Devlin's simultaneous betrayal of Alicia and himself in his posture; through the image of a body progressively hunching over as after the absorption of body blows, Grant displays his ceding of his individual character to his professional superiors. Both Rothman ("North by Northwest," 12–15) and Cavell ("North by Northwest," 251) suggest that in North by Northwest Hitchcock is redeeming Grant from the "guilt" incurred in his previous Hitchcock roles. For an extremely rich, impressively compressed discussion of the cultural meaning of the persona Cary Grant enacts during the course of his career, emphasizing his capacity to explode a narrowly constructed version of masculinity, see Andrew Britton, Cary Grant: Comedy and Male Desire (Newcastle upon Tyne: Tyneside Cinema, 1983).

17. Stanley Cavell emphasizes the curative or renovative theme of the film in his reading, suggesting that it asks us to become aware of, and reconsider, our present "fetishistic, scopophilic, . . . or narcissistic 'mode of attachment' " toward experience. For Cavell, such a renovation is achieved and exemplified by the reaffirmation of marriage; I am arguing that the film proposes that an awareness of the ideological is the crucial curative element. See Cavell, "North by Northwest," 260–61, 263.

18. I have in mind the puritanical tone of some film criticism, which zealously demonstrates the ideological "complicity" of the movies analyzed but betrays no awareness that academic film criticism might itself be interestingly "imbricated" in the history of middle-class discourse—in which the rhetorical production of a "liberation" achieved by the condemnation of the entrapment of others has played a distinguished role.

19. Marian Keane assembles a useful list of these self-referential elements, on behalf of a different argument about the meaning of Hitchcock's self-consciousness, in "Designs of Authorship."

20. See Leff, "Hitchcock at Metro," 52–53.

8

Hitchcock's Revised American Vision
The Wrong Man *and* Vertigo

Paula Marantz Cohen

The Wrong Man and *Vertigo*, released in 1956 and 1958 respectively, are important transitional works in Hitchcock's repertory. Both show the film-maker cutting loose from novelistic and familial influences that had informed his earlier films and that were the legacy of Victorian culture. Hitchcock's move to Hollywood in 1939 and the influence of David O. Selznick, a specialist in the character-centered "woman's picture," had initially given new form and vigor to this legacy. But Hitchcock was also an observer of the American scene, and he found in the images and social conventions of mid-twentieth-century America a new direction for representation that could give expression to changes in himself. By the early 1960s, the conditions of Hitchcock's life in America had led him to abandon a Victorian notion of character. *The Wrong Man* and *Vertigo* can be read as two stages in a process of letting go. They represent a bridge between the character-centered films of the 1940s and 1950s and the character-effacing films of the 1960s and 1970s. They launch him in the direction of a postmodern American esthetic.

AT ITS RELEASE, *The Wrong Man* was widely publicized as the authentic rendering of a true story. Publicity posters for the film proclaimed it to be "the first Hitchcock film taken from life. Every twist and turn of it is true," and Hitchcock himself made an unprecedented appearance on screen, before the film began, announcing that "this is a true story—every word of it." In his later conversation with Truffaut, he repeated the claim, insisting that the drive for "authenticity" had motivated him throughout: "Everything was minutely reconstructed with the people who were actually involved in that drama."[1] He even let it be known that he had Vera Miles buy her wardrobe at the thrift shops where Rose Balestrero (the woman she portrays in the film) had actually shopped.

Nonetheless, claims of truth and authenticity must be taken with a grain of salt. The actual case, as reported in the *Life* magazine article, did not follow the inexorable downward spiral that the film records.[2] Indeed, the film can hardly be said to reflect a documentary approach. Despite the on-location footage and sparse dialogue, the images are as artfully arranged and the structure of the plot as schematic as any in the Hitchcock repertory. Bernard Hermann's score and Robert Burks's cinematography both contribute substantially to setting a mood for the film, and the use of black-and-white film stock at a time when color had become the norm suggests a calculated pursuit of effect (to be employed again in *Psycho*). Hitchcock is reported to have told Burks that he "wanted it to look like a newsreel shot,"[3] though even this claim is disingenuous when one considers the inordinate use of crosshatched shadow—an effect that consistently invokes the dominant theme of imprisonment and, more melodramatically, of crucifixion.

What *The Wrong Man* does, in fact, is manipulate familiar Hitchcockian techniques, images, and themes so as to suggest a realistic treatment. Picturesque locales, lavish color photography, glamorously turned-out performers, exciting action punctuated by humorous business, and, of course, a piquant love interest—elements that were central to the appeal of *To Catch a Thief*, released the year before—are all subverted or eliminated. This reflects more than a simple attempt to deglamourize the film and thereby produce an illusion of reality. The reversal of conventional effects that characterizes *The Wrong Man* strikes at the literary core of Hitchcock's cinematic enterprise. Hitchcock's drive of the 1940s and 1950s had been the attempt to reclaim novelistic (i.e., psychological), character for cinematic representation and to accommodate gender complementarity to this reclamation process. *Rear Window* had been about the construction of subjectivity for its male protagonist, while *The Man Who Knew Too Much* meshed the gender characteristics of the couple. *The Wrong Man* reverses the drive of both these films. It moves relentlessly to strip the protagonist of an active identity without substituting a compensating subjective identity. By the same token, female subjectivity, as embodied in Manny's wife Rose, becomes an encumbrance rather than an aid to the protagonist and to the working out of the plot. In discarding the notion of character and couple that had increasingly lent weight and complexity to his Hollywood films, Hitchcock unsurprisingly sought the cover of documentary realism. The claim of realism acquitted him of responsiblity for a change in perspective—one he must have realized would be unpopular with his traditional audience and one he was perhaps not yet prepared to own, even to himself. Hitchcock also distanced himself from the film after it was made. "The industry was in a crisis at the time," he explained to Truffaut, "and since I'd done a lot of work for Warner Brothers, I made this picture for them without taking any salary for my work. It was their property."[4] The statement might be compared to disclaimers made about *Rope* (where he attributed the film's peculiarities wholly to his experimentation with technique). *Rope*, however, stands out as an isolated experiment, while *The Wrong Man* sets the direction for the remainder of his career. Among subsequent films, only *North by Northwest* would be a throwback to the style and tone of his earlier Hollywood films.

The lengthy opening sequence of *The Wrong Man* deserves examination for the methodical way in which it both invites and subverts our expectations about meaning. As the credits begin, we see the elegantly dressed patrons of the Stork Club dancing and sitting at tables. The music, produced by a small band at the back of the room, is a lively rhumba. Watching these opening shots, one imagines that the hero and heroine will be drawn from the couples on the dance floor or seated at the tables. As the crowd thins to suggest that the hour is getting late (an effect obtained through a series of lap dissolves), this impression is reinforced: One of the few remaining couples will surely be the focus of the narrative. But once the credits end, the camera shifts to the band, formerly only glimpsed in the background, where Manny is playing the bass fiddle. After teasing us with one more shot of the remaining couples in the club, the camera returns to Manny as the music ends, definitively taking him as its object. It records him putting aside his instrument and walking away from the band area and out the door. He says goodnight to the doorman and walks briskly to the subway entrance. The camera follows, and we are once again given a false lead as two policemen on their beat stroll behind Manny, the backs of their dark uniforms symmetrically placed on either side as though about to close in for an arrest. But as Manny descends into the subway, the policemen are cropped from the shot, obviously continuing on their way on the sidewalk. There is a quick overhead shot from the top of the subway steps showing Manny at the bottom, then a shot of him on the platform as the train arrives. As he takes a seat inside, he pulls a newspaper from his pocket, turns briefly to the racing page, then to an ad for a Ford automobile, showing a family around a car and the title "Family Fun," then to another for New York Savings Bonds. A close-up of his face shows him glance somewhat furtively to the side for a moment and then turn back to the racing page. The train stops, and we see him emerge and enter a subway coffee shop. He converses briefly with the man behind the counter, orders a cup of coffee (the exchange indicates that he is known to stop here at this hour). He takes the coffee to a nearby table and returns to the newspaper, this time taking out a pen and marking the list of horses on the racing page. The next shot shows him on the sidewalk, approaching his home. He mounts the steps, takes a milk bottle from the stoop, unlocks the door and enters the dark hall. He looks in at the first door, where two boys are shown sleeping in one bed, smiles slightly, then continues down the hall, depositing the milk in the refrigerator. Finally, he slips into his bedroom. The shot is dark for a second, then the room is illuminated—the light is switched on by his wife, who is lying in the bed, kept awake by a toothache. Only now, as his conversation with her begins, do we finally learn the true nature of the man whom the camera has been so doggedly tracking up until now.

What we learn about Manny is decidedly at odds with the impression that the opening sequence, with its virtual absence of dialogue, has created. Each image registered by the camera has been charged with potential dramatic meaning as we reflexively fill it in based on our conditioning in the conventions of the suspense film. The Stork Club is a posh nightclub, and Manny's association with it casts an aura of glamour onto him (his familiarity with the doorman reinforces the sense of his insider status). The scene with the policemen creates a vague climate of suspicion, and the maneuver with the newspaper on the subway suggests this man is a gambler with something to hide. The service in the coffee shop ("the usual?)" supports the idea that he "hangs out" here, and, of course, his marking the racing page reinforces the suggestion of morally dubious behavior. There is even a portentousness about his entering his house at such a late hour, especially given the muted score and the emphasis on darkness and shadow (although the milk bottle that he picks up outside the door begins the countermovement that will be completed when Manny begins his conversation with his wife and reveals himself to be a wholesome family man).

As we watch Manny, we expect to find something that will justify our interest in him and set the plot in motion. The effect resembles that of the first panning shot in *Rear Window* that settles on Jeffries's sleeping face and causes us to expect his awakening to coincide with the activation of an exciting narrative—an expectation thwarted when the second panning shot ends by tracking from the sleeping face down to the leg cast. The effect of the camera's concentration on the details of Manny's trip home also resemble the false suspense moments (Hitchcock called them "suspense effects") that spotted earlier films (the use of the threatening dog on the stairs in *Strangers in a Train* prior to Guy's entry into Bruno's father's bedroom, for example). Only here the context has been stretched so that not just the particular supposition that the image evokes is revealed to be false but also the very terms under which we have been operating to deduce meaning. In other words, we are being schooled in a climate of being in which signifiers do not fit into the master narrative that we have been made to anticipate. This, we may recall, was the way Doyle responded to experience in *Rear Window*. Whereas Jeffries sought to build meaning by extrapolating from the visible to the invisible, Doyle stubbornly opposed this. "Did you ever own a saw?" he asked, refusing to see Thorwald's saw as different from anyone else's. This literalizing tendency is the premise of a documentary approach to experience. It announces in advance that what will be represented will not fit neatly within a narrative structure—the importance of "things" being not in what they suggest about what we don't know but in what they are in themselves. Meaning gets constructed by induction—by simple accretion—rather than by deduction. However, what keeps *The Wrong Man* from fully conforming to this documentary method is that its thwarting of narrative meaning is ultimately a form of foreshadowing for a more all-encompassing narrative of mistaken meaning. The details of Manny's homeward journey are not arbitrary; they are signifiers that help explain how he will be interpreted by other eyes later. His admission to occasionally playing the horses leads the detectives to see him as a gambler; his association with the Stork Club suggests to them that he is a "high roller"; and his family responsibilities and debts are used to support a portrait of a man desperate for money.

It would seem that the very act of focusing on the surface details of this man's existence is conducive to a narrative supporting his guilt. In life, surface meanings in a case like this would tend to work in contradictory ways—some signifiers supporting guilt, others innocence. In *The Wrong Man*, however, Hitchcock is concerned with a series of accidents in which the accrual of meaning occurs in the mistaken direction only. The initial impetus that appears to set the faulty interpretation of Manny in motion involves a number of coincidental elements: his need to borrow money on his wife's insurance policy, his entrance into the company's office with his hand in his pocket, and his slight resemblance to the man who had robbed the company. Yet even if these occurrences precipitated the mistaken identity plot, it is questionable whether they would have been enough to have kept that plot on course. What seems to have made this possible is something about Manny himself—something in his self-presentation. Whenever he is shown alone or interacting with strangers, his body is remarkably still, his face without apparent expression. The impassivity of his manner supports interpretation without offering a corrective as the interpretation continues to take shape. This is what fueled our speculation about his possibly illicit activity early in the film. The effect is repeated in the insurance office where, by simply standing and waiting his turn, he attracts the nervous attention of the female clerk. Hitchcock stages the scene with this contrast in mind: the jumpy tremulous reaction of the woman (who gathers other women to her, all of whom quickly dissolve into a similar hysteria) against Manny's stony-faced immobility. He is the tabula rasa upon which the clerk projects her imagination of excitement and danger. The scene bears comparison to the recognition scene in *Strangers on a Train*. The close-up shot of the clerk as she stares at Manny (eyes panicky behind glasses, lips parted, body temporarily paralyzed) resembles the close-up of Barbara (played by Hitchcock's daughter) as she "saw" the true identity of the villain in the earlier film. Only here, of course, the woman recognizes the wrong man, a fact that Hitchcock takes care to bring home to us at the end of the film when the same woman meets Manny's gaze after she has identified the "right" man—her look no longer one of emotional intensity but of guilt and embarrassment.

Why does Manny's tentative figure and impassive face produce this kind of false recognition in those who look at him? The answer seems to be a function of what it is his self-presentation "really" means. In other words, there is a connection between the "wrong" identity ascribed to Manny and his "right" identity.

For the very details that at first encourage us to produce a false narrative can actually be shown to produce a true one if we apply a consistently opposite interpretation. Thus, for example, Manny's work at the Stork Club is not to gain access to the "fast lane" but to provide for his family, despite the late hours and the long commute (indeed, his lawyer notes that the club will vouch for his character at the trial). The marking of the racing sheet that initially looks like a guilty act is, we later learn, only a game which, when he explains it to his wife, becomes a tribute to his self-control and his sense of responsibility concerning how to use his money. Similarly, the coffee at the diner, far from being the expression of possibly illicit solitary habits, becomes, retrospectively, a way of dramatizing Manny's later assertion to the detective that he doesn't drink. In short, the trip home first encourages us to read Manny as the detectives will do, while it also subsequently acts to discredit the detectives' interpretation and to refer us to another narrative—that of the exemplary family man. The correct reading of the details of Manny's homeward journey shows him to be not only *not* guilty—a condition he shares with the other mistaken-identity heroes in Hitchcock—but also profoundly innocent.

Manny's innocence has important implications for the structure and style of the film. Mistaken-identity victims in earlier Hitchcock's films always harbored some guilt and could therefore be said to reap some form of justice in the ordeals they were made to suffer. Guy Haines is the most extreme example, but a suggestion of guilt clings even to Father Logan in *I Confess*. Manny's fate, however, is wholly unwarranted. On the one hand, this can be understood as Hitchock's way of dramatizing the basically flawed nature of human justice (and, if one is convinced by the ending, the role of faith in bringing about individual salvation). Yet while this may thematically explain the unrelenting quality of Manny's ordeal, it does not explain the peculiarly unsettling quality of the characterization on us and others within the film. To explain this, it becomes necessary to link the very exemplary nature of Manny's life to the fact of his victimization.

It seems that in performing his roles of husband, father, and son so well, Manny has disappeared within them. Our tendency to read illicit meaning into the Stork Club, the racing sheet, and the diner are all attempts to affix onto Manny's life a "masculine" plot of adventure and irresponsibility—the sort of life that Jeffries led prior to his accident. Instead, these same variables actually bespeak a narrative that goes unnoticed because its continuity suggests repetition rather than linear progression of the kind we are conditioned to want from our heroes. The "outside" world, the symbolic site of action and variety within the lexicon of narrative film, is not really available to Manny. It exists only as a passage back to a domestic space. The image of the subway train and of the tunnel that Hitchcock shows stretching in front of the train expresses the idea vividly, as does the image of the house whose door Manny must unlock to enter (it is as he fumbles for his key, in fact, that the detectives first arrest him). In *Rear Window*, Jeffries, cut off from a life of action due to his accident, felt compelled to find a domestic plot and to fashion a subjectivity within it. Manny, by contrast, has already been so conditioned to a variety of constraints that the imposition of another does not produce resistance, only a numbing fatigue: When released on bail, his overwhelming need is to sleep.[5]

Hitchcock takes pains to dramatize the way an absence of resistance in the character is taken advantage of, first through the imposition of a false identity, then through the physical humiliation of booking and imprisonment. The film chronicles, with excruciating deliberation, the process of incarceration: the fingerprinting, the emptying of the pockets, the physical search, and finally the removal of the tie—the last access to a means of self-assertion—before the actual jailing. This sequence is, to my mind, practically unwatchable, both tedious and painful at the same time. Yet Hitchcock would remark to Truffaut that this was the portion of the film he was most proud of, frankly acknowledging his emotional investment in it: "I did fancy the opening of the picture because of my own fear of the police."[6] This, then, is the enactment of the nightmare-fantasy that Hitchcock so often told, of being locked up as a child in the local prison on his father's orders. Critics of the film, including Truffaut, argued that it was unrealistic in failing to register the emotion of the victim. But Hitchcock's point appears to be that he is reenacting a childhood event (or fantasy about such an event)—and it is a characteristic of the child that he cannot take in and hence cannot resist, either physically or emotionally, what is happening to him. We may recall that an early, unpopular death in Hitchcock had been the death of the boy in *Sabotage*. Part of the different kind of discomfort one feels in watching the first half of *The Wrong Man* is connected to the fact that this is not a child but a grown man suffering a similarly gratuitous victimization. During his ordeal, Manny is continually ordered, as if he were a child, to remove his hat. He is also addressed, like a child, by his first name—a name that itself suggests his status as an infantilized man.[7]

The Wrong Man depicts a condition of vulnerability and helplessness for its male protagonist that can be said to correspond to the self-conception that led Hitchcock into filmmaking. His career in film acted as a defense: It gave him access to technological expertise and to a means of manufacturing fantasies that could bolster a fragile and insecure self-image. His personal story can be connected to the larger story of patriarchal culture, as it too sought to bolster itself against an increasingly powerful feminine literary culture. Narrative film shaped the world to the male gaze and clarified and empowered that gaze in the process. *The Wrong Man* depicts a world where such shaping is absent. It is what the man fears he could be reduced to were the magnified images of the movie screen not present to convince himself and others of the importance of his role.

Whereas the fantasy of being locked up that the film records would seem to have its roots in Hitchcock's early life, *The Wrong Man* can also be said to encode a crisis occurring at the time the film was made. Indeed, it may be a personal crisis that he was invoking when he referred so unconvincingly to a crisis in the industry. America's devotion to conformity, its drive for material success, and its support for rigid stereotypes and conventions appear as central themes in Hitchcock's films of the 1950s, but only in *The Wrong Man* do they emerge as overriding, destructive forces. The film seems to mark a pivotal moment in Hitchcock's development when his social observations became extensions or analogues for stress in his personal life.[8]

Two scenes are especially revelatory with respect to this self-conception. The first introduces Manny to us as the film's protagonist. The camera, having concentrated on the elegantly dressed patrons of the Stork Club, cuts to him, in the shadowed background space where the band plays. He is shown in profile, holding the bass fiddle, mechanically doing his job. The glamour and festivity of the club are rendered so as to highlight his status behind the scenes, present but virtually invisible to those whom he is entertaining. The second noteworthy scene takes place when Manny is brought up before a group of police officers to be registered prior to his arraignment. He stands on a bare platform, an oversized microphone practically obliterating his features. He is told curtly to remove his hat, is asked to recite his name and address, and is perfunctorily dismissed.

These scenes can be read as metaphors for the filmmaker's conception of himself in the eyes of his audience. One is equated with a sense of invisibility, the other with a sense of callous misrecognition (Hitchcock's unusual appearance at the beginning of the film on an empty sound stage both invokes and seeks to counter the scene in which Manny is displayed but "misrecognized" by the audience of police officers).[9] In Hitchcock's British films, character asserted itself: The look that would seek to misrepresent met resistance. Richard Hannay in *The 39 Steps* is the early prototype of the active, resisting hero. Faced with being misread by the world, Hannay determines to find the real villain and prove his innocence. But if such a character reflects Hitchcock's newly empowered self-conception at the outset of his career, then Manny is his disempowered self-conception at a later point. Manny offers no resistance to the look of the sales clerks, merchants, detectives, and policemen, and they are free to impose the meanings they choose. When not being misread, he simply fades into the background, content not to be looked at at all—hidden in the shadows, behind the bass fiddle at the Stork Club, and shuttling home from work underground.

The shift in vision registered in *The Wrong Man* is also connected to an apparent loss of faith in the power of the couple to sustain meaning in the face of adversity. In the 1940s and 1950s, Hitchcock introduced the woman's responding gaze as a complement and corrective to male action. In *Spellbound*, Constance's power to revise meaning saves Ballantine. Barbara's look at the villain in *Strangers on a Train* causes him to lose control and resets the balance that will lead eventually to a just resolution of the plot. Francie's (Grace Kelly) brazen come-ons to Robie

(Cary Grant) in *To Catch a Thief* ultimately help to clear him of robbery charges, while they also "catch" him in marriage. Manny's wife originally seems to occupy a role like that of past Hitchcock heroines. She is determined to counteract the world's misidentification of her husband, overcoming her shyness in order to call a lawyer to defend him and eagerly grasping at the leads they can pursue together to prove his innocence. But as his tentative efforts at action prove futile against the crushingly authoritative and indifferent social bureaucracy, her emotional support wears itself out. "How do I know you're not guilty?" she asks as she sinks into depression and paranoia, finally turning against herself all the energy that would otherwise have been directed to propping him up and staring down his accusers. Ben's sedation of Jo in *The Man Who Knew Too Much* had been an enactment of power relations within the couple that would be gradually revised in the course of that film. But Manny's initial character is too tentative and feeble to warrant this kind of revision. Indeed, the institutionalization of Rose after her breakdown can be viewed as a kind usurpation of what, in the earlier film, had been Ben's role. The society, in the form of the psychiatrist, takes over from the husband the management of the wife. It is as though the more democratic conception of the couple that is achieved at the end of *The Man Who Knew Too Much* exists at the outset of *The Wrong Man*, but with the result that the couple can no longer endure as a functioning complementary structure in the face of crisis. His plodding activity and her wellspring of imagination and feeling—plot and character—now exist without recourse to each other.

In the end the film returns to a superficial assertion of old values in order to produce a sense of closure: The right man is ultimately caught, and Rose, we are told in the written text superimposed on the screen, recovers. Yet these events, affixed in the final minutes, seem unconvincing and incidental to the larger feel of the film. The appearance of the right man is made as though an answer to Manny's prayers—a highly contrived implication in a film that has not previously invoked religion, except as a resource for imagery. Rose's recovery is even more untenable, since the film fails to represent it visually. The last dramatic scene in the film occurs when Manny visits Rose in the mental hospital. He is positioned between the dark, huddled figure of his wife in the corner and the cheerful, white-garbed nurse at the door. Hermann's emotional score swells in the background. This is about as far from a documentary scene as one can get, yet it is also aggressively subversive of classical cinematic convention. It shows the wife refusing her complementary role in the couple and hoarding her subjectivity. "It's fine for *you*," she intones in response to the news that he has been acquitted, a statement that opposes the marital convention whereby what's fine for him is also fine for her. The scene also depicts the world "outside," in the figure of the waiting nurse, as another version of the authority figures who have victimized Manny. Here, authority is masked by a certain routinized optimism and cheerfulness ("Your husband's going now, Mrs. Balestrero. Couldn't you speak to him? He

Rose cracks up: the couple without recourse to each other

brought you good news"), but it remains programmed and impersonal. Couched in the pleasant rhetoric is the order that Manny leave (like those earlier orders that he take off his hat). The two women in the scene thus merely reduplicate the two kinds of looks—one unseeing, the other misrecognizing and potentially oppressive—that have been directed at Manny from the beginning. When the film moves in again to salvage this vision of indifference and menace with its written text, assuring us that Rose does recover and rejoin her family in Florida, we are made aware of how much such endings owe to a literary tradition where male action and female subjectivity were conceived of as each other's reward. The superimposed written text represents Hitchcock's way of fulfilling the studio's demand for a happy ending, but he manages to get the last image for himself (and in cinema, this is obviously better than getting the last word). This is of a family, filmed in very long shot, strolling down a Florida street. The image both glosses the written text and unsettles it. For how do we know that these are the Balestreros any more than the detective knew that Manny was the "right" man? On the other hand, the distance at which we are placed from the figures recalls the documentary premise of the film, suggesting that these are, in fact, the real Balestreros (as opposed to the actors who played them) and, as such, prefer to remain in long shot, having returned to the background where they feel safe: Better to be invisible than to be misrecognized and coerced. But surely, however we interpret this last image, an ending in which the principal players are calculatedly reduced to pinpoints on the screen would seem to be saying something about the future of character for this filmmaker. The way has been prepared for *Vertigo*, a film that will continue to dismantle the nineteenth-century legacy of character and gender complementarity without resorting to the pretense of documentary truth.

THE OPENING SCENES OF *Vertigo*, with their quick pace, witty dialogue, and lush color photography, bear far more of a superficial resemblance to *Rear Window* than to the drab and humorless landscape of *The Wrong Man*. The appearance of Stewart in the leading role also makes us expect that this will be another film about self-improvement. The first scene, a chase over the roofs of San Francisco, establishes the same sort of antecedent life of action and danger for the hero that the photograph of the burning sports car established for Jeffries in the earlier film. The next scene shows Scottie visiting with his friend Midge, who, like Lisa Fremont at the beginning of *Rear Window*, cares more for the protagonist than he does for her. Scottie also complains of the corset he wears for his sprained back. "Tomorrow's the big day [when the corset comes off]," he announces to Midge at one point, recalling Jeffries's anticipation of being liberated from his leg cast.

But these correspondences to the earlier film are false leads, versions of the "suspense effects" Hitchcock enjoyed setting in the path of his audience. Their falseness lies in giving us a message out of synch with a film no longer interested in affirming an idea of the self and of the complementary couple. The opening scene is not a simple reference to reckless action designed to provide a contrast to the subjective exertions of the invalid to follow. It is an invocation of existential horror. The chase is almost immediately eclipsed by the image of Scottie, having lost his footing, hanging to the roof of the building. His glance downward in panic is what appears to trigger an attack of vertigo that in turn triggers (not in a causal but in an associative sense for Scottie) the death of the policeman who tries to rescue him. Hence the encoded equation: "action" leads to "abyss" leads to "vertigo" leads to "death." Midge, who appears in the next scene, is not, in this context, introduced as the heroine in disguise—a girl destined to be "reseen" by a more mature hero later on. She is the woman whom we soon sense he cannot love—her literalism and practical sense are the antithesis of what he is searching for after his harrowing ordeal. As for the corset, it is incidental. Not the sprained back but the vertigo has caused Scottie to retire from the police force and abandon his ambition to be chief of police.

Scottie is suffering not from a temporary handicap but from a condition with no apparent cure. In this he resembles Manny, whose daily life, with its tedious routine and financial burdens, is such a condition (the subway tunnel and the locked house metaphorically express this). Yet *The Wrong Man* is far narrower in its focus than *Vertigo*. For all that Manny can be equated with Hitchcock and with 1950s masculinity in general, the film's insistence that it is based on a true story provides an escape from its harshest and most general implications. At the end of *The Wrong Man*, the right man is apprehended, a substitution of right for wrong that Hitchcock emphasizes by filming the criminal in long shot superimposed upon a close-up of Manny's face and then showing the figure move toward the camera until his face entirely fits and replaces Manny's in a dissolve. Even if we remain skeptical about the institutions of justice portrayed in the film, justice is enacted in this shot, which expresses the ideas of both divine intervention (Manny has just been shown reciting a prayer in front of a picture of Christ) and intervention by a seer filmmaker. Indeed, in billing itself as a true story, *The Wrong Man* becomes its own proof that truth exists.

Vertigo abandons the true-false structure of *The Wrong Man* and, in the process, makes explicit the underlying skepticism about meaning that *The Wrong Man* hints at but draws back from. Manny is imprisoned and then finally liberated. Both states, while they suggest his status as a pawn to forces outside him, also suggest the continued existence of a framework within which truth and falsehood, justice and injustice, can be distinguished. Scottie, by contrast, moves on uncharted terrain, navigating his own search. He announces to Midge his intention to "wander," then decides to follow the wandering Madeleine. It becomes difficult to imagine an outside to this kind of aimless, circuitous movement.

Much of the effect of *Vertigo* is a result of its artificial presentation, which, unlike the insistence on realism in *The Wrong Man*, works to confuse the boundaries of the real and the dream image and to disorient us with respect to conventional coordinates of plot development.[10] Concrete consideration of how things happen are calculatedly marginalized. For example, we never learn how Scottie got down from the roof to which he was clinging at the beginning of the picture; or how Madeline was able to bypass the hotel clerk who claimed not to have seen her enter; or what actual role Judy played in planning Madeleine Elster's death. Yet even obviously explanatory shots—like that in the redwood forest that locates Madeleine leaning against a tree after she seemed to have magically disappeared—do not have the effect of canceling the original enigmatic impression. Nor does the later explanation that Judy is really Madeleine dissipate the confusion of identity surrounding the character. The question of meaning is detached from the literal and causal, so that even when logical explanations are given, they cease to be fully elucidating. The opening credit sequence encodes the film's open-ended project: It begins with a close-up of a generic woman's face, tracks in to the pupil of the woman's eye, and then produces the graphic image of a spiral emerging from the eye. The image raises these questions: Who is this woman (we try unsuccessfully to connect her to someone inside the film), and what does she represent—that is, what narrative attaches to the spiral that emerges from her eye? Where the first question is akin to the question posed in *The Wrong Man* and correlates with the film's concern with a literal series of impersonations (Judy pretending to be Madeleine pretending to be Carlotta), the second refers to the subjective narrative attached to each of these impersonations, culminating finally in the unanswerable question: Who is Judy?[11]

What initially draws Scottie to accept Elster's request to investigate his wife appears to hinge on Elster's question "Do you believe that someone out of the past, someone dead, can enter and take possession of a living being?" Scottie says no, but his manner announces that the question has drawn him in: He is ready to take on the job that he had earlier refused. According to Spoto, Scottie is "a man drawn ineluctably into the past,"[12] but it would be more correct to say that he is a man seeking a past in another to compensate for the lack of one in himself. In *The Wrong Man*, Manny's routinized existence reflected the absence of a narrative of subjectivity (a past encoded in the unconscious that would have given inflection to his behavior). Hitchcock makes the same point about Scottie with more dramatic immediacy in the opening scene of *Vertigo*: A male prototype of action, a detective (one recalls the active, literalist Doyle in *Rear Window* as a possible precursor), is brought face-to-face with the abyss. There is a strikingly cartoonish quality to this scene. The criminal is dressed in white, the policeman in black, but otherwise they share a square-jawed physical resemblance. Scottie, by contrast, wears a gray suit (his face softened as well by his gray hair) and seems to be distinguished from the other two figures as the odd or extra man, the "real" one, lagging behind their highly conventionalized chase. When Scottie loses his footing and clings to the edge of the roof, their function as metaphorical reflections of himself becomes clear: One falls to his death (the fall will be reenacted as his own in a dream later), while the other races off out of sight (that part of himself that symbolically "gets away" and will be tracked for the remainder of the film). In presenting the chase in a highly condensed, surreal form early in the film, Hitchcock has abandoned all interest in its conventional function as a hinge for plot. *Rear Window* had used the chase motif—in Jeffries's pursuit of Thorwald—to lend structure to the story. *Vertigo* introduces the chase only as a point of departure—an event that produces the "condition" of the protagonist. After the opening scene, the protagonist abandons pursuit of the "right man" and soon embarks on the alternative project of trying to plumb the meaning of a woman.

Hitchcock summarized the film's theme to Truffaut as the story of a man who "wants to go to bed with a woman who's dead; he's indulging in a form of necrophilia."[13] But Madeleine appears to be possessed not so much by a nineteenth-century woman as by a narrative of subjectivity associated with such a woman. The painting displayed in the museum and the grave located at the local mission are fragments of that woman's narrative. Scottie makes it his job to piece these fragments together—to learn the whole story. He finally gets this from the local bookseller, Pop Liebl: Carlotta Valdes, the old man tells him, was a beautiful but poor woman taken up by a wealthy man who later abandoned her and took away her daughter. Driven mad with grief, she killed herself. The story might be the plot of a George Eliot or Thomas Hardy novel. However, it was not the plot but the emotions and imaginings that the plot encouraged that constituted the lure and the threat of novels within nineteenth-century culture. It is this subjective aspect of narrative that Scottie is seeking. Madeleine thus becomes for him the carrier of the subjective content of a lost text, the physical embodiment of a psychological narrative. This is the role that Hitchcock had assigned to women in many of his most successful Hollywood films. But where these films had employed the image uncritically, *Vertigo* deconstructs it.

Feminist critics who insist that Scottie's love of Madeline is based on a patriarchal power fantasy are, of course, right, but they miss the countervailing impulses at work in the obsession. What appears to be propelling the protagonist in this film is the sudden recognition of a "lack" in himself—that abyss that stretches dizzily beneath him as he hangs from the building. Once that recognition is experienced, Scottie gives up his old job and his competitive aspirations without apparent regret. With Madeleine, he seeks a relationship that, while it holds to hierarchical aspects of gender complementarity, also includes a desire for the "daughter's effect"—for self-revision.

Although an important portion of the film records Scottie's efforts to refashion what is apparently another woman into his lost love, it has not been noted that Scottie has himself been refashioned in his relationship with Madeleine. His response to meaning has been altered. The basic skepticism and sarcasm with which he approached life—the hallmark of his interactions with Midge—have fallen away. He is willing to feel deeply and to be tolerant of the irrational and ambiguous. What enrages him in the end is the revelation that the woman whom he has allowed to refashion him is actually a male construction.[14] Indeed, not only is Madeleine constructed by Elster, but the story that she requisitioned as her own (Carlotta's story) is also constructed by men: Elster, Pop Liebl, and the museum curator are its narrators. This is a deconstructive insight of sorts into the way nineteenth-century male novelists can be said to have constructed female subjectivity and then passed it on to filmmakers like Hitchcock as the real thing. The revelation that other men have shaped Scottie's fantasy places him—and, by extension, Hitchcock—in precisely the position of imitative subordinate that constituted Brandon's role with respect to Rupert in *Rope*. Insofar as the audience is made to share Scottie's desires, it is placed in this position as well.

The revelation to the audience that Judy and Madeleine are the same person might seem intended to take us out of the spiral in which we have been confined with Scottie. But the revelation also draws us into that spiral on another level by making us want Scottie to love the "real" Judy. In Judy, the film continues to hold out the hope that an authentic self exists. She is represented as the opposite of the woman whom we learn has been constructed by another man and, in keeping with the technique, already explored in *The Wrong Man*, whereby an illusion of reality is created through the negation of a fictional convention, she appears more real and unmediated than Madeleine or even Midge (a male imitation rather than a male construction who presents herself as Scottie's buddy and whose rule of life seems to be to keep a stiff upper lip). But, of course, Judy is no less a construction than Madeleine. Her behavior is dictated by what predatory urban life requires of the poor shop girl, and her appearance is more overtly designed to attract men than Madeleine's. Indeed, part of Scottie's drive to transform her involves toning down the heavy makeup and explicitly sexy clothes. Knowing that Hitchcock's feminine ideal was the polished Grace Kelly type, we can see how calculatedly Judy has been designed as the antithesis of that ideal. The paradoxes of her self-presentation are multiplied if we also consider the actress behind the role. Novak, discovered by Columbia Pictures as a replacement for Rita Hayworth, was by most critical standards a bad actress. Her "badness" consisted of a false elegance of manner and a kind of breathy socialite diction (it is quite possible that Novak was imitating Marilyn Monroe). In the Madeleine role, Novak's affected style fit well with the character of a constructed ideal. In the Judy role, she appeared to overlay a false elegance with a false vulgarity—the layer of artifice doubled rather than halved. We get an almost painful sense of a bad actress striving to be real, more exposed as a bad actress but also appearing more real in being so exposed. But in trying to glimpse the real Novak, the Novak without the veneer of acting altogether, we find ourselves not closer but farther away from what this might be. Ultimately, we must ask what the idea of the real woman behind the actress really means—whether such an idea is anything more than the idea of Madeleine cherished by Scottie. We seem only to be able to talk in terms of the good or the bad actress, turns of the screw on the imagined idea of the real person behind the acting.[15]

In *Marnie*, made six years after *Vertigo*, the protagonist will explore his wife's past and give voice to this desire: "I want to know what happened to the child, the little girl, the daughter." The plea expresses both the particularized desire of Hitchcock, the father of a daughter grown up and left home, and the more general desire of a culture, no longer secure in a stable, gender-differentiated identity. As early as *Rear Window*, the plea had been there, buried in Jeffries's desperate, though impersonalized, declaration: "I just wanted to know what happened to the salesman's wife." *Vertigo, Psycho, The Birds*, and *Marnie* will struggle to come to terms with the realization that the daughter—the knowable "other" and perfect complement to the father—is gone.

SPOTO HAS WRITTEN that "if one seeks a single word to describe the world of Hitchcock's films of this time it might indeed be 'loss.' "[16] Certainly, the tone of *Vertigo*, like that of *The Wrong Man*, is profoundly melancholy, and both end with dramatic scenes that are explicitly tragic. But *Vertigo* (unlike *The Wrong Man*, which carries the finality that we associate with a one-time "true" experience) is a film that spirals back upon itself, making it possible to return to it in a later context and see the seeds of a new orientation. Consider, for example, how one scene that might be viewed as no more than a simple transitional moment can give rise to a line of thought totally at odds with the film's dominant tone. The scene I have in mind directly follows the famous vertiginous embrace, where Scottie, having convinced Judy to physically transform herself, has his fantasy realized. The scene in question shows Scottie chatting with Judy/Madeleine as she sits before the vanity, putting on her earrings. This is actually the first time in the film in which he seems relaxed and content. The fact that Judy's voice and manner inhabit Madeleine's image seems not to bother him at all. She too is represented as happy at this moment—so much so, in fact, that her frank references to her own constructedness ("Don't touch; I just put on my face") put a new spin on the idea of what it means to be one's own woman. Her assumption of the hybrid Judy/Madeleine persona and his willingness to accept the mix seem a triumph for the accommodating potential of the couple.[17]

However, as Scottie fastens the necklace around Judy's neck and realizes that it had belonged to Madeleine, he suddenly understands the plot to which he has been a dupe, and the moment of ease is destroyed. I assume that some others have experienced what I did at this moment: a wave of irritation that that necklace gave it all away. Had the additional piece of knowledge not been presented (had Hitchcock not felt constrained to make his protagonist "see," or had Scottie let the hint go and not pushed to find the true meaning behind the illusion), everyone might have lived happily ever after. The desire aroused in us to let well enough alone has its source, I suspect, less in a desire to be deluded than in a postmodern recognition, which the film itself teaches, that experience is, by definition, constructed and hence delusionary. The "true" Judy behind the role is only another facsimile of our own desire, cohabiting uneasily with what does not quite fit the mold of that desire. If the world is nothing but the constructions we place on it, then we would do well not to push too hard for additional meanings that are likely to topple whatever structure we have put in place. This is a vision of meaning as bricolage rather than psychological truth, and it will be the guiding spirit of Hitchcock's last films.

Notes

1. François Truffaut, *Hitchcock*, rev. ed. (New York: Touchstone, 1985), 237.

2. See Marshall Deutelbaum, "Finding the Right Man in *The Wrong Man*," in *The Hitchcock Reader*, ed. Deutelbaum and Leland Poague (Ames: Iowa State University Press, 1986), for a fuller discussion of how Hitchcock's film deviated from the facts of the case.

3. Quoted in Deutelbaum, "Finding the Right Man," 214.

4. Truffaut, *Hitchcock*, 242. Although the studio system was breaking down during this period, Warner Brothers had expanded into television and was apparently doing well.

5. Critics tend to compare Manny's situation to that of Joseph K. in Franz Kafka's *The Trial*. Kafka, however, manages to entwine a social critique with a critique of individual consciousness. Since we are brought into contact with the character's thoughts, his self-delusion and paranoia seem to play a part in his condition. By contrast, the film's wholly external orientation works to deny the very idea of consciousness for its character and hence to produce a far more complete picture of human passivity.

6. Truffaut, *Hitchcock*, 243.

7 Hitchcock includes a sequence in which the detectives who come to Manny's home to make the arrest assume, based on their knowledge of his full name (Christopher Emmanuel Balestrero), that his nickname is Chris. When they call out, "Chris," this not only anticipates the string of mistaken identifications to follow, it also acts subliminally to highlight our association of Manny's name with his character. For another angle on the name, see Robert Stam, "Hitchcock and Buñuel," in *Hitchcock's Rereleased Films: From Rope to Vertigo*, ed. Walter Raubicheck and Walter Srebnick (Detroit: Wayne State University Press, 1991), 125.

8. See David Sterritt, *The Films of Alfred Hitchcock* (Cambridge: Cambridge University Press, 1993), chap. 4, for a discussion of the relationship of *The Wrong Man* to 1950s conformism (and to the conventions of film noir). See my *Alfred Hitchcock and the Legacy of Victorianism* (Lexington: University Press of Kentucky, 1995), for an analysis of Hitchcock's daughter's role in his cinematic development.

9. Ironically, Hitchcock's appearance at the beginning of the film may be considered its most documentary aspect. Despite the fact that that appearance involves a claim that the film is an authentic transcription of reality, the appearance itself introduces an element of self-reflexivity that conforms with contemporary documentary practice, encouraging us to see the ensuing film as the filmmaker's construction. See Jeanne Allen, "Self-Reflexivity in Documentary," in *Explorations in Film Theory: Selected Essays from Cine-Tracts*, ed. Ron Burnett (Bloomington: Indiana University Press, 1991).

10. Katie Trumpener, in her postmodern reading of *Vertigo*, "Fragments of the Mirror: Self-Reference, Mise-en-Abime, *Vertigo*," in Raubicheck and Srebnick, *Hitchcock's Rereleased Films*, 183, addresses this confusion as part of the film's larger project of deconstruction: "The distinctions between levels of vision collapse in *Vertigo* along with all our other distinctions, our accustomed hierarchy of actor and audience, fiction and reality; as we lose our illusions, we simultaneously lose our bearings, our depth perception, our ability to tell apart the two-dimensional and the three."

11. Sterritt, *The Films of Alfred Hitchcock*, 84, notes that the spiral emerging from the eye in the opening credits "evokes the notion of birth, connoting all kinds of creation—

among them synthesis, fabrication, performance—and linking them intimately with the act of seeing."

12. Donald Spoto, *The Art of Alfred Hitchcock: Fifty Years of His Motion Pictures*, 2d and rev. ed. (New York: Anchor Books, 1992), 279.

13. Truffaut, *Hitchcock*, 244.

14. Tania Modleski, *The Women Who Knew Too Much* (New York: Methuen, 1988), 91, also notes that the early scene in which Midge shows Scottie a brassiere designed by an engineer is playing on the notion of femininity as the product of a male design.

15. Truffaut noted that Novak wasn't Hitchcock's original choice for the role but suggested that the film "was even more intriguing in light of the fact that the director had compelled a substitute to imitate the actress he had initially chosen for the role" (*Hitchcock*, 325). For a related discussion of character and performance, see Wendy Lesser, *His Other Half: Men Looking at Women through Art* (Cambridge: Harvard University Press, 1991), 132–44. For an interesting counter-argument to mine, see Marian E. Keane, "A Closer Look at Scopophilia: Mulvey, Hitchcock, and *Vertigo*," in Deutelbaum and Poague, *A Hitchcock Reader*. Keane sees Novak's "metaphysical integrity" pushing through the role and asserting itself as a corporeal reality when the character looks directly at the camera before falling (jumping?) from the tower. I would also like to thank Rosemary Abbate for her observations on Novak's bad acting.

16. Spoto, *The Art of Alfred Hitchcock*, 280.

17. Molly Haskell, *From Reverence to Rape: The Treatment of Women in the Movies* (Chicago: University of Chicago Press, 1974), 352, argues that both Madeleine and Judy are unreal extremes and calls for a more realistic " 'fusion' woman." I posit the existence of such a woman not as some more natural hybrid but as a compromise construction in the Madeleine/Judy composite.

9

Fearful Cemetery

Michael Wood

> And *Wuthering Heights* is a good case of double plot in the novel, both for covert deification and telling the same story twice with the two possible endings.
>
> William Empson, *Some Versions of Pastoral*

Family plot. The double meaning in the title of Alfred Hitchcock's last completed film (1976) seems too obvious at first. The conspiracy and the cemetery. The family plot, like the paths of glory, leads but to the family plot. Isn't this where all paths lead in Hitchcock? And wasn't the old gentleman a little tired?

"I think of *Family Plot* as a curtain-call," William Rothman says in *The Murderous Gaze*,[1] "light, assured, intended for pleasure ... a medium's intimate salute to a medium." Slavoj Žižek, dividing Hitchcock's films into five periods, sees "isolated touches of brilliance" in the last group and mentions "the use of parallel narration in *Family Plot*" but generally regards the late films as "post"-everything, including the postmodernism of the previous period, that of "the big films of the 1950s and early 1960s."[2] What's striking here is the critical plot of lateness, the acceptance of time as structure and story, the eager sense of an ending; and then the infection of the punning in Rothman, where the joke about the medium makes even the curtain call look like a gangster's gag about death. Rothman may not have intended this, but like the rest of us watching this movie, he has entered a world where puns are unavoidable; we stumble on them at every turn. We respond not to their intention or subtlety but to their profuse possibility, the skittering multiplication of meaning they represent. The obvious double sense of the title of *Family Plot* is just a start. It's not as late as we think.

What about the other, narratological meaning of the word "plot," for example? And what about the meanings of the word "family"? Is a plot as storyline always a conspiracy against someone—the viewer or the reader, perhaps? Do all stories lead to the grave, as Roland Barthes thought all stories went back to Oedipus?[3] Is a family plot a form of entertainment, announcing, a little ahead of time, the celebration of family values, or is it just the family romance, Oedipus again? What happens when the family plot is a double plot? And is there an American inflection to all this in Hitchcock's film, a suggestion that although plots are everywhere, American plots represent a (mildly or extravagantly) shocking excess of order, a cancellation of the freedom of movement that seemed to be promised by all that space?

Family Plot was written by Ernest Lehman, who was also the screenwriter for *North by Northwest*, a film where several American myths turn out to be traps or threats. Who would have thought the empty prairies would be so crowded—since a man trying to kill you is always one man too many? What are the faces on Mount Rushmore for, if not to fall from? The allegories are very playful, but they are not hollow. You can't hide in open country, and you're not alone even in a scene of great apparent isolation. It's always dangerous to hang around monuments, animal or mineral. Much American literature, Andrew Delbanco suggests, is dedicated to "the idea that individual human beings can break free of the structures of thought into which they are born and that, by reimagining the world, they can change it."[4] It is a form of tribute to that idea to keep picturing its improbability, as late-arriving Americans like Chandler and Hitchcock do. You can reimagine the world, their work suggests, and you have to, but you can't change it, and old structures of thought can dog you like an inheritance. Chandler's characters, like the chief criminal character in *Family Plot*, have buried their old lives, but their old lives then get up and walk, like those characters in Poe who scarcely ever manage to stay in their graves.

We need a slightly stronger sense of plot than Forster offers us, when he distinguishes it from story, and indeed stronger than the one the Russian Formalists and their followers use in their opposition of *fabula* to *szujet*. To help us here, a plot has to be not only the arrangement of story events but an arrangement felt as such, a scheme pointing to its own scheming, so that the narrative signals both its conspiracy and its organization. A plot is story showing its hand, we might say—a little theology. It invites us to understand the order of a fiction and to compare it to the orders and disorders of the world.

Hitchcock's film is based on an elegant novel by Victor Canning, *The Rainbird Pattern* (1972), where the parallel narration is already beautifully executed. Hitchcock makes it even more prominent, turns double story into double vision, and of course shifts the whole thing to an American location, so that the Thames and Chelsea and the Wiltshire countryside become a riverless San Francisco and the dry, dusty hills of California. What attracted his interest in this material, Hitchcock said, "was the structural image of those two separate plots and separate groups of characters coming gradually, inevitably together." Hitchcock was responding to a question from John Russell Taylor about whether there has "ever been anything specific you wanted to say in your films." The answer was carefully shaded: "Now we're back to Sam Goldwyn, aren't we?—messages are for Western Union. Of course in each specific subject there is something I want to say, in the sense that there is something which attracts my interest, and I want to bring that out in my treatment of the subject. It may be something technical, as in *Family Plot*."[5]

It may be something technical. We know what it means for characters or sets of characters to meet, in stories and in material reality, but what does it mean for two plots to come together, gradually, inevitably, or anyhow? Think of the shock of certain famous moments in novels, where Konstantin Levin shows up in Anna Karenina's story, for example, or Tertius Lydgate shows up in Dorothea Brooke's. Children often feel enormous, almost unmanageable excitement when a character from one television program makes an appearance on another. It's as if an important rule were being broken, or a divisive fact were revealed to be a fiction. Unconnected, insulated worlds turn out to be connectable after all, like the two ways of the child's walks in Proust, toward Swann's house or the Guermantes' place, landscapes that come to represent idealized instances of different flora and views, and indeed become metaphors for life's options, the choices of love or society. The grown man is astonished to discover that the walks are not opposed to each other, do not indicate drastic alternatives, but are just figures drawn among rural possibilities. If you wanted to switch your walk from Swann's way to that of the Guermantes, you could do it at any time.

Hitchcock speaks of a structural image, and structure is important here. Walks, television programs, and plots, or rather the accounts we give ourselves of these things, consciously or not, are arrangements of the world, forms of symbolic geography. The longer the arrangements last, and the more intimate we become with them, the more exclusive and self-sustaining they seem. Their protagonists can't go anywhere else, and no new protagonists are needed, unless they are born into and entirely dedicated to this arrangement. Early on in a novel, for instance, or in our walks or our watching of the program, we feel that anything could happen. It seems quite likely that a romance will develop between the twin idealists Dorothea and Lydgate—it would be a fine thing, far better than the unfortunate marriage each of them makes. But then we realize it's not going to happen, the separate lives settle into separate shapes, and we concentrate on reading the double plot as double, two stories that reflect and comment on each other but can do this only because there are two of them, their resemblances and differences adding up and crisscrossing: They are the same and not the same. The shock occurs when the two stories momentarily become one; that is, not when the characters happen to meet—they could do that at any time within the world of the book, and sometimes have—but when they meet at a moment of narrative tension, when they are able to have an effect on each other's lives. Even more dramatic than the effect, though, is the sense of their (and our) escape from a plot that seemed inescapable. There is always magic in the air at such moments, and this, or something even broader, is what the children are responding to when characters momentarily migrate into other television countries. The magic, I think, is not simply that of liberation, the discovery that our categories are only categories, that the seeming transgression is not even a transgression. This experience needs to be recognized and is certainly part of whatever the overall feeling is. But there is magic in the very idea of the old person in the new place, in the possibility of switching walks. Our imagination receives a shock, because our thinking was a little too stiff; but the world itself now seems endlessly multiple and mobile—more multiple and mobile than it is, no doubt. Behind the rebuke to our limitations—and I think it unlikely that children feel this rebuke as strongly as adults do—is the sheer thrill of seeing what our limitations almost made us miss. In Hitchcock, of course, this thrill turns to fear, but the principle is the same. What the double plot always tells us is that there is another plot, that our own is not the only one. What meetings between plots tell us is that we could be in that other plot, perhaps already are; the other plot is waiting for us, if not in a studio or an English or Russian drawing room, then in an American cemetery.

Our first encounter with the double plot in Hitchcock's film looks like a strange loss of control or direction. Blanche (Barbara Harris), a medium, and Lumley (Bruce Dern), her taxi-driver boyfriend, are riding home in his cab, discussing a scheme they have for making $10,000. They are to discover the lost nephew of one of Blanche's clients, the elderly Miss Rainbird. The nephew is to become the old lady's heir, and the money is to be Blanche's reward for finding him. Turning back to look at Blanche, Lumley almost runs over a pedestrian crossing the road. It is Fran (Karen Black), and the film now follows her rather than staying with Blanche and Lumley. Fran is going to pick up a diamond and, in return, to tell the city authorities where they can collect a kidnapped politician. She does this; rides a helicopter to the spot; and is met by her boyfriend, Adamson (William DeVane), owner of a jewelry story and mastermind of the kidnapping scheme. They return home, tidy up the place where they kept the victim, and go upstairs to bed, amid much banter about the aphrodisiac possibilities of danger.

Adamson sticks the diamond to a chandelier, where it gleams brightly among the dangling glass drops.

The narrative principle at this stage could be that of Luis Buñuel's *Phantom of Liberty* (1974), where a minor character in one story, say a nurse at the doctor's office, becomes the main character in the next story, only to be abandoned in her turn when the film follows a man who was staying at the same inn as the nurse. And so on. Buñuel doesn't return to any of these people, so the effect is that of a potentially infinite unfolding of narratives, a series of plots that undo the idea of plot and are never collected into any finalizing conspiracy. The comparison is instructive, because Hitchcock's move is exactly the opposite. From the Fran and Adamson story he returns to Blanche and Lumley, and he zigzags between the two stories for most of the rest of the film. And not only do the stories keep bumping into each other; they are, as we learn long before the characters do, the same story—the lost nephew is the kidnapper. The man Blanche and Lumley are seeking in order to give him the good news of his inheritance is also the man the police are seeking in connection with a series of brilliant crimes. Needless to say, Adamson doesn't imagine anyone is trying to bring him good news: He has murder and arson in his past as well as kidnapping in his present life. In the novel, the narrative interest centers on the double hunt of the same man; but Hitchcock, after a brief scene that suggests he was at one time more attached to the police pursuit than he later became, concentrates on Blanche and Lumley's benevolent if self-interested quest and its contrast with Fran and Adamson's criminal activities, increasingly hampered by their sense that someone is after them.

The meeting point of the two plots, the place where they cease their crisscrossing and become one, is a cemetery, and Hitchcock's (for him rather unusual) recourse to an extreme high-angle shot allows us to see the meeting as if we were God—or had become God for a moment. On Adamson's instructions, a man called Maloney has tried to kill Blanche and Lumley and has died in the attempt. At the cemetery Lumley spots Maloney's widow, who he thinks can provide him with the missing piece of his puzzle. Lumley has unearthed a lot about the past of the lost nephew, including a faked death and a phony gravestone, but not the man's present name or whereabouts. The widow, knowing that Lumley is on Adamson's trail but of course not knowing why, tries to make off down a cemetery path. Lumley moves to join her down another path, as if they were caught in a labyrinth without walls, and the camera rises very high on its crane. The widow could avoid Lumley if she left her path and made for the parking lot, but that doesn't appear to be permitted in this particular narrative game. She is not really fleeing, and Lumley is not hurrying, as if they both know that the labyrinth can only bring them together; that labyrinths contain many paths, but no escape— either from the labyrinth or from encounters with others in the same maze. The paths run parallel; the widow's at the top of the screen, Lumley's at the bottom.

The widow's path takes a right angle, returns to parallel Lumley's; the two almost meet but then continue round the sides of another, final square. The widow does leave the path at this point but takes only a few steps, then stands waiting. Doomed by geometry, so to speak, she tells Lumley the name he needs to know. The cemetery is ragged, half-overgrown, untidy, the pattern of the paths irregular. On the soundtrack the priest's voice continues with the burial service, and a lightly spooky music suggests that we are present at a piece of magic.

We are looking, clearly, at a picture of parallel narration, Hitchcock's image for his own interest in this film. Lesley Brill compares the scene to the "converging rails at the beginning of *Strangers on a Train*," which is also "an emblem of plot,"[6] and the connection helps us to see all kinds of things. There are interesting differences, though. The rails in *Strangers on a Train* converge and diverge, making a letter X. A little later, possessed of Guy Haines's lighter, and knowing how his own plot is supposed to unfold, the psychopathic Bruno murmurs to himself, "Crisscross." If you exchange murders, there will be no perceptible motive, and your two paths, having intersected, will continue off in their own directions. Unless of course, something goes wrong, as it must. But the visual image here is of crossing; in *Family Plot* it is of parallel lines that do not converge but take a sudden turn and run straight into each other. There is nowhere else to go.

The ragged cemetery suggests a world that is closed and ordered but not neat, a sort of wilderness with a design. It is a picture not of a destiny but of a joking symmetrical pattern of chances—or, more precisely, of Hitchcock's careful simulation of such chances. Outside of chance, there is no reason why the news of Adamson's good fortune should turn out to be his undoing; we can't moralize this into any sort of comeuppance. But of course the picture is not meaningless just because we can't moralize it. It means what it shows: not that paths must meet but that they can, and that a picture of paths is a picture of how we have drawn the world.

Armed with Adamson's name, Blanche and Lumley have one more move to make. They have to find the right Adamson among the many wrong Adamsons in San Francisco. Blanche tears a page out of the telephone book and starts on her quest. A number of candidates are eminently unsuitable—wrong age, wrong sex, wrong color, and so on. But then she finds him. Or, rather, finds his trace— his jewelry store, his house. She rings the bell. Fran and Adamson are inside, not answering. They have recognized her, because like Mrs. Maloney, they know Blanche and Lumley are pursuing them but don't know why. Blanche appears to leave, and Fran and Adamson continue with their business, which happens to concern the transportation of a kidnapped (and drugged) archbishop to a drop-off point. The archbishop is in the car; we see Fran's face in the darkness of the garage as she operates the device to open the door, which folds upward slowly to reveal the sidewalk, and Blanche is standing there, framed, as if in a movie, her car behind her, blocking the way out.

The story moves in wonderfully intricate stages from here, but I want to stay with this shot, which completes, I think, the proposition of the cemetery and closes Hitchcock's "structural image" for him. It's not just that Blanche has found Adamson, come face to face with him, which is plainly the most immediate narrative point. It's that Blanche has been found, by the camera and by Adamson, in the path of Adamson's plot. Or to put that slightly differently, we have discovered through Blanche that in the world of this film you can't complete your own story without intruding dangerously on someone else's. Blanche's appearance in this frame, her startled but ignorantly delighted face, is the pure thrill of double plot, a terrific instance of its blossoming, that is, of its collapse into a larger plot that swallows all doubleness. Here the result is danger, and Blanche almost gets killed—in the novel she does get killed. But beyond the danger there is something else. Blanche's standing in Adamson's way means not only that her life has gotten entangled with his but also that his own old life, through her and unknown to her, has come back to him: that the structure of thought into which he was born, to paraphrase Delbanco, has gotten up and walked here with her from the cemetery, with its phony grave and family plot. And what we have seen, who are neither Blanche nor Adamson, is a kind of diagram of ironies. You don't want to find what you think you want to find. This person apparently pursuing your past is actually pursuing your present—although, even then, not the part of your present you might think. This deck of chances runs so smoothly together it looks as someone had planned the whole thing—a grinning God, let's say, or a mischievous movie director. Why are we so startled? What image of our desire or our fear stares out of the frame?

"What *Family Plot* allows us to witness," Fredric Jameson writes,

> "as though in a small-scale laboratory situation, is the mechanism whereby the thriller generates a secondary representation of daily life by absorbing the peculiarities of the overhead garage door into the plot proper, and exploiting the subliminal anxiety aroused by the lack of windows in the door panel by situating the telepathic heroine outside it in the street."[7]

This comment follows a brilliant discussion of overhead garage doors as markers of "daily life in San Francisco," and of Hitchcock, along with Chandler and Nabokov, as one of "the great foreigners, the great European exiles" who "work by dissassemblage, taking the American misery apart" and who use plot as a form of lure for the public, giving us what we think we want, while allowing us to focus, in a state of Benjaminian "distraction," on the real business of the details of an "everyday life" we are always about to lose in generalities. Plot in the sense I am after, and even more so double plot, feeds on these details, can't do without them. But then the details feed the plot, and the garage in San Francisco, or more precisely, the sidewalk outside the garage, becomes the scene of a tremendous illumination, like the understanding of the passage between the two ways in Proust, or the children's excitement at the migration of television personalities.

If the double plot tells us there is always another plot, the American double plot turns the screw by conscripting the most exact and ordinary features of everyday life for its truly lurid manifestations, liberating or intimately imprisoning. In Buñuel, for instance, the camera could shift, or a garage door could open, to reveal virtually anything—a couple of dead donkeys draped across a piano; why not? In Hitchcock, and not only because he is working within a recognizable genre, a garage door can open only to reveal whatever it is you don't want to see, waiting on the sidewalk like doom disguised as a dippy lady trying to stretch her psychic talents a little farther than they will go.

Notes

1. William Rothman, *Hitchcock: The Murderous Gaze* (Cambridge: Harvard University Press, 1982), 250.

2. Slavoj Žižek, ed., *Everything You Always Wanted to Know about Lacan (But Were Afraid to Ask Hitchcock)* (London: Verso, 1992), 5.

3. Roland Barthes, *Le Plaisir du texte* (Paris: Editions du Seuil, 1973), 75: "Tout récit ne se ramène-t-il pas à l'Oedipe? Raconter, n'est-ce pas toujours chercher son origine?"

4. Andrew Delbanco, *Required Reading* (New York: Farrar Straus and Giroux, 1997), ix.

5. Sidney Gottlieb, ed., *Hitchcock on Hitchcock: Selected Writings and Interviews* (Berkeley and Los Angeles: University of California Press, 1995), 61.

6. Lesley Brill, *The Hitchcock Romance* (Princeton: Princeton University Press, 1988), 77.

7. Fredric Jameson, *Signatures of the Visible* (New York: Routledge, 1992), 110.

Filmography

Hitchcock's American Films

1940

Rebecca
Selznick Studios, 1939
Screenplay: Robert E. Sherwood and Joan
    Harrison, adaptaption by Philip
    MacDonald and Michael Hogan,
    based on the novel by Daphne du
    Maurier
Music: Franz Waxman
Featured performers: Laurence Olivier, Joan
    Fontaine, Judith Anderson, George
    Sanders

Foreign Correspondent
Wanger Productions
Screenplay: Charles Bennet, Joan Harri-
    son
Music: Alfred Newman
Featured performers: Joel McCrea, Laraine
    Day, Herbert Marshall, George
    Sanders

1941

Mr. And Mrs. Smith
RKO, 1940
Story and screenplay: Norman Krasna
Music: Edward Wand
Featured performers: Carole Lombard, Rob-
    ert Montgomery

Suspicion
RKO
Screenplay: Samson Raphaelson, Joan
    Harrison, and Alma Reville, based
    on the novel *Before the Fact* by Fran-
    ces Iles
Music: Franz Waxman
Featured performers: Joan Fontaine, Cary
    Grant, Sir Cedric Hardwicke,
    Dame May Whitty

1942

Saboteur
Universal, 1941
Screenplay: Peter Viertel, Joan Harrison,
    Dorothy Parker, based on an idea
    by Hitchcock
Music: Frank Skinner
Featured performers: Robert Cummings,
    Priscilla Lane, Otto Kruger, Alma
    Kruger

1943

Shadow of a Doubt
Universal, 1942
Screenplay: Thornton Wilder, Sally Ben-
    son, Alma Reville, based on a story
    by Gordon McDonnell
Music: Dimitri Tiomkin
Featured performers: Joseph Cotten, Teresa
    Wright, MacDonald Carey, Patri-

cia Collinge, Henry Travers, Hume Cronyn

1944

Lifeboat
20th Century-Fox, 1943
Screenplay: Jo Swerling, based on a story by John Steinbeck
Music: Hugo W. Friedhofer
Featured performers: Tallulah Bankhead, John Hodiak, William Bendix, Walter Slezak, Mary Anderson, Hume Cronyn, Henry Hull, Heather Angel, Canada Lee

1945

Spellbound
Selznick Studios, 1944
Screenplay: Ben Hecht, adaptation by Angus MacPhail, based on the novel *The House of Dr. Edwardes* by Frances Beeding
Music: Miklos Rozsa
Featured performers: Ingrid Bergman, Gregory Peck, Leo G. Carroll

1946

Notorious
RKO, 1945–46
Screenplay: Ben Hecht
Music: Roy Webb
Featured performers: Ingrid Bergman, Cary Grant, Claude Rains, Leopoldine Konstantin

1947

The Paradine Case
Selznick-Vanguard, 1946–47
Screenplay: David O. Selznick, adaptation by Alma Reville, based on the novel by Robert Hichens
Music: Franz Waxman

Featured performers: Alida Valli, Gregory Peck, Ann Todd, Charles Laughton, Ethel Barrymore

1948

Rope
Transatlantic
Screenplay: Arthur Laurents, adaptation by Hume Cronyn, based on the play by Patrick Hamilton
Music: Francis Poulenc, Leo F. Forbstein
Featured performers: James Stewart, John Dall, Farley Granger, Sir Cedric Hardwicke, Constance Collier

1949

Under Capricorn
Transatlantic, 1948
Screenplay: James Bridie, adaptation by Hume Cronyn, based on a play by John Colton and Margaret Linden
Music: Richard Addinsell
Featured performers: Joseph Cotten, Ingrid Bergman, Michael Wilding, Margaret Leighton

1950

Stage Fright
Warner Brothers-First National, 1949
Screenplay: Whitfield Cook, adaptation by Alma Reville, based on the novel *Man Running* by Selwyn Jepson
Music: Leighton Lucas
Featured performers: Marlene Dietrich, Jane Wyman, Michael Wilding, Richard Todd, Alastair Sim, Sybil Thorndike

1951

Strangers on a Train
Warner Brothers-First National, 1950

Screenplay: Raymond Chandler and Czinzi Ormonde, adaptation by Whitfield Cook, based on the novel by Patricia Highsmith

Music: Dimitri Tiomkin

Featured performers: Robert Walker, Farley Granger, Laura Elliott, Ruth Roman, Patricia Hitchcock

1953

I Confess

Warner Brothers-First National, 1952

Screenplay: George Tabori and William Archibald, based on the play *Nos Deux Consciences* by Paul Anthelme

Music: Dimitri Tiomkin

Featured performers: Montgomery Clift, Anne Baxter, Karl Malden

1954

Dial "M" for Murder

Warner Brothers-First-National, 1953

Screenplay: Frederick Knott, based on his play

Music: Dimitri Toimkin

Featured performers: Ray Milland, Grace Kelly, Robert Cummings, Anthony Dawson

Rear Window

Paramount, 1953

Screenplay: John Michael Hayes, based on the story by Cornell Woolrich

Music: Franz Waxman

Featured performers: James Stewart, Grace Kelly, Thelma Ritter, Wendell Corey, Raymond Burr

1955

To Catch a Thief

Paramount, 1954

Screenplay: John Michael Hayes, based on the novel by David Dodge

Music: Lyn Murray

Featured performers: Cary Grant, Grace Kelly, Jessie Royce Landis

The Trouble with Harry

Paramount, 1954

Screenplay: John Michael Hayes, based on the novel by J. Trevor Story

Music: Bernard Herrmann

Featured performers: Edmund Gwenn, John Forsythe, Shirley MacLaine, Mildred Natwick, Mildred Dunnock, Jerry Mathers

Films made for TV: *Breakdown, Revenge, The Case of Mr. Pelham*

1956

The Man Who Knew Too Much

Paramount, 1955

Screenplay: John Michael Hayes and Angus Macphail, based on a story by Charles Bennett and D.B. Wyndham Lewis

Music: Bernard Herrmann

Featured performers: James Stewart, Doris Day, Christopher Olsen, Bernard Miles, Brenda de Banzie

The Wrong Man

Warner Brothers-First National

Screenplay: Maxwell Anderson and Angus MacPhail, based on a story by Anderson

Music: Bernard Herrmann

Featured performers: Henry Fonda, Vera Miles, Anthony Quayle

Films made for TV: *Back for Christmas, Wet Saturday, Mr. Blanchard's Secret*

1957

Films Made for TV: *One More Mile to Go, The Perfect Crime, Four O'Clock*

1958

Vertigo
Paramount, 1957
Screenplay: Alec Coppel and Samuel Taylor, based on the novel *D'Entre les morts* by Pierre Boileau and Thomas Narcejac
Music: Bernard Herrmann
Featured performers: James Stewart, Kim Novak, Barbara Bel Geddes, Tom Helmore

Films made for TV: *Lamb to the Slaughter, Dip in the Pool, Poison*

1959

North by Northwest
MGM, 1958
Screenplay: Ernest Lehman
Music: Bernard Herrmann
Featured performers: Cary Grant, Eva Marie Saint, James Mason, Leo G. Carroll, Martin Landau

Films made for TV: *Banquo's Chair, Arthur, The Crystal Trench*

1960

Psycho
Paramount, 1959–60
Screenplay: Joseph Stefano, based on the novel by Robert Bloch.
Music: Bernard Herrmann
Featured performers: Anthony Perkins, Janet Leigh, Vera Miles, John Gavin, Martin Balsam

Films made for TV: *Incident at a Corner, Mrs. Bixby and the Colonel's Coat*

1961

Films made for TV: *The Horseplayer, Bang! You're Dead*

1962

Film made for TV: *I Saw the Whole Thing*

1963

The Birds
Universal, 1962
Screenplay: Evan Hunter, based on the story by Daphne du Maurier
Music: Remi Gassman, Oskar Sala, Bernard Herrmann
Featured performers: Tippi Hedren, Rod Taylor, Jessica Tandy

1964

Marnie
Universal, 1963–64
Screenplay: Jay Presson Allen, based on the novel by Winston Graham
Music: Bernard Herrmann
Featured performers: Tippi Hedren, Sean Connery, Diane Baker, Louise Latham

1966

Torn Curtain
Universal, 1965–66
Screenplay: Brian Moore
Music: John Addison
Featured performers: Paul Newman, Julie Andrews, Lila Kedrova

1969

Topaz
Universal, 1968–69

Screenplay: Samuel Taylor, based on the novel by Leon Uris

Music: Maurice Jarre

Featured performers: Frederick Stafford, John Forsythe, Dany Robin, John Vernon, Karen Dor

1972

Frenzy

Universal, 1971

Screenplay: Anthony Shaffer, based on the novel *Goodbye Picadilly, Farewell Leicester Square* by Arthur La Bern

Music: Ron Goodwin

Featured performers: Jon Finch, Barry Foster, Barbara Leigh-Hunt, Anna Massey

1976

Family Plot

Universal, 1965

Screenplay: Ernest Lehman, based on the novel *The Rainbird Pattern* by Victor Canning

Music: John Williams

Featured performers: Karen Black, Bruce Dern, Barbara Harris, William Devane

Index